desserts
BY PIERRE
HERMÉ

Also by

DORIE GREENSPAN

Sweet Times: Simple Desserts for Every Occasion

Waffles: From Morning to Midnight

Pancakes: From Morning to Midnight

Baking with Julia

desserts

BY PIERRE HERMÉ

WRITTEN BY

DORIE GREENSPAN

photographs by

HARTMUT KIEFER

LITTLE, BROWN AND COMPANY

Boston New York Toronto London

A ma femme Frédérick,
écrivain-cuisinière.
P. H.

To my husband, Michael,
and my son, Joshua.
D. G.

Acknowledgments x

Introduction xi

BASIC RECIPES 1
FRUITS, CREAMS, AND COOKIES 41
TARTS AND TARTLETS 113
CAKES 161

A Dictionary of Terms, Techniques, Equipment, and Ingredients 265

Mail-Order Sources 282

Index 284

ACKNOWLEDGMENTS

Over the two years that we worked on this book, we had help from many people. We are grateful to Jane Dystel, our agent, for introducing us to Jennifer Josephy, our editor. From the moment we met Jennifer, we knew we had been placed in exceptional hands: Our book is better for her intelligence and insight, our lives better for her friendship and humor. Many thanks to the team at Little, Brown, especially Julia Sedykh, the book's designer, Beth Davey and Katie Long, our publicists, and Emily Fromm, Jennifer's assistant, for their tireless efforts and unflagging enthusiasm. And a chocolate kiss to Judith Sutton, our all-knowing copyeditor.

In New York, warmest thanks to Nick Malgieri, who said he'd be the project's *parrain,* and, good to his word, he proved the ideal godfather; François Payard, for his knowledge and beyond-the-call-of-friendship help; and our recipe testers, Jeremy Meyers and David Nussbaum, for their talent, precision, patience, and perfect testing notes.

In Paris, a thousand *merci*s to Charles Znaty for his consistently wise advice; Harmut Kiefer for his brilliant photographs; Birgit Kiefer for the just-right props; and Richard Ledu for preparing picture-perfect desserts.

At Ladurée, many thanks to Francis and David Holder for their confidence.

And, as always, we are thankful for the love and encouragement of Frédérick Grasser-Hermé and Michael and Joshua Greenspan.

PIERRE HERMÉ

and

DORIE GREENSPAN

INTRODUCTION

Nonstop "sweet talk" is what I remember most from my first meeting with Pierre Hermé. It was 1993, I was in Paris on a working holiday, and he was the chef-pâtissier of the fabulous specialty shop Fauchon. All I'd wanted was a recipe by him for a piece I was writing on chestnuts and, he'd told me, all I had to do was come to Fauchon to pick it up. That morning, I got the recipe, as planned, but I also got nibbles of innumerable desserts with incomparable tastes, and three hours of conversation that careered into *cannelés* (soft pastries from Bordeaux), fleur de sel (Pierre's favorite salt), chocolate, caramel, cinnamon, and almonds and always seemed to return to the chef's favorite topic, the pleasures of dessert.

I left dizzy with new ideas and clutching a present, the dazzling Cherry on the Cake, Pierre's now-mythic milk chocolate extravaganza. It seemed to me that this cake, which, sadly, can't be replicated at home, was the dessert that epitomized the range and character of Pierre's gifts. The cake was risky — Pierre used milk chocolate at a time when chefs were competing to find the darkest, bitterest chocolate. It was complex but seamless — he combined crunchy meringue, creamy ganache, crackly shards of praline cookies, thin sheets of chocolate, and crispy toasted nuts. It was groundbreaking — he had collaborated with a celebrated designer, Yan Pennor's, to create the dramatic fall-away box and the plaster mold for the cake, a wedge that looked like a slice from a giant cake. And it was whimsical, if not downright silly — Pierre capped his masterpiece with a huge, glossy, clown's-nose–red cherry, its stem tilted at the jauntiest angle.

I was smitten, inspired, and hungry for more of Pierre's desserts. I wanted to taste everything he made and find out about everything he did. Why did his lemon cream, which looked like every other French lemon cream, have an otherworldly lightness? How did he get that just-right balance between sweetness and acidity in his chocolate-raspberry dessert? Had he really dared to use Rice Krispies and Nestlé's chocolate crunch candy in that elegant charlotte? I had a million questions. I couldn't wait to find out more.

I didn't have to look hard — or far — to get the rundown on Pierre. In France, the creations of a brilliant pastry chef make headlines; just by scanning the newspapers, I quickly discovered that the modest, soft-spoken, puckish man I'd met had so beguiled French journalists that they'd run out of words to describe him. In countless stories in the daily papers and the numerous glossy monthly food magazines, if writers didn't call him a genius, they pegged him as a wizard or magician. Even the buttoned-down *Le Monde,* France's newspaper of record, followed Pierre's creations. In 1993, Pierre Hermé was worshipped among the cognoscenti in France, sought after to teach in Japan and Spain, and well known across the continent. In America, it was primarily pastry chefs who knew his name, but they, too, had a way of talking about him in hushed, reverent tones, and many had made the pilgrimage to Paris to learn at his side.

Who was this man who, at the age of thirty-two, was France's most acclaimed — and beloved — pastry chef?

He was a wunderkind — and that's said without exaggeration. Pierre was born in Colmar in 1961 and was, from birth, surrounded by the aromas of butter and sugar, of rising bread and melting chocolate, that wafted from his father's pâtisserie. He teasingly says that his passion for pastry, and it is a passion, was encoded in his DNA — and maybe it was. Certainly, by the time he was three he knew that he'd become a pastry chef, the fourth generation to do so in his family.

Before he turned fourteen, Gaston Lenôtre, who was then France's best known pastry chef, would request that the young Pierre be apprenticed to him. We don't have this kind of system in the United States, so it's hard to understand how monumental the request was. Think of it as being tapped for the major leagues when you're only in junior high school. Of course, Messrs. Hermé senior and junior were in accord and, at fourteen, Pierre left home for this apprenticeship. Later, in what people still talk about as a startling turn of events, he was given command of Lenôtre's most prestigious boutique, on Avenue Victor Hugo. Pierre was just nineteen, but he'd shown a sensitivity to the nuance of desserts and a mastery of organization, one of the least talked about but most important skills a chef can have. It was a stunning start.

After military service and work in Brussels's most famous pastry shop, Witamer, Pierre returned to Paris to take over the pastry kitchen at Fauchon. Then twenty-four years old, he was given free rein to create new desserts. Overseeing a staff of thirty-five and responsible for everything from the window displays, which became so fantastical you could barely see the glazed chocolate cakes for the nose prints left by admirers, to the plated desserts served in Fauchon's restaurants, Pierre turned out a hundred and fifty different specialties each day. And, like a top fashion designer, he presented a new collection of sweets twice yearly.

Just when it seemed as if there couldn't be more, Pierre's first book, *Secrets Gourmands,* was published and promptly won France's most coveted cookbook prize. (Pierre has published four books in France; this is his first book for America.) It was also at about this time that Jeffrey Steingarten, writing in *Vogue,* called Pierre the "Picasso of Pastry," and the moniker, so apt, stuck.

Pierre remained at Fauchon for eleven years, creating cakes like the Riviera (page 215), a perfectly balanced chocolate and lemon cake, and desserts like the Gourmandise (page 49), an ingenious combination of pineapple, coconut milk, and pearl tapioca, now a "hall of famer." Then, as his thirty-fifth birthday neared, he announced that he would go to Paris's oldest pâtisserie-tea salon, Ladurée, to direct the opening of their grand new outpost on the Champs-Élysées.

The new "Ladurée by Pierre Hermé" opened in the fall of 1997. It is filled with antiques, paneled with marble from the Louvre's former Salle Rubens, and entered through a greenhouse designed by Gustave Eiffel. And, in addition to a pastry shop and tea salon, a chocolate boutique, and a bread counter, there is a two-hundred-seat restaurant at which guests take breakfast, lunch, dinner, and, of course, dessert, all from menus both sweet and savory conceived by Hermé. The chef-pâtissier has donned a second toque and become chef-cuisinier too.

It was during this time of tremendous change that Pierre was decorated as a Chevalier of Arts and Letters, the only pastry chef ever to attain this honor (usually reserved for the likes of Colette), and named France's Pastry Chef of the Year, the youngest ever.

It was also when we began working on this book. To start, we set aside a no-interruptions-no-matter-what week. I had expected to spend the week in the kitchen, but Pierre insisted we go to the beach. And so it was that I ended up facing the tranquil Arcachon Basin in Bordeaux, tasting ingredients and talking about desserts into the night. We read recipes with the precision of grammarians parsing sentences, dissected the merits of flavor combinations, and discussed texture until I found myself rubbing my tongue against the roof of my mouth, imagining I could feel the crunch of a streusel and the suppleness of a pound cake's fine crumb. But we didn't make a single dessert — nor did we even talk much about what it would take to make one.

"Technique is not so significant," claimed Pierre. "Anyone can make my recipes. But it's important to understand the taste."

And, indeed, for Pierre, taste is key. Although he realizes that we feast with our eyes first, he doesn't put too much stock in the package. He dislikes superfluous decorations — he never tosses a mint sprig here or there; if an ingredient's only purpose is appearance, it's out — and he disapproves of architectural food, skyscrapers of ingredients that have to be deconstructed before they can be eaten. Instead, Pierre holds to the "architecture of taste," his expression to describe the way he builds flavor and uses texture to enhance and sustain it.

Naturally, the best way to appreciate Pierre's genius for flavor is to taste his desserts. But even before you bake, you can get a feel for his style by doing what we did that first week — reading through the recipes. Skim these pages and you'll find a homey coconut loaf cake (page 165) with the unexpected — and inspired — addition of coriander; a simple dessert of carpaccio-thin pineapple made spectacular with a speckling of salt, pepper, and sugar (page 75); a chocolate tart (page 120) that conceals caramelized bananas and rum-soaked raisins; a made-in-a-flash assemblage of grapefruit slices, ruby port, and mint granité (page 77); and a remarkable creation of soft circles of ladyfinger cake, impossibly light mascarpone mousse, sweet blueberries, and slightly browned meringue (page 189). Nothing about the recipes is typical. Pierre has even redefined the classics: His pâte brisée (page 62) is made crisper with the addition of milk, yolks, and more butter; his meringue (page 5) is baked longer than usual so that it emerges from the oven with a light caramel flavor, a thin, shatter-at-a-touch crust, and a chewy interior; and his puff pastry (page 21) is, literally, turned inside out — reversing convention, he puts the lion's share of the butter on the outside, rendering the dough easy to roll and the pastry exceedingly flaky and capable of rising to extreme heights.

It is these refinements in taste and texture and these extraordinary flavor marriages that capture Pierre's imagination and bring him such pleasure. And they are what will please you, too, when you make these desserts.

Pierre's claims notwithstanding, to make these recipes you do need some technical skill. However, none of the recipes is beyond the capabilities of an average home baker, although some, because they take a while to prepare, require above-average patience. What the recipes demand is an attention to detail. Pay attention, and you'll always be rewarded with a sensational dessert — you'll usually learn something too. As you work your way through these recipes, you'll discover scores of Pierre's *trucs,* tricks, and techniques. You'll be more conscious of the temperature of ingredients than ever before. You won't add butter to a cooked mixture until it has cooled to $140°F$, so that the butter will maintain its best flavor and texture, and you'll wait for chocolate to cool to $104°F$ before you blend it with a batter — the instant-read thermometer will become your steady, trusted companion. You'll put aside some of your traditional cake pans to do as the pros do and construct cakes in bottomless metal rings so that they always look pastry-shop perfect, even on the first try. You'll add salt to caramel and black pepper to berries and wonder why you hadn't thought to do this sooner.

Most of all, you'll have the pleasure of working with the ingredients and the satisfaction of making something with your own hands. One day, I was trying to describe to Pierre the pleasure I derived from making his Tarte Tropézienne (page 201). I tried to explain that it was not just that the cake tasted wonderful, but that it was a joy to make, and that I was delighted when I served it to friends. He smiled his quiet smile, nodded with understanding, and said, "I know. I feel that every day."

This treasury of recipes with something from every part of Pierre's repertoire will let you, too, "feel that every day." I have translated, adapted, written, and tested these recipes with the home baker in mind, organizing and presenting them so that they'll work for you in your own kitchen with American ingredients.

You'll find everything you need to get started in the first and last chapters. To begin, there's "Basic Recipes," those cornerstones of the pastry chef's repertoire that, once mastered, become the foundation for so many other cakes, tarts, and desserts. All the classics (at least the classics as Pierre interprets them) are here, including a downy but quite sturdy génoise, France's favorite sponge cake; meltingly sweet meringue; ladyfingers; silken crème anglaise and its cousin, pastry cream; Pierre's one-of-a-kind lemon cream; tart doughs sweet and not so sweet; a flourless chocolate cake that you'll use in many other cakes but also make solo over and over again; and glazes, syrups, and sauces. At the back of the book, there's "A Dictionary of Terms, Techniques, Equipment, and Ingredients." This is where you'll learn about chocolate in all its forms, find out about cake rings, discover fleur de sel and Tahitian vanilla beans, and look up the definition of *"à la minute."* For some this will be a refresher, for others an introduction to the language of sweets, but I think everyone will find it a useful reference if ever a question comes up mid-mousse. You can think of these two chapters as a brief course in pastry and dessert making. They're just what's needed to get you ready to delve into the middle three chapters, the heart of the book.

There's a far-ranging collection of "Fruits, Creams, and Cookies," including crème brûlée and a brilliant crème brûlée ice cream; a luxurious chocolate cream guaranteed to supplant pudding in your affections; linzer cookies filled with homemade red raspberry jam; and a grand assortment of simple, easy-to-prepare fresh fruit desserts. Following are the "Tarts and Tartlets," a compilation without rival. From the Mirliton-Citrus Tart with its soothing almond filling and the Coconut and Dried Cherry Flan with its haunting aroma to the mile-high Caramelized Cinnamon Tart and the tiny Passionately Chocolate Tartlets that pack a punch, there are tarts to match every occasion and mood, as well as every level of expertise — but most of the tarts can be mastered by beginners. And to finish, the rich and varied "Cakes" chapter.

The first six cakes are easy, a tyro's paradise. You'll find lemon, coconut, chocolate, spice, and carrot loaves whose simple forms belie their sophisticated flavors, as well as a round raspberry-dotted Ligurian Lemon Cake that I urge everyone who loves lemon to make straightaway. The next group of cakes highlights fruits and nuts, and includes such notables as the Philadelphia Almond Cake with its cream cheese mousse and blue-ribbon streusel, the elegant Coffee-Walnut Cake, and the brioche-based Tarte Tropézienne, the chef's luscious rendition of a cherished Côte d'Azure specialty. Anyone with an affinity for chocolate should start with the chocolate cakes in this chapter, recipes that explore — and celebrate — each facet of chocolate's enduring appeal. The group encompasses everything from the Chocolate Dome, a shiny, through-and-through chocolate igloo constructed of chocolate mousse, chocolate cake, and chocolate glaze, to the Crispy and Creamy Rice Treat, a charlotte filled with rice pudding and topped with a layer of thick, velvety chocolate cream. (This is the dessert in which Pierre was audacious enough to use caramelized Rice Krispies and Nestlé's chocolate crunch candy — it's fabulous!) Finally, just as fashion shows close with a wedding dress, the book closes with "The Wedding Cake," one as timeless as the ritual it marks.

If baking is new to you, start with the "Fruits, Creams, and Cookies" chapter. Most of these recipes are exceptionally easy — actually, many need no baking — but all are stamped with Pierre's signature style. Then move on to the easy cakes, at the start of the "Cakes" chapter. If a question comes up, turn to the Dictionary for a quick answer. And if the excitement of early success or the craving for a more elaborate creation strikes you, succumb and skip ahead. For the most part, the long recipes for fancy cakes are complex but not complicated. Read the directions through at least twice before you set to work, then jump in and enjoy.

And if you're a professional — and I know that many of you have waited for Pierre's recipes to be adapted for the American kitchen — I can only hope you will be inspired to try everything and have the same pleasure preparing, tasting, and serving these sweets as I had.

Here, for the first time in America, are Pierre Hermé's recipes, each delicious proof that, as Brillat-Savarin said, "The discovery of a new dish does more for the happiness of mankind than the discovery of a new star."

DORIE GREENSPAN

New York City

BASIC RECIPES

Génoise

The génoise is the "Old Faithful" of French pastry chefs. It is the most basic cake in the repertoire, the first that apprentice pastry cooks master and the one they turn to throughout their careers when they're looking for an ideal layer cake or a base for petit fours. A member of the sponge-cake clan, the génoise is a firm cake whose prime leavener is whole eggs. The eggs are mixed with sugar and warmed in a pan of simmering water, the better to help them achieve maximum — and magnificent — volume. In fact, before the flour and melted butter are added to the batter, the egg mixture is beaten until it is triple its original volume and as light and airy as a ribbon of whipped cream.

Because it is a dry cake, drier than most American sponge cakes or any American butter cake, the génoise is the ultimate sopper-upper — its tight, springy cell structure can absorb a splash of liqueur or a soaking of flavored syrup and, in an instant, take on innumerable tastes. Make a génoise for the Carioca (page 241) and soak it with a punchy espresso syrup and you'll see how easily this culinary chameleon goes from French to Brazilian, and from plain to potently flavorful.

A final note on the nature of this cake: It's a tad temperamental but rarely out of control. If all goes well — if you heat everything to the right temperature, beat everything to the right volume, fold everything in with the right touch, and appease the right kitchen witches — your batter may be so ethereally light that it will bake over the top of your two-inch-deep cake pan. On other, less-perfect days, the batter may just reach the top or come out of the oven a half inch or so shy of the rim. Fortunately, given the way génoise is used, any of these cakes, tall or short, will be fine. However, if your batter is consistently over the top, you may want to use it to bake two nine-inch cakes instead of one. Neither will be particularly high, but each one will yield as much cake as you'll need for any of Pierre's recipes.

Génoise has always been important to French baking as a base or foundation for cakes with several elements. I still remember — I can almost taste — my father's Strawberry Diplomat, a cake he made every Friday. It was a single layer of génoise soaked with kirsch syrup and finished with whipped cream, fresh strawberries, and a strawberry glaze. It was one of my favorites.

Makes one 9-inch round cake

Génoise is still being used like that, but in addition to making plain génoise that gets its flavor from a soaking syrup, today pastry chefs often flavor the batter itself with nuts, spices, or herbs — providing a good example of something classic becoming something modern. ≫ — P.H.

- **4 tablespoons (2 ounces) unsalted butter**
- **6 large eggs**
- **1 cup sugar**
- **1⅓ cups all-purpose flour, sifted**

1. Before you start mixing the batter, check the specific recipe in which you'll be using the génoise or read the baking instructions on page 4 for information on preheating the oven and preparing the pan.

2. Pour a few inches of water into a skillet large enough to hold the bowl from your mixer. Bring the water to a gentle simmer and keep it at the ready. Melt the butter and set it aside to cool — it should be just warm when you're ready for it.

3. Whisk the eggs and sugar together in the mixer bowl. Place the bowl in the skillet of simmering water and, whisking without stop, heat the mixture until it is foamy, slightly pale, and between 130°F and 140°F, as measured on an instant-read thermometer, about 4 minutes; remove the bowl from the water. Working in the mixer fitted with the whisk attachment, beat the mixture on high speed until it cools to room temperature and triples in volume, about 5 to 8 minutes. You'll know it's just right if when you lift the whisk, the batter falls back into the bowl and forms a ribbon that remains on the surface for 10 seconds before it dissolves.

4. Stir about 2 tablespoons of batter into the slightly cooled butter and set it aside. Now, working with a large flexible rubber spatula, gently fold the flour into the batter in two or three additions (you might find it most convenient to add the flour to the bowl by shaking it through a strainer), taking care to handle the batter gently in order to maintain its bubble structure. (The batter will lose volume as you fold in the flour and later the butter. This reaction is inevitable and shouldn't jeopardize the success of the finished cake, but be careful just the same.) Still working with the spatula, fold in the butter mixture. At this point, the batter must be used immediately.

to bake

Recipes calling for génoise will tell you what size cake you need but, in general, génoise batter is baked in a 9-inch round cake pan with sides at least 2 inches high.

Center a rack in the oven and preheat the oven to 350°F. Butter the pan, dust the interior with flour, and tap out the excess. Pour the batter into the pan and bake for 28 to 33 minutes, or until the top is golden and springy to the touch and a toothpick inserted in the center of the cake comes out clean. Transfer the cake to a cooling rack, then unmold after 5 minutes. Turn the cake right side up to cool to room temperature on the rack.

4

Keeping

While the batter cannot be kept, baked génoise can be wrapped in plastic and kept at room temperature for a day or two, or packed airtight and frozen for a month.

Meringue Batter

Whipped egg whites and sugar may not sound like much, but as meringue, they're one of the great wonders of the pastry kitchen. Whether smoothed on a cake and baked at ultrahigh heat for just seconds to make a soft, elegant frosting, or piped into disks, cookies, or rosettes and baked (actually dried) for hours at the oven's lowest setting until firm yet still fast to melt on your tongue, meringue may be the egg white's greatest achievement.

There are three kinds of meringue: French, or plain, in which egg whites and sugar are beaten together until firm and glossy; cooked, in which the whites and sugar are heated before they are beaten; and Italian, in which a hot sugar syrup is beaten into the whites. Each is used differently, but all depend on the egg white's remarkable expanding cell structure to capture and retain air.

This recipe is for French uncooked meringue. Although it is traditionally made with a blend of granulated and confectioner's sugar, Pierre prefers to use only granulated sugar — half of it beaten into the whites, the other half folded in gently — so that the baked meringue has a light caramel flavor, a crackly exterior, and a soft, chewy interior. In other words, this is perfect meringue.

« Since eggs separate most easily when they are fresh and chilled, but whites whip better when they are old and warm, it's good to separate the eggs as soon as you take them from the refrigerator, then let the whites come to room temperature before you make the meringue. Ideally, you should separate the whites and, if the eggs are very fresh, keep them covered in the refrigerator for a day before whipping them. "Aged" whites are more liquid than "young" whites, so they whip to greater volume and don't fall as easily. » — P.H.

- 4 large egg whites
- 1 cup sugar
- ¾ teaspoon pure vanilla extract

*Makes enough for three 9-inch disks
and some cookies or rosettes*

1. Before you start mixing the batter, check the specific recipe in which you'll be using the meringue or read the baking instructions below for information on preheating the oven and preparing the pan.

2. In an impeccably clean, dry mixer bowl with a clean, dry whisk attachment in place, whip the egg whites on high speed until they turn opaque and form soft peaks. Still whipping on high, gradually add half of the sugar and continue to beat until the whites are glossy and hold firm peaks. Beat in the vanilla.

3. Working with a large rubber spatula, gradually fold in the remaining sugar. Work as quickly and delicately as you can to incorporate the sugar without deflating the whites. The meringue is now ready to be piped into whatever shapes or forms your recipe requires.

to pipe and bake

The following are general directions for piping and baking meringue batter. If anything more specific is needed, you'll find it in the individual recipes that use a meringue base.

1. Position the racks to divide the oven into thirds and preheat the oven to 250°F. Line two large baking sheets with parchment paper and fit a pastry bag with a plain ½-inch tip.

2. To make disks, pencil the outline of a 9-inch disk on one piece of parchment and the outline of two 9-inch disks on the other; turn the sheets of paper over. (If you can't see the outline of the circles clearly now that the paper is flipped over, darken the pencil lines.) Gently spoon one third of the batter into the pastry bag and begin piping the batter at the center of a circle. Work your way in a spiral to the penciled edge and try to have each coil of batter touch the preceding coil. Pipe with light, consistent pressure and try to keep the disks thin — they shouldn't be more than ⅓ inch high. Refill the bag twice more to pipe the remaining disks. If you have any leftover meringue, use it to make another disk, if there's enough, or switch to a star-shaped tip and pipe out rosettes — they'll make great cookies for espresso or tea.

3. If there are any spaces or uneven sections in the disks, give them a once-over-lightly with a metal spatula. Place the baking sheets in the oven and insert the handle of a wooden spoon into the oven to keep the door slightly ajar. Bake the disks for 1½ to 2 hours, until firm and very lightly caramel colored, rotating the pans front to back and top to bottom two or three times during the baking period. Turn off the oven and continue to dry the meringues for another 8 hours (or overnight) with the door closed.

4. Transfer the meringues, parchment and all, to a counter. Run an offset spatula under the disks to loosen them from the paper.

Keeping
Stored in a cool dry place, such as an airtight metal tin, meringues will keep for at least a week.

Ladyfinger Batter

This batter is a cornerstone of French baking. Light, airy, and spongy, it is often spiraled into rounds to serve as cake layers, formed into bands flexible enough to be wrapped around cakes, or piped into the traditional plump biscuits, ladyfingers, that give the batter its name. As ladyfingers, the biscuits are served with tea, used as the base and border of fancy charlottes, or broken into pieces and laid into the bottom of a fruit tart — the perfect sponge to absorb the fruits' flavorful juices and the tastiest assurance of a stay-crisp crust.

If you're making ladyfinger bands and disks, it's best to pipe out the bands (the part that will show in the finished cake) first, while the batter is at its fullest.

When I'm making a band of ladyfingers to go around a charlotte, or if I'm piping individual ladyfingers to eat by themselves or with ice cream, I like to dust them with confectioner's sugar before I bake them. Then I let the piped bands or biscuits rest on the counter for 15 minutes, dust them again — very lightly — and bake them. As they bake, the sugar beads, giving the ladyfingers a slight crust that I think is an important part of the cake's texture. — P.H.

- 6 large egg whites
- ⅔ cup plus 2 tablespoons sugar
- 5 large egg yolks
- 1 cup minus 1 tablespoon all-purpose flour, sifted

1. Before you start mixing the batter, check the specific recipe in which you'll be using the ladyfingers or read the baking instructions on page 8 for information on preheating the oven and preparing the pan.
2. In an impeccably clean, dry mixer bowl with a clean, dry whisk attachment in place, whip the egg whites on high speed until they turn opaque and form soft peaks. Still whipping on high,

*Makes enough batter for two 9-inch disks
and two 9-inch bands of biscuits*

gradually add ⅔ cup of the sugar. Continue beating until the whites are glossy and hold very firm peaks. It's important that the whites develop into a really firm meringue — this is what will allow the batter to rest on the counter for 15 minutes and still maintain its shape. Set aside for the moment.

3. In another bowl, whisk the yolks and the remaining 2 tablespoons sugar together until they are well blended, about 1 to 2 minutes. Working with a rubber spatula, gently fold the yolk mixture into the beaten whites. Then fold in the flour, sifting the flour over the mixture in a few additions and incorporating it gingerly. (No matter how delicately you fold in the flour, the batter will deflate. Don't worry, but do be gentle.) The batter is now ready to be piped and baked according to your recipe's particular instructions.

to pipe and bake

The following are general directions for piping and baking ladyfinger batter. If anything more specific is needed, you'll find it in the individual recipes that use a ladyfinger base.

- **Confectioner's sugar**

1. Position the racks to divide the oven into thirds and preheat the oven to 450°F. fit a large pastry bag with a plain ½-inch tip and set aside until needed. Cut two pieces of parchment paper to fit two large baking sheets. On each sheet of paper, draw a 9-inch circle and, across one of the ends of the sheet, draw a band that's 8 inches long and 4 inches wide. Turn the sheets of paper over and place each piece of parchment on a baking sheet. (If you can't see the outlines clearly now that the paper is flipped over, darken the pencil lines.)

2. Gently spoon a little more than half the batter into the pastry bag. Position a baking sheet so that the top and bottom lines for the 8-inch-long band run from your left to your right. Start making a ladyfinger band by piping plump logs of batter from top to bottom within the pencil lines. Pipe one ladyfinger log right next to the last one — they'll touch, and they're supposed to. Keeping firm and steady pressure on the pastry bag, you should end up with ladyfingers that are about 1 inch wide and about ⅔ to ¾ inch high. When you've piped the full 8-inch band, dust it lightly with confectioner's sugar and pipe the second band in the same fashion; dust it with confectioner's sugar too. Refill the bag when you run out of batter. (The bands will probably take about two thirds of the batter.) Next, pipe the disks, keeping in mind that the disks should be only about half as high as the plump ladyfinger bands, so you should exert less pressure on the pastry bag. For each disk, begin piping the batter at the center of the circle. Work your way in a spiral to the penciled edge and try to have each coil of batter touch the preceding coil. If you have any holes, you can run an offset spatula very

lightly over the disks to fill in the spaces. Let the piped batter rest on the counter for 15 minutes, during which time the confectioner's sugar will pearl, or form beads.

3. Give the bands a second light dusting of confectioner's sugar (there's no need to sugar the disks) and slip the baking sheets into the oven. Insert the handle of a wooden spoon into the oven to keep the door slightly ajar. Bake for 8 to 10 minutes, just until the disks and bands are very lightly golden — you don't want the cake to take on much color. Slide the parchment off the baking sheets and transfer the cakes, on their parchment sheets, to racks. Allow the cakes to cool to room temperature.

4. When the cakes are cool, run an offset spatula under the disks and bands to loosen them from the paper. If you want individual biscuits, separate the cookies with a sharp knife or pizza cutter. If you want a decorative ladyfinger band that can be wrapped around cakes or charlottes, keep the cookies intact but cut the band in half lengthwise, or according to the measurements given in the specific recipe.

9

Keeping

Once mixed, the batter should be used immediately. Once baked, the cakes can be wrapped well in plastic or packed in an airtight tin and kept at room temperature for 2 days or frozen for a month.

Flourless Chocolate Cake Batter

Unlike the flourless chocolate cakes that were the rage in America in the 1970s and '80s — cakes that were exceedingly moist and seemed almost unbaked — this cake is flat as a flapjack and exceedingly dry. In fact, the first time you bake this you'll probably think you've overbaked it (it will look and feel that dry), but it will be perfect, since this deeply chocolaty, pleasantly chewy cake is always combined with other ingredients that soften and moisten it.

《 *You can use this batter to make a dessert that's like a fallen soufflé cake. Pour the batter into a buttered 9-inch cake pan, one with high sides (butter the rim too), and bake it in a 350°F oven with the door propped open with a wooden spoon for about 40 to 45 minutes — the cake will rise and then fall. Cool it on a rack and refrigerate it overnight before serving. I serve the cake cold, right from the refrigerator, with ice cream. If you want, you can add chopped nuts, small pieces of dried fruit, or some finely chopped orange zest to the batter.* 》 — P. H.

- 4 ounces bittersweet chocolate (preferably Valrhona Manjari), finely chopped
- 6 tablespoons (3 ounces) unsalted butter, softened
- ½ cup sugar
- 1 teaspoon Dutch-processed cocoa powder
- 2 large egg yolks, at room temperature
- 1 large egg, at room temperature
- 6 large egg whites, at room temperature

1. Before you start mixing the batter, check the specific recipe in which you'll be using the cake or read the baking instructions opposite for information on preheating the oven and preparing the pans.

2. Melt the chocolate over simmering water or in a microwave oven and allow it to cool to 114°F, as measured on an instant-read thermometer.

Makes enough batter for four 9-inch disks

3. In a mixer fitted with the paddle attachment, beat the butter, 3 tablespoons of the sugar, and the cocoa powder together until the mixture is creamy. Add the yolks and beat until well blended. Add the egg (don't worry if the mixture looks curdled) and then the melted chocolate, beating only until the mixture is smooth, satiny, and blended. As is true with all chocolate preparations, it's best not to overwork the mixture once the chocolate is added. Set the bowl aside for the moment.

4. In an impeccably clean, dry bowl, whip the egg whites until they form soft peaks. Gradually add the remaining 5 tablespoons sugar and beat until the peaks are firm and shiny. Using a large rubber spatula, stir about one quarter of the egg whites into the chocolate mixture, just to lighten it; gently fold in the remaining whites. The batter is now complete and must be used immediately.

to pipe and bake

The following are general directions for piping and baking the batter. If anything more specific is needed, you'll find it in the individual recipes that use this cake as a base.

1. Position the racks to divide the oven into thirds and preheat the oven to 350°F. Line two baking sheets with parchment paper and fit a pastry bag with a plain ¼-inch tip.

2. To make disks, pencil the outline of two 9-inch circles on each piece of parchment; turn the sheets of paper over. (If you can't see the outline of the circles clearly now that the paper is flipped over, darken the pencil lines.)

3. Gently spoon half the batter into the pastry bag and begin piping the batter at the center of one circle. Work your way in a spiral to the penciled edge and try to have each coil of batter touch the preceding coil; if there are any spaces, you can fill them in by running a metal spatula gently over the disk. Repeat for the second disk on the same sheet. Refill the bag and pipe the remaining disks — you'll have just enough batter for four thin circles.

4. Bake the disks for 25 to 30 minutes, rotating the pans top to bottom and front to back halfway through the baking period. The edges will be very brown and the cakes will seem drier and more baked than those you're accustomed to, but that's just the way these should be. Transfer the cakes, parchment paper and all, to racks to cool to room temperature.

5. To release the cakes, run a spatula between the cakes and the parchment.

11

Keeping
Once mixed, the batter must be baked immediately; once baked, the cakes can be wrapped airtight in plastic and stored at room temperature for 2 days or frozen for a month.

Perfect Tart Dough

Pierre's Perfect Tart Dough, or pâte brisée, bakes to a crispness and melting goodness that places it delightfully between a flaky pie crust and a tender one. Although the dough is made in minutes, you'll need to allow chilling time — four hours before you roll it out and then at least thirty minutes before you bake it. These refrigerated rests give the gluten in the flour a chance to relax — just what's needed to keep the dough from shrinking under the oven's heat. Chilling also maintains the dough's friability, something you'll appreciate with the first forkful.

This recipe makes enough dough for three large or four smaller tarts — which may be more than you'll want for any one baking session — but if you work with smaller quantities, you won't get the lovely consistency that makes the dough so special. Extra dough can be shaped into disks and frozen.

Pâte brisée can be made in a mixer with the paddle attachment or in a very large capacity food processor.

《 *This is not a classic pâte brisée, which is usually made with water and without eggs. I added milk, yolks, and additional butter to give the dough the crisper texture I love. This dough can be used to make savory tarts too. It's what I use for quiches.* 》 — P. H .

- 3 sticks plus 2 tablespoons (13 ounces) unsalted butter, softened
- ⅓ cup plus 1 tablespoon milk, at room temperature
- 1 large egg yolk, at room temperature, lightly beaten
- 1 teaspoon sugar
- 1 teaspoon salt
- 3½ cups all-purpose flour

Makes enough for three 10¼-inch or four 8¾-inch tarts

to make the dough in a mixer

Put the butter in the bowl of a mixer fitted with the paddle attachment and beat on low speed until creamy. Add the milk, yolk, sugar, and salt and beat until the mixture is roughly blended. (At this point, the mixture will look curdled — it's not pretty, but it's inevitable and OK. Further mixing won't make it look any better, so just stop after a minute or two.) With the mixer still on low, add the flour in three or four additions (add it steadily — there's no need to wait for the flour to be incorporated thoroughly after each addition) and mix just until the ingredients come together to form a soft, moist dough that doesn't clean the sides of the bowl completely but does hold together. Don't overdo it.

to make the dough in a large-capacity food processor

Place the butter, milk, yolk, sugar, and salt in the work bowl of a food processor fitted with the metal blade. Pulse on and off a few times to break up the butter and start the blending, then process until the mixture is roughly blended. Add the flour and pulse until the mixture just starts to come together. When the dough forms moist curds and clumps and then starts to gather into a ball, stop! — you don't want to overwork it.

to shape and chill

No matter the method you used to make the dough, gather it into a ball and divide it into three or four pieces: three pieces for $10\frac{1}{4}$-inch tarts, four for $8\frac{3}{4}$-inch tarts. (Of course, you can press the dough into one large disk and cut off as much as you need at the time that you need it.) Gently press each piece into a disk and wrap each disk in plastic. Allow the dough to rest in the refrigerator for at least 4 hours or for up to 2 days before rolling and baking. *(At this stage, the dough can be wrapped airtight and frozen for up to a month.)*

to roll

1. For each tart, place a buttered tart ring on a parchment-lined baking sheet and keep close at hand. Work with one piece of dough at a time; keep the remaining dough in the refrigerator.
2. Working on a lightly floured surface (marble is ideal), roll the dough between $\frac{1}{16}$ and $\frac{1}{8}$ inch thick, lifting the dough often and making certain that the work surface and the dough are amply floured at all times. (Because this dough is so rich, it can be difficult to roll, but a well-floured surface makes the job easier. If you are a novice at rolling, you might find it easier to tape a large piece of plastic wrap to the counter and to roll the dough between that and another piece of plastic. If you do this, make sure to lift the top sheet of plastic wrap from time

13

to time so that it doesn't crease and get rolled into the dough.) Roll the dough up and around your rolling pin and unroll it onto the tart ring. Fit the dough into the bottom and up the sides of the ring, then run your rolling pin across the top of the ring to cut off the excess. If the dough cracks or splits as you work (as it may, since it is so fragile), don't worry — patch the cracks with scraps (moisten the edges to "glue" them into place) and just make certain not to stretch the dough that's in the pan. (What you stretch now will shrink later.) Prick the dough all over with the tines of a fork (unless the tart will be filled with a runny custard or other loose filling) and chill it for at least 30 minutes in the refrigerator or freezer. Repeat with the remaining dough, if necessary.

to bake

When you are ready to bake the crust(s), preheat the oven to 350°F. Fit a circle of parchment paper or foil into each crust (cut the paper or foil large enough to extend above the top of the tart) and fill with dried beans or rice. To partially bake the crust(s), bake for 18 to 20 minutes, or until lightly colored. If the crust needs to be fully baked, remove the parchment and beans and bake for another 5 to 8 minutes, or until golden. Transfer the crust(s) to a rack to cool.

Keeping

The dough can be kept in the refrigerator for up to 2 days or wrapped airtight and frozen for a month. Frozen disks of dough take about 45 minutes to an hour at average room temperature to reach a good rolling-out consistency. Baked crusts can be kept uncovered at room temperature for about 8 hours.

Sweet Tart Dough

This sweet cookie-like dough, pâte sucrée, used for dessert tarts and tartlets, benefits from Pierre's untraditional addition of ground almonds, vanilla, and confectioner's sugar and is at once crunchy and melt-in-your-mouth smooth. Like pâte brisée, it can be made in a very large capacity food processor or a mixer, and it needs a long refrigerated rest. Also as with pâte brisée, you'll get the best results if you make a larger quantity than you might need at the moment — the crust's consistency depends on this; you can cut the dough into portions and freeze the extras.

« Work this mixture as little as possible so that you'll get a nice, crumbly texture. If everything seems mixed but you still have a few large pieces of butter, it's best to leave them. It's preferable to have pieces of butter rather than an overworked dough. » — P.H.

- 2½ sticks (10 ounces) unsalted butter, softened
- 1½ cups confectioner's sugar, sifted
- ½ cup (lightly packed) ground blanched almonds (see page 277)
- ½ teaspoon salt
- ½ teaspoon vanilla bean pulp (see page 281) or ¼ teaspoon pure vanilla extract
- 2 large eggs, at room temperature, lightly beaten
- 3½ cups all-purpose flour

to make the dough in a mixer

Place the butter in the bowl of a mixer fitted with the paddle attachment and beat on low speed until creamy. Add the sugar, almonds, salt, vanilla, and eggs and, still working on low speed, beat to blend the ingredients, scraping down the paddle and the sides of the bowl as needed. The dough may look curdled — that's all right. With the machine still on low, add the flour in three or four additions and mix only until the mixture comes together to form a soft, moist dough — a matter of seconds. Don't overdo it.

*Makes enough for three 10¼-inch
or four 8¾-inch tarts*

to make the dough in a large-capacity food processor

Place the butter in the work bowl of a food processor fitted with the metal blade and pulse and process, scraping down the sides of the bowl as needed, until creamy. Add the confectioner's sugar and process to blend well. Add the almonds, salt, and vanilla and continue to process until smooth, scraping the bowl as necessary. Add the eggs and process to blend. Add the flour and pulse until the mixture just starts to come together. When the dough forms moist curds and clumps and then starts to gather into a ball, stop! — you don't want to overwork it. The dough will be very soft, pliable, and Play-Doh-ish, more like your favorite butter-cookie dough than traditional pie dough — that's just the way it should be.

to shape and chill

No matter the method you used to make the dough, gather it into a ball and divide it into three or four pieces: three pieces for $10\frac{1}{4}$-inch tarts, four for $8\frac{3}{4}$-inch tarts. (Of course, you can press the dough into one large disk and cut off as much as you need at the time that you need it.) Gently press each piece into a disk and wrap each one in plastic. Allow the dough to rest in the refrigerator for at least 4 hours or for up to 2 days before rolling and baking. *(At this stage, the dough can be wrapped airtight and frozen for up to a month.)*

to roll

1. For each tart, place a buttered tart ring on a parchment-lined baking sheet and keep close at hand. Work with one piece of dough at a time; keep the remaining dough in the refrigerator.
2. Working on a lightly floured surface (marble is ideal), roll the dough into a round between $\frac{1}{16}$ and $\frac{1}{8}$ inch thick, lifting the dough often and making certain that the work surface and the dough are amply floured at all times. (Because this dough is so rich, it can be difficult to roll, but a well-floured surface makes the job easier. If you are a novice at rolling, you might find it easier to tape a large piece of plastic wrap to the counter and to roll the dough between that and another piece of plastic. If you do this, make sure to lift the top sheet of plastic wrap from time to time so that it doesn't crease and get rolled into the dough.) Roll the dough up and around your rolling pin and unroll it onto the tart ring. fit the dough into the bottom and up the sides of the ring, then run your rolling pin across the top of the ring to cut off the excess. If the dough cracks or splits as you work (as it may, since it is so fragile), don't worry — patch the cracks with scraps (moisten the edges to "glue" them in place), and just make certain not to stretch the dough that's in the pan. (What you stretch now will shrink later.) Prick the dough all over with the tines of a fork (unless the tart will be filled with a

runny custard or other loose filling) and chill it for at least 30 minutes in the refrigerator or freezer. Repeat with the remaining dough, if necessary.

to bake

When you are ready to bake the crust(s), preheat the oven to 350°F. Fit a circle of parchment paper or foil into each crust (cut the paper large enough to extend above the top of the tart) and fill with dried beans or rice. To partially bake the crust(s), bake for 18 to 20 minutes, or until lightly colored. If the crust needs to be fully baked, remove the parchment and beans and bake for another 5 to 7 minutes, until golden. Transfer the crust(s) to a rack to cool.

Keeping

The dough can be kept in the refrigerator for up to 2 days or wrapped airtight and frozen for a month. Frozen disks of dough take about 45 minutes to an hour at average room temperature to reach a good rolling-out consistency. Baked crusts can be kept uncovered at room temperature for about 8 hours.

Cinnamon Dough

Here's a crumbly, delicate, cinnamon-and-almond-flavored crust characterized by delectability, fragility, and finesse. Its memorable texture, a cross between a sweet pastry dough and a butter cookie, is related in part to the addition of finely sieved hard-boiled egg yolks, used often by Austrian pastry chefs, rarely by the French. Given the crust's heritage, it's not surprising that it forms the base of Austrian Linzer Cookies (page 108) and the layers of the Mozart (page 221), the apple-filled cake that Pierre named after the celebrated Austrian composer.

To roll a thin layer of this dough, you'll need to keep your work surface and the dough very well floured. If the dough cracks during rolling, as can happen, fold it up and start over again — although fragile when baked, the raw dough can stand a little rough play. And if the dough gets too soft to work, put it back in the refrigerator for a brief chill, then try again.

- 2 sticks plus 5 tablespoons (10½ ounces) unsalted butter, softened
- ⅓ cup plus 2 tablespoons confectioner's sugar
- ⅓ cup plus 1 tablespoon finely ground blanched almonds (see page 277)
- 3 hard-boiled large egg yolks, cooled to room temperature and pressed through a fine strainer
- 2 teaspoons cinnamon
- Pinch of salt
- 1 tablespoon dark rum
- Pinch of double-acting baking powder
- 2¼ cups all-purpose flour

to make the dough in a food processor

Place the butter in the work bowl of a food processor fitted with the metal blade and process until creamy, scraping down the sides of the bowl as needed. Add the confectioner's sugar, al-

Makes enough for three 9-inch rounds

monds, egg yolks, cinnamon, and salt. Continue to pulse and process until smooth, scraping the bowl as necessary; add the rum and pulse to blend. Whisk the baking powder into the flour and add to the work bowl, pulsing until the mixture is blended completely. (Unlike pâte brisée or pâte sucrée, this dough can be worked past the clump-and-curd stage.) The dough will feel soft and look like the dough you'd use to make peanut-butter cookies.

to make the dough in a mixer

Place the butter in the bowl of a mixer fitted with the paddle attachment and beat until creamy. With the mixer on medium-low speed, blend in the confectioner's sugar, almonds, egg yolks, cinnamon, and salt. Continue to mix until smooth, scraping down the sides of the bowl as necessary; mix in the rum. Whisk the baking powder into the flour and gradually add the dry ingredients to the bowl, mixing until the flour is incorporated. The dough will feel soft and look like the dough you'd use to make peanut-butter cookies.

to make the dough by hand

Place the butter in a large mixing bowl and, using a large flexible rubber spatula, beat it until creamy. Add the confectioner's sugar, almonds, egg yolks, cinnamon, and salt. Continue to mix until smooth, scraping down the sides of the bowl as necessary; mix in the rum. Whisk the baking powder into the flour and gradually add the dry ingredients to the bowl, mixing until the flour is incorporated. The dough will feel soft and look like the dough you'd use to make peanut-butter cookies.

to shape and chill

No matter which method you used to make the dough, gather it into a ball and divide it into thirds. Gently press each piece into a disk, and wrap the disks in plastic. Allow the dough to rest in the refrigerator for at least 4 hours or for up to 2 days before rolling and baking. *(At this stage, the dough can be wrapped airtight and frozen for up to a month.)*

to roll

The following are general directions for rolling and baking. If anything more specific is needed, you'll find it in the individual recipes that use this dough.

I. Line two baking sheets with parchment paper and keep them close at hand. Working with one piece of dough at a time — keep the remaining dough refrigerated until needed — and keeping the work surface and the dough well floured, roll the dough into a round between

$1/16$ and $1/8$ inch thick. (If the dough softens as you work and sticks excessively to the work surface, it's best to chill it for about 30 minutes before continuing.) Brush any excess flour off the dough with a pastry brush and cut the dough to size. If you're making $8\frac{3}{4}$-inch/22-cm rounds, as is often the case with this dough, use that size tart or dessert ring as you would a cookie cutter to cut the dough: Press the ring firmly against the dough, lift the ring, and pull away the excess dough by lifting it off the work surface with an offset spatula; use a small sharp knife to clean the edges as needed. Lift the dough onto a parchment-lined baking sheet with the aid of a lightly floured metal circle — the removable bottom from a large tart pan is perfect for this job. When the dough is on the sheet, prick it all over with the tines of a fork, cover with a sheet of plastic wrap, and chill for at least 30 minutes; repeat with the remaining dough.

2. You can gather the leftovers into a ball, flatten the dough into a disk, chill it, reroll it, and cut out cookies. Baked cookies are delicious sandwiched with jam (see the recipe for Linzer Cookies on page 108).

to bake

When you're ready to bake, position the racks to divide the oven into thirds and preheat the oven to 350°F. Remove the plastic wrap and bake the pastry for about 18 to 20 minutes, rotating the pans from top to bottom and front to back halfway through the baking period. The disks should be honey brown. Transfer the pastry, paper and all, to racks to cool to room temperature. Once baked, this pastry is extremely fragile, so take care when assembling your dessert. (But don't worry if a layer cracks. Since most recipes use two or three layers, but only one for "show," salvaging a single perfect layer is usually all that's needed to carry the day. The hidden layers can be patched — no one will know.)

Keeping

The dough can be kept in the refrigerator for up to 2 days or wrapped airtight and frozen for a month. Frozen disks of dough take about 30 minutes at average room temperature to reach a good rolling-out consistency.

Inside-Out Puff Pastry

In French, puff pastry is sometimes called *mille-feuille,* for the one thousand leaves or layers that are created when the dough is rolled and folded over on itself several times. It's called puff pastry because it does, indeed, puff — dramatically. When the oven's heat hits the hundreds of layers of cold butter in the dough, the water in the butter melts, turns to steam, and pushes the pastry up, up, up. This pastry is one of the best reasons for having a window in your oven — its meteoric rise is mesmerizing.

Because of its extremely high butter content — and you've got to use butter; nothing else will give you the rise or the flavor — puff pastry can be difficult to handle if you're not used to its ways. Your best friend when you're working with puff is your refrigerator: A quick chill cures most ills. If you find that the dough is getting soft and sticking to your work surface, just pop it into the refrigerator — the cold will work wonders. And keep in mind that this is not a dough to hurry along. It needs at least four sixty-minute chills, so what's a few more minutes here and there? This is also a dough for which neatness counts. Because you are working to create layers of lean dough and buttery dough — that's what the rolling and folding is all about — it's important to roll the dough evenly in every direction (except over the edges; you'll glue them together if you run them over), and to keep the alignment of the dough as straight as possible. When you're folding the dough over into a rectangle or square, keep the layers in line and you won't have to deal with a lopsided rise.

As you're sure to have noticed from the name, this puff pastry is not the usual. In classic puff pastry, a flour-and-water dough (to which a little butter is occasionally added) is used to encase a block of butter and then the package is rolled and folded a half dozen times until the eponymous thousand or so layers are achieved. But Pierre has literally turned the dough inside out: He puts the lion's share of the butter on the outside and makes a mix of flour, water, and melted butter for the inside bundle. The result? A puff pastry whose texture Pierre describes as "at once melting and crisp."

Makes about 2½ pounds dough

You can use this dough in any of your recipes calling for puff pastry. It's the dough of choice for Pierre's Apple Galette (page 126) and it makes delicious sugar-coated twisty, turny Grissini (page 111). Whatever you do, don't toss away the scraps. Piece them together, trying to keep the layers in line, and roll them out again to use as the base for sweet or savory tarts or canapés. Even though the rerolled dough never puffs as proudly as fresh dough, its lovely buttery flavor never fades.

first mixture

- 3 sticks plus 4 tablespoons (14 ounces) unsalted butter, softened
- 1¼ cups all-purpose flour

Put the butter in a mixer fitted with the paddle attachment and work the butter just until it is smooth. Add the flour and mix just until the ingredients come together. There's always a little flour left in the bottom of the bowl — just mix that into the butter with a spatula. Scrape the soft dough out onto a large sheet of parchment or wax paper and, working with a dough scraper, flatten the mixture into a square about 6 by 6 inches. Wrap the mixture well and refrigerate it for at least 1½ hours.

second mixture

- ¾ cup water
- 2 teaspoons salt
- ¼ teaspoon white vinegar
- 3 cups all-purpose flour (maybe a bit more)
- 1 stick (4 ounces) unsalted butter, melted and cooled

Mix the water, salt, and vinegar together and keep it at the ready. Put the flour into the mixer bowl (you can use the same bowl you were using; no need to wash it) and fit the mixer with the paddle attachment. With the mixer at medium-low speed, add the melted butter to the flour and mix until the flour is moistened. The dough will look bumpy and lumpy, like the topping for a fruit crisp. With the mixer still on medium-low speed, gradually add the water mixture by pouring it down the sides of the bowl a little at a time. Add the water very slowly and keep a little of it in reserve — because the absorbency of flours differs, it's hard to predict whether you'll need all of the water or not. Keep mixing, scraping down the bowl and adding water until you have a dough that cleans the sides of the bowl. The dough will be soft, rather like an elastic tart dough, and that's fine. If the dough doesn't come together, it may need a tad more flour — add flour, up to about a tablespoon, in sprinkles — or a tablespoon or two more water. Turn the soft dough out onto a sheet of parchment or wax paper and shape it into a square that's about an inch or two smaller than the butter-flour square. Wrap well and chill for at least 1½ hours.

to roll and turn

1. Place the chilled first mixture on a very well floured work surface (marble is ideal) and dust the top of the dough with flour. If the dough is too hard to roll, press your rolling pin against it to create a series of parallel indentations that will soften the dough and help you get it going. Roll the dough out into a rectangle that's roughly 12 inches by 7 inches, rolling in all directions and on both sides, and making sure to lift and turn the dough as you roll; dust the work surface and the dough with flour as necessary. Position the chilled second mixture so that it covers the bottom half of the rolled-out dough. Fold the top half of the rolled-out dough over it and press the dough to form a neat, sealed package. Make sure that the second mixture extends into each of the corners of this square. If you have to, smoosh the second mixture into the corners with your fingertips so that the package is an even thickness throughout. Tap your rolling pin against each of the sides of the dough to square the bundle (which will probably be about 7 or 8 inches on a side). Wrap the dough well in plastic and re-frigerate for at least an hour.

2. To make the first double turn, place the dough on a well-floured work surface and dust the top of the dough with flour. Again rolling the dough in all directions and on both sides, taking care not to roll over the edges and keeping the work surface and the dough as well floured as needed, roll the dough until it is about three times longer than it is wide, about 7 or 8 inches wide and about 21 to 24 inches long. (Don't worry if your dough isn't exactly the specified measurements. Dough widens as you roll it — it's only natural. What's important is to roll the dough to three times its width, whatever its width — keep a ruler nearby.) If, as you're rolling, the dough cracks, just patch it as best you can and keep going. To create what's called the double turn or the wallet turn, fold the bottom quarter of the dough up to the center of the dough, then fold the top quarter of the dough down to the center. Now, fold the dough in half at the center. You'll have four layers of dough. Brush off any excess flour and wrap the dough well. Chill it again for at least 1 hour.

3. For the second double turn, position the dough so that the closed fold, the one that looks like the spine of a book, is to your left, and repeat the rolling and folding process as above, always keeping the dough and the work surface amply floured. When you have folded the dough into its double turn, brush off the excess flour. Wrap the dough in plastic and chill it again for about an hour. *(The dough can be made to this point and kept refrigerated for up to 48 hours. In fact, at this point, it is good to give the dough a rest of more than 3 hours.)*

4. The morning of the day that you are going to use the dough, or a short while before you need the dough, give it its last turn, a single turn. To do this, position the dough with the closed fold to your left and roll the dough out as before. This time, fold the dough like a business letter: Fold the bottom third of the dough up so that it covers the middle third of the dough and then fold the top third over so that it meets the edge of the already folded dough. (If your dough was in fact three times longer than it was wide, this fold should result in a square; if not, it will still be fine.) Brush off any excess flour. Wrap the dough well and chill it for at least 30 minutes before rolling it out to use in any recipe. If you can, it's best to give the dough a longer chill now, and then, after you've rolled the dough out for your recipe (you'll probably cut this large piece to divide it and roll out only a portion of it), let the rolled-out dough chill for about 30 minutes before cutting and baking. The best plan is to roll the dough out, transfer it to a baking sheet, cover, and chill it on the sheet, then, with the chilled dough still on the sheet, do the actual cutting.

Keeping

The refrigerator life of this dough is about 3 days from the time you make the mixtures to the time you use the dough for a dessert. You can roll and turn the dough and then wrap it and let it stay in the refrigerator for several hours rather than the minimum 1½ hours — it can be rolled around your schedule. Once the dough is made, it can be divided into portions, wrapped airtight, and kept in the freezer for up to a month. Thaw, still wrapped, in the refrigerator overnight before rolling out to cut and bake.

Crème Anglaise

Sometimes called English cream or pouring custard, crème anglaise is the accompaniment of choice for many cakes and tarts — try it with Warm Chocolate and Banana Tart (page 120) — and the base for the best ice creams. It is a flawlessly smooth and deliberately rich amalgam of egg yolks, cream, and whole milk. Don't even think about using a low-fat milk or cutting back on the heavy cream — you won't get the exquisite taste or texture with anything less than the richest ingredients.

Traditionally, crème anglaise is cooked and then quickly cooled over ice. However, by removing the cream from the heat and allowing it to "poach" in the pan a few minutes before cooling it, as you do in this recipe, you get a smoother cream. Similarly, refrigerating the cream for twenty-four hours before using it is just the ripening period that's needed to create a perfect osmosis between the eggs and the lactates in the milk. — P.H.

- 1 cup whole milk
- 1 cup heavy cream
- 2 plump, moist vanilla beans, split lengthwise and scraped (see page 281)
- 6 large egg yolks
- ½ cup sugar

1. In a small saucepan, bring the milk, cream, and vanilla beans (pulp and pods) to a boil over medium heat (or do this in the microwave oven). Cover the pan, remove from the heat, and allow the mixture to rest for 10 minutes, time enough for the liquids to be infused with the warm flavor of vanilla.

2. Fill a large bowl with ice cubes and set aside a small bowl that can hold the finished cream and be placed in this ice bath. Set aside a fine-meshed strainer too.

3. Put the yolks and sugar in a heavy-bottomed medium saucepan. Whisk them together until thick and pale, about 3 minutes. Whisking without stop, drizzle in the hot milk and cream. After about one third of the liquid has been added and the yolks are acclimated to the heat,

Makes about 2½ cups

add the liquid in a steadier stream. When all the liquid has been whisked into the yolks, remove and discard the pods (or save them for another use — see page 281), put the saucepan over medium heat, and, stirring constantly with a wooden spatula or spoon, cook the cream until it thickens slightly, lightens in color, and, most important, reaches 180°F, as measured on an instant-read thermometer — which will take less than 5 minutes. (Alternatively, you can stir the cream and then draw your finger down the spatula or the bowl of the wooden spoon — if the cream doesn't run into the track you've created, it's done.)

4. Immediately remove the saucepan from the heat and allow the cream to rest or "poach" until the temperature reaches 182°F — again, just a matter of minutes. Immediately strain the crème anglaise into the reserved small bowl and place the bowl into the ice bath (you can add some cold water to the cubes now). Keep the cream over ice, stirring occasionally, until it has cooled completely. When it is cold, cover it with plastic wrap, pressing the plastic against the custard's surface, and refrigerate for at least 24 hours before using.

Keeping
Covered tightly with plastic wrap pressed against its surface to create a seal, crème anglaise can be kept in the refrigerator for up to 3 days. Do not freeze this custard.

Vanilla Pastry Cream

Pastry cream, a crème anglaise (page 25) thickened with cornstarch and enriched with butter, is a good base for fillings like the featherweight Cognac cream in the Golden Pearl Brownie Cake (page 231) and the liqueur-scented nut cream in the Poached Pear and Walnut Tart (page 129), and a great all-purpose filling for fruit tarts — a fully baked crust, a thin layer of pastry cream, a topping of freshly glazed fruit, and you've got an infinitely variable classic dessert.

《 *I let the pastry cream cool before adding the butter, a small step that ensures that the cream doesn't separate and the butter doesn't lose its smooth texture. It also gives you a pastry cream with a better, more buttery taste.* 》 — P.H.

- 2 cups whole milk
- 1 plump, moist vanilla bean, split lengthwise and scraped (page 281)
- 6 large egg yolks
- ½ cup (slightly rounded) sugar
- ⅓ cup cornstarch, sifted
- 3½ tablespoons (1¾ ounces) unsalted butter, softened

1. In a small saucepan, bring the milk and vanilla bean (pulp and pod) to a boil over medium heat (or do this in the microwave oven). Cover the pan, remove from the heat, and allow the mixture to rest for 10 minutes, time enough for the liquids to be infused with the warm flavor of vanilla.

2. Fill a large bowl with ice cubes and set aside a small bowl that can hold the finished cream and be placed in this ice bath. Set aside a fine-meshed strainer too.

3. Whisk the yolks, sugar, and cornstarch together in a heavy-bottomed medium saucepan. Whisking all the while, very slowly drizzle a quarter of the hot milk into the yolks. Still whisking, add the rest of the liquid to the tempered yolks in a steady stream. Remove and discard the pod (or save it for another use — see page 281).

Makes about 2 cups

4. Place the saucepan over high heat and, whisking vigorously and without stop, bring the mixture to the boil. Keep at the boil, whisking energetically, for 1 to 2 minutes, then remove the pan from the heat and press the cream through the sieve into the reserved small bowl. Set the bowl in the ice bath (you can add some cold water to the cubes now) and, stirring frequently so that the mixture remains smooth, cool the cream to 140°F, as measured on an instant-read thermometer. Stir in the butter in three or four additions. Keep the cream over ice, stirring occasionally, until it is completely cool. The cream can be used now or refrigerated.

Keeping

*Covered tightly with plastic wrap
(press the plastic against the cream's
surface to create an airtight seal),
pastry cream can be refrigerated
for 2 days.*

Vanilla Buttercream

Smooth and satiny, rich and elegant, this classic cooked-syrup buttercream is indispensable as a filling and frosting (see the Tarte Tropézienne on page 201) and can be flavored in ways both subtle and intense. To use liqueurs and brandies to lend a light aroma and mellow taste to the basic vanilla buttercream, add about one third cup of Cognac, dark rum, Grand Marnier, or kirsch to the finished recipe (less, of course, if you're using just a portion of the batch). You can also flavor the buttercream with nut paste to produce a hazelnut, almond, or pistachio cream, or with a coffee syrup made by dissolving instant espresso in an equal amount of water. Because these flavorings are added after the vanilla buttercream has been whipped to perfection, you can always add them "to taste." See page 30 for instructions on how to make a chocolate buttercream.

« People think buttercream is heavy, but when it's properly made, when the butter is blended into the mixture very well, it's light on the palate. And, of course, buttercream must have butter — nothing else works. » — P.H.

- 3 cups sugar
- 1 cup water
- Pulp from 1 plump, moist vanilla bean (see page 281)
- 7 large egg yolks, at room temperature
- 4 sticks plus 2 tablespoons (17 ounces) unsalted butter, softened

I. Pour the water and sugar into a small saucepan and add the vanilla bean pulp. Bring the mixture to the boil, swirling the pan occasionally to help melt and mix the sugar. Wash down any splatters on the sides of the pan with a pastry brush dipped in cold water, and cook the syrup, without stirring, until it reaches 245°F, as measured on an instant-read or candy thermometer, 10 to 15 minutes.

Makes about 6 cups

2. While the sugar and water are cooking, place the yolks in the bowl of a stand mixer fitted with the whisk attachment. Beat just to break up the yolks.

3. When the sugar has reached 245°F, beat the yolks in the mixer at medium-high speed and slowly pour the sugar syrup into the bowl, trying to pour the syrup down the side of the bowl so that it doesn't get caught in the spinning whisk. (If it does splatter, just carry on. You won't have lost much syrup and it's better to leave it on the side of the bowl than to try to mix it into the eggs — you'll get lumps.) Once the syrup is incorporated, increase the mixer speed to high and continue beating until the mixture is completely cool, 10 to 15 minutes. (Poke your finger into the mixture — it should feel close to room temperature; touch the bottom of the bowl — it should feel cool too.)

4. While the eggs and syrup are cooling, put the butter in another mixing bowl and work it with a flexible rubber spatula until it is creamy, or work it until smooth by pushing it against a counter with the heel of your hand. (Whatever you do, don't allow the butter to melt or become oily and gooey.) When the eggs are absolutely cool, decrease the mixer speed to low and add the softened butter in about twelve additions. Once all the butter is incorporated, the mixture may look curdled — don't panic. Keep mixing on low speed and the cream will become smooth. (If it still looks curdled after about 5 minutes, you can give it a super-high-speed whir in the food processor.) The cream can be flavored now. If the cream is very soft, it should be chilled until it is spreadable. *(At this point, the buttercream can be packed airtight and stored in the refrigerator or freezer.)* Buttercream that has been chilled until firm will have to be beaten to bring it back to its satiny consistency (see directions below).

VARIATION

CHOCOLATE BUTTERCREAM

The best way to make chocolate buttercream is to do a little math. Measure out the amount of vanilla buttercream you need for your recipe and then weigh it. Figure out what 20 percent of the buttercream's weight is and melt that much bittersweet chocolate. Allow the chocolate to cool to 114°F and then whisk it gently into the finished buttercream. If you don't have a scale, you can always add melted bittersweet chocolate to taste.

Keeping

Buttercream can be wrapped airtight and kept in the refrigerator for 2 to 3 days or in the freezer for a month. To thaw, place it, still wrapped, in the refrigerator overnight. When you remove the buttercream from the refrigerator (whether or not it has been frozen), it will need to be whipped before you use it. Put the chilled buttercream in the mixer with the whisk attachment in place and beat at high speed until it returns to its original creamy consistency, a transformation that can take as long as 8 to 10 minutes to accomplish.

Lemon Cream

Although it contains the same ingredients as those used to make lemon curd, and is used in much the same way as curd, this cream's exquisite silky texture and true lemon flavor set it apart. Its splendid texture is achieved by cooling the cream significantly before adding the butter, and then giving the cream a high-speed finish in a blender. While it is sublime in crêpes (page 88), tarts (page 115), and desserts (pages 59 and 65), and stunning paired with chocolate mousse in the Riviera (page 215), just a spoonful spread on a piece of toast is a simple but special pleasure.

« *The crucial moment in this recipe is when you add the butter to the lemon cream — you must cool the cream to 140°F before adding the butter. (Indeed, butter should never be added to any mixture that's over 140°F.) If the cream is too hot and the butter melts too much, you won't get the smooth texture this lemon cream should have. Finally, it's the beating in the blender that helps to incorporate the butter thoroughly and make the cream airy.* » — P.H.

- 1 cup sugar
- Zest of 3 lemons — removed with a zester and finely chopped (see page 281)
- 4 large eggs
- ¾ cup freshly squeezed lemon juice (from 4 to 5 lemons)
- 2 sticks plus 5 tablespoons (10½ ounces) unsalted butter, cut into tablespoon-sized pieces, softened

1. Put a saucepan of water over heat and bring the water to the simmer. Place the sugar and lemon zest in a large metal bowl that can be fitted into the pan of simmering water. Off the heat, rub the sugar and zest together between your fingers until the sugar is moist, grainy, and very aromatic. Whisk in the eggs and then the lemon juice.

2. Fit the bowl into the pan of simmering water (making certain that the water doesn't touch the bottom of the bowl). Cook, stirring with the whisk, until the cream thickens and reaches 180°F, as measured on an instant-read thermometer. As you cook the cream, whisking all the

Makes 2½ to 3 cups

while to keep the eggs from overheating and scrambling, you'll see that at first the cream is light and foamy, then the bubbles get larger, and finally, as the cream starts to thicken, the whisk leaves tracks. Pay particular attention at this point — the tracks mean the cream is almost ready. Keep whisking, keep checking the temperature, and keep your patience — depending on how much water you've got simmering beneath the bowl, it could take as long as 10 minutes for the cream to reach 180°F.

3. Pull the cream from the heat as soon as it is cooked and strain it into the container of a blender or food processor, or into a clean bowl large enough in which to beat it with an immersion blender. Let the cream rest at room temperature, stirring occasionally, until it cools to 140°F, about 10 minutes.

4. Working with the blender on high speed, or using a food processor or immersion blender, beat the cream while adding the pieces of butter, about five at a time. Scrape down the sides of the container or bowl as needed. When all the butter has been incorporated, continue beating the cream for another 3 to 4 minutes — extra insurance for a light and perfectly smooth lemon cream. (Depending on your blender's power, you may need to adopt a beat-for-a-minute-wait-for-a-minute pattern to keep your machine from overheating. Check the manufacturer's instructions.)

Keeping

Lemon cream can be used as soon as it is finished or it can be packed airtight and refrigerated for up to 4 days or frozen for a month.

Twenty-Hour Apples

Slow cooking and equally slow cooling turn out deeply satisfying, soft, sweet, buttery apples. Although you start with a mound of fruit in the baking dish, you finish with a mere two inches or so of juicy *pommes confites*. Don't skimp on the ten-hour chill — it's as important as the ten-hour bake in giving you a perfect texture: apples so compacted they can be unmolded, yet so thoroughly "candied" that each thin slice is completely infused with butter, sugar, orange zest, and its own juice.

The measurements for this recipe are approximate, which is unusual in baking but appropriate here, where you brush the apples with butter and sprinkle them with sugar. A little more, a little less, no matter — these apples are foolproof.

I adapted this recipe from Edouard Nignon's L'Heptaméron des Gourmets, *a cookbook from the early twentieth century. It yields more than you'll need for any one recipe, but the cooking method works best with large quantities and extras aren't a problem. With a little cream, the apples make a simple dessert; with yogurt, they're nice for breakfast.* — P.H.

- 4 to 4½ pounds (about 8 to 10 large) apples, such as Golden Delicious, Fuji, Granny Smith, or other tart-sweet apples
- 4 to 6 tablespoons (2 to 3 ounces) unsalted butter, melted
- About ½ cup sugar
- Zest of 1 orange — removed with a zester (see page 281)

1. Position a rack in the center of the oven and preheat the oven to 175°F. (If your oven doesn't have markings for as low as 175°F, preheat it at its lowest setting.) Line a jelly-roll pan with parchment or aluminum foil (to facilitate cleanup), and butter an 8 by 8-inch baking dish (ovenproof glass or ceramic is ideal); set aside.
2. Peel the apples, cut them in half from stem to blossom end, and remove the core with a melon baller. Working with the apples cut side down, cut each half crosswise into very thin slices, about ¹⁄₁₆ inch thick; keep the slices in place to retain the form of each apple half.

Makes about 5 cups

Working with one half-apple at a time, press the apple between your palms to fan the slices; lay the slices in the pan. Continue fanning and arranging apple halves until you've covered the bottom of the pan. (If there are holes here and there, just fill them with apple slices. You want to get as even a layer as you can, but it doesn't make any difference if the apples are in a line, perpendicular to one another, or just helter-skelter.) Brush the layer generously with butter, sprinkle evenly with a thin layer of sugar, and toss on a few strands of orange zest. Continue making layers until you have used all the apples, at which point the ingredients may mound above the top of the pan.

3. Double-wrap the pan with plastic film, stretching the plastic around the pan, top and bottom, to make certain that it is well sealed. Prick the plastic on the top in 6 to 8 places with the point of a knife, and weight the top with a couple of ovenproof plates or bowls, taking care not to cover all of the air holes you've created. Nesting two soufflé dishes on top of the pan is a perfect arrangement — it's OK that a portion of the surface won't be weighted. Place the weighted pan on the lined jelly-roll pan and bake for 10 hours. (Don't be concerned — the oven temperature is so low there's no danger of the plastic wrap melting or burning.) Remove the apples from the oven to a cooling rack and, keeping the plastic wrap and weights in place, cool to room temperature.

4. Chill the apples, still wrapped and weighted, for at least 10 hours before using them. When you are ready to use the apples, unmold or spoon them from the pan.

Keeping
The apples can be kept wrapped airtight in the refrigerator for about 5 days.

Strawberry Juice

Vibrantly flavored and brilliantly colored, this translucent juice is not quite a syrup, not quite a sauce. Made by cooking sugar and fresh strawberries slowly over very low heat, the sweet crimson juice adds the essential flavor of strawberries to summery Strawberry-Rhubarb Soup (page 53 — double this recipe so you'll have enough), and shares top billing with blueberries in the luscious sauce for French Toast (page 45). And hold on to the cooked strawberries — they make a great addition to Strawberry Ice Cream (page 87). You can use this same technique to make raspberry or currant juice.

- **3 pints strawberries, hulled**
- **½ cup sugar**

1. Mix the strawberries and sugar together in a heatproof bowl that can be placed over a deep casserole to make a double boiler; cover the bowl tightly with plastic wrap. Set over the simmering water, making sure that the water doesn't touch the bottom of the bowl, and cook over low heat for 1 hour and 15 minutes, at which point the berries will be floating in liquid.

2. To obtain the juice, drain the berries in a rustproof mesh strainer over a large bowl. Leave the berries in the strainer over the bowl for about 2 hours, after which time whatever solids may have passed through the mesh will have settled to the bottom of the bowl. Pour off the translucent red juice and use it immediately, or store it in a tightly covered jar in the refrigerator. Discard any solids at the bottom of the bowl. Although it was the juice you were after, don't toss away the soft, sweet berries — they're an optional but delicious ingredient in Strawberry Ice Cream (page 87) and wonderful in yogurt or on breakfast cereal.

Keeping
The juice can be stored in the refrigerator in a tightly covered jar for 2 to 3 days. Packed airtight, it can be frozen for a month.

Makes about 1 cup

Chocolate Sauce

This sauce, satiny and not terribly sweet, is an important component of both the shiny Chocolate Glaze (opposite) and the mousse that layers the Autumn Meringue Cake (page 247), but it is wonderful on its own. Keep a jar in the refrigerator and serve it either warm, when it's pourable, or cold, when it's spoonable, over ice cream or plain cakes.

« I never use cocoa powder to make a chocolate sauce — it gives it a disagreeable dusty taste. » — P. H .

- 4½ ounces bittersweet chocolate (preferably Valrhona Guanaja), finely chopped
- 1 cup water
- ½ cup crème fraîche, homemade (page 272) or store-bought, or heavy cream
- ⅓ cup sugar

Place all the ingredients in a heavy-bottomed 2-quart saucepan and bring to the boil over medium heat, stirring constantly. Reduce the heat to low and simmer, stirring frequently, until the sauce thickens very slightly and coats the back of a spoon. It doesn't really thicken much, but it does really coat the spoon. You can use the draw-a-line test to check: Dip a wooden spoon into the sauce and draw your finger down the back of the spoon — if the sauce doesn't run into the track created by your finger, it's done. Be patient — this can take about 10 to 15 minutes and shouldn't be rushed. Use the sauce immediately, or allow it to cool; chill until needed.

Makes about 1½ cups

Keeping
The sauce will keep in a tightly sealed jar in the refrigerator for 2 weeks, or it can be packed airtight and frozen for 1 month.

Chocolate Glaze

Pierre's dark chocolate glaze maintains its sheen because it is heated, cooled before the butter is added, and then cooled even more before it's used, steps that trick the chocolate into believing it has been tempered.

So that you don't beat too much air into this glaze, add the chocolate little by little, always stirring in circles. Start with small circles in the center of the bowl and then slowly and gently enlarge the circles. You're creating an emulsion by working this way, just the way you would if you were making mayonnaise. — P.H.

37

- ⅓ cup heavy cream
- 3½ ounces bittersweet chocolate (preferably Valrhona Guanaja), very finely chopped
- 4 teaspoons unsalted butter, cut into 4 pieces, softened
- 7 tablespoons Chocolate Sauce (opposite), warm or at room temperature

1. In a small saucepan over medium heat, bring the heavy cream to a boil. Remove the saucepan from the heat and, little by little, add the chocolate, stirring the mixture gently with a spatula. Start at the center of the pan and stir slowly in a small circle. As you add more chocolate, continue to stir gently in a circular fashion, gradually increasing the size of the circle. Measure the temperature of the mixture with an instant-read thermometer: It should be 140°F. If it is too cool — as will often be the case — warm it in a microwave oven or scrape the mixture into a mixing bowl or the top of a double boiler and warm it over (not touching) simmering water; remove from the heat as soon as the mixture reaches 140°F. If it is too hot, let it cool to 140°F.

2. Stirring gently, blend in the butter and the chocolate sauce. Once again, take the temperature of the glaze: You're aiming for 95°F to 104°F, the temperature at which the glaze attains prime pourability. If the glaze is too cold, it can be warmed in a water bath or a microwave oven at a low setting. The glaze is now ready to use.

Keeping

The glaze can be made up to 3 days ahead and kept in a tightly covered jar in the refrigerator, then brought up to the proper spreading temperature in the top of a double boiler over *simmering water or in a microwave oven at a low setting. If you reheat the glaze, don't stir it a lot — working the glaze can dull its beautiful sheen.*

Makes about 1 cup

Transparent Glaze

All transparent glazes give tarts and cakes a polished finish, but this one actually gives them a spark of fresh flavor too.

- ½ cup sugar
- 1 package Oetker Clear Glaze for fresh fruit tarts or cakes (see Mail-Order Sources, page 282)
- 1¼ cups water
- Zest of ½ lemon — removed with a peeler or knife and cut into strips
- Zest of ½ orange — removed with a peeler or knife and cut into strips
- ½ plump, moist vanilla bean, split lengthwise and scraped (see page 281)
- 1 tablespoon freshly squeezed lemon juice
- 5 fresh mint leaves

1. Mix the sugar and glaze together in a small bowl and set aside. In a large deep casserole, heat the water, zests, and vanilla bean (pod and pulp) until just warm. The temperature should be 104°F, as measured on an instant-read thermometer. Remove the casserole from the heat and add the sugar and glaze mixture in a steady stream, stirring all the while. Return the pot to the heat and bring the mixture to the boil. Allow the glaze to boil for 2 to 3 minutes over low heat, stirring constantly with a wooden spoon. The glaze may bubble a lot — just keep stirring. Add the lemon juice and bring to a boil again. Remove the casserole from the heat, add the fresh mint, cover the pot, and let the mixture infuse for 15 minutes. Strain the glaze into a container and let it cool to room temperature.

2. The glaze can be used as soon as it cools, or it can be stored in the refrigerator or freezer. If the glaze has set (at which point it will mound and jiggle like Jell-O), liquefy it again by heating it in the microwave oven on low power. But take care — the glaze should never be heated above 104°F.

Makes about 1 cup

Keeping
The glaze can be stored airtight in the refrigerator for a week or the freezer for a month. If you're going to freeze the glaze, it's most convenient to freeze it in two portions.

Simple Syrup

A mix of sugar and water that's brought to the boil, then cooled, this syrup is the base for many sorbets and poaching preparations.

- ⅓ cup sugar
- 6 tablespoons cold water

Stir the sugar and water together in a heavy-bottomed saucepan, place over medium heat, and bring to the boil. As soon as the syrup comes to the boil, remove it from the heat. Cool to room temperature.

Keeping
The syrup can be used as soon as it cools, or it can be poured into a jar with a tight-fitting lid and stored in the refrigerator for several months.

Makes about ½ cup

Egg Wash

This simple glaze gives pastry a golden finish.

- 1 large egg
- 1 large egg yolk
- 1½ teaspoons sugar

Whisk the ingredients together in a small bowl until well blended.

Makes about ¼ cup

Keeping
The glaze can be kept tightly covered in the refrigerator for 2 days.

FRUITS, CREAMS, AND COOKIES

deep chocolate cream

with

RASPBERRY COULIS

Pierre calls this dessert *"crème onctueuse"* (creamy cream), but you're bound to call it the best chocolate pudding you've ever tasted. Unlike American chocolate pudding, which is usually made with cornstarch, this silky concoction is really a crème anglaise, really *onctueuse,* and really terrific.

Here, the pudding is served with a raspberry coulis, a sauce made by whirring berries and sugar together in the blender. This is a complete and wholly satisfying dessert, but Pierre suggests that if you have a little brioche (page 202) on hand, it's nice to toast some slices and serve them too. Then, ever unstoppable when it comes to pairing one good thing with another, Pierre goes on to suggest that perhaps you should sprinkle a nonstick pan with some sugar, put that leftover brioche in the pan, sprinkle the top of the brioche with a little more sugar, and then pop the whole thing into a 475°F oven and let it bake just until the brioche takes on some color and the sugar starts to caramelize. Normally made as a pastry chef's midmorning snack, it would be sensational with this dessert.

« *For many years I wasn't a fan of raspberry with chocolate. It wasn't until I discovered Manjari chocolate — very aromatic, a little acidic, and not too strong — that I discovered how good the combination can be.* **»** — P.H.

43

Makes 6 to 8 servings

the cream

- 9½ ounces bittersweet chocolate (preferably Valrhona Manjari), finely chopped
- 1⅔ cups whole milk
- 1½ cups heavy cream
- 5 large egg yolks
- ⅔ cup sugar

1. Put the chocolate in a bowl large enough to hold all of the ingredients; set aside. (If you have a mixing bowl with a spout, it would be perfect for this.) Bring the milk and heavy cream to a boil in a saucepan over medium heat or in a microwave oven.

2. While the liquids are coming to a boil, whisk the yolks and sugar together in a heavy-bottomed 2-quart saucepan until thick and slightly pale. Whisking without stop, slowly drizzle about one quarter of the hot liquid into the yolk mixture. When the yolks are acclimatized to the heat, add the remainder of the liquid in a steadier stream.

3. Place the saucepan over medium-high heat and, stirring energetically and constantly with a wooden spoon or spatula, cook the custard until it thickens slightly, lightens in color, and, most important, reaches 180°F, as measured on an instant-read thermometer —which will take less than 5 minutes. (Alternatively, you can stir the crème anglaise and then draw your finger down the bowl of the wooden spoon or spatula — if the cream doesn't run into the track you've created, it's done.) Remove the saucepan from the heat.

4. Strain half of the crème anglaise over the chocolate and, working with a small spatula, slowly stir it into the chocolate. Start by stirring in a small circle in the center of the bowl and then slowly work in increasingly larger concentric circles. Add half of the remaining crème anglaise through the strainer, stirring in the same fashion, and then add the remainder. Pour the cream into small cups or soup plates and chill for at least 2 hours; cover the cups once the chocolate cream has cooled. If you don't want the chocolate cream to form a skin, you can press a piece of plastic wrap against the top of the cream as soon as you pour it into the cups. *(The cream can be made up to 2 days ahead and kept covered in the refrigerator.)*

the coulis

- 1½ pints raspberries, plus extra for garnish
- ⅓ cup sugar, or more to taste

1. Place the raspberries and sugar in the container of a blender or food processor and whir until puréed. Taste, and blend in more sugar if you think it needs it. Press the coulis through a strainer. *(The coulis can be made a day ahead and kept covered in the refrigerator.)*

2. When you're ready to serve the cream, pour the coulis over and top each serving with a few fresh berries.

Keeping

Both the chocolate cream and the coulis can be made ahead and kept, wrapped airtight, in the refrigerator, but once the coulis is poured over the cream, the dessert should be served.

FRENCH TOAST
with *blueberry sauce*

In France, French toast is called *pain perdu*, or lost bread, since it is made from stale bread that would otherwise be "lost" to the table. Not surprisingly, the French use "French bread," or baguettes, for their toast, but you can use whatever bread is at hand — this is, indeed, memorable with cut-on-the-bias slices of baguette, but it's good with thick pieces of white or whole-grain bread, and out of this world made with hunks of brioche (page 202), challah, or other egg-rich bread. If you're serving the French toast for breakfast (something that's rarely done in France, where this is a traditional dessert), you can offer it with the all-American fixings, butter and maple syrup. But when the toast is taking a dessert turn, spoil everyone and make the Blueberry Sauce, a syrupy, sweet-and-tart sauce that's great with the French toast and just as welcome with pancakes, waffles, slices of pound cake (try it with a piece of Lemon Loaf Cake, page 163), or even a wedge of Lemon Tart (page 115). Happily, this recipe makes more than you'll need for the French toast.

For a change, serve the pain perdu *with caramelized chocolate mousse [page 68] — the combination is very, very, very delicious.* ❯❯ — P. H.

the sauce
- 2½ tablespoons sugar
- ¾ cup Strawberry Juice (page 35), at room temperature
- 2½ cups blueberries
- 2 tablespoons freshly squeezed lemon juice

Makes 6 servings

- Pinch of salt
- Freshly ground black pepper

To give the sauce its depth of flavor, the sugar needs to be caramelized. Working in a large heavy-bottomed skillet, preferably nonstick, caramelize the sugar bit by bit: Heat the pan over medium-high heat and then sprinkle about 2 teaspoons of the sugar into the center of the pan. Start stirring the sugar with a wooden spoon or spatula as soon as it begins to melt. When the sugar is completely melted, bubbly, and caramelized, add 2 teaspoons more sugar and cook, stirring constantly, until it, too, caramelizes. Repeat with two more additions of sugar, cooking until the sugar is a deep amber color — test the color by dropping a bit on a white plate. Still stirring, add the strawberry juice and bring the mixture to a full boil. (If the juice is cool, the mixture may seize and clump — just keep heating and stirring and it will even out.) Add the berries and cook for another 3 to 5 minutes, or until the berries pop and the sauce reduces and thickens. Add the lemon juice, salt, and 3 turns-of-the-peppermill's worth of black pepper; remove the pan from the heat. (The hint of heat you'll get from this small amount of pepper is delightful, particularly when the sauce is paired with the eggy French toast.) Spoon the sauce into a sauceboat, pitcher, or bowl, and set it aside while you make the toast.

46

the toast

- 4 large eggs
- ½ cup sugar
- 2 tablespoons whole milk
- 2 tablespoons orange flower water
- Pulp from 1 plump, moist vanilla bean (see page 281)
- Twelve 1-inch-thick slices of bread (if you're using a baguette, slice the bread on the bias)
- Butter for sautéing

I. In a large shallow bowl, whisk together the eggs, sugar, milk, orange flower water, and vanilla bean pulp. Add as many slices of bread to the bowl as will fit comfortably in a single layer and soak the bread on both sides until the slices are saturated.

2. Working in a large skillet, preferably one with a nonstick finish, melt 1 tablespoon butter over medium-high heat. When the bubbles subside, add the bread, adding only as many slices as will fit in a single layer. Sauté the bread until it is golden on both sides, adding more butter to the skillet as needed. Soak and cook the remaining bread. Serve the French toast immediately, passing the sauce.

Keeping

While the sauce can be made up to 2 weeks ahead and kept tightly covered in the refrigerator (it can be served at any temperature), the French toast is best served as soon as it comes out of the skillet. However, if you must hold the toast for a short time — no more than 10 minutes — place it on a baking sheet in a preheated 200°F oven and cover it loosely with foil.

GOURMAND*i*SE

The name is grand, but the dessert is simple, a cross between a treat for children and one for sophisticates. Its centerpiece is a mound of thinly sliced pineapple, surrounded by a chilled blend of small-pearl tapioca and coconut milk. Not really sweet and not really rich, the dessert falls into that rarely explored realm between refreshing and comforting. The coconut tapioca — its consistency like that of a bisque, its floating pearls just right for popping against the roof of your mouth — is mild, milky, soupy, and soothing, while the pineapple, glistening with bittersweet marmalade and spiked with lime zest, is all sparkle and zip. The dried pineapple rings are optional, but they're fun to make, a good addition to this dessert, and a tasty snack to keep in the cupboard.

This is one of my favorite desserts. I love the many relationships that play out between the flavors and the textures, and am happy when each spoonful is a mixture of crispy and creamy. — P.H.

the dried pineapple (optional)

- ¼ pineapple
- Confectioner's sugar

I. Peel the pineapple and cut 6 slices, core and all; ideally, the slices should be less than ⅛ inch thick. (If you have a meat slicer, you'll find it's perfect for getting a very thin slice of fruit.) Cut the core from each slice (this is easily done with a small cookie or biscuit cutter) and place

Makes 6 servings

the slices on a triple thickness of paper towels. Cover with three layers of paper towels and allow the pineapple to drain for an hour or two.

2. Preheat the oven to 200°F. Dust a nonstick baking sheet with a light coating of confectioner's sugar; have another baking sheet at hand.

3. Place the pineapple rounds on the baking sheet dusted with the confectioner's sugar, cover with the other baking sheet (it will serve as a weight), and bake for about 1 hour, with the oven door held slightly ajar with a wooden spoon, until the pineapple is dried. Cool on a rack and then store in an airtight tin. *(The pineapple can be made a few days ahead and kept in a tin at room temperature, safe from humidity. This same technique works for oranges, lemons, apples, and pears.)*

the tapioca

- 1 cup whole milk
- 2 tablespoons sugar
- Strip of orange zest
- 3 tablespoons small-pearl tapioca (not granulated or instant)
- ⅓ cup heavy cream, boiled (it can be hot or at room temperature)
- 1 cup unsweetened coconut milk, at room temperature

1. Bring the milk, sugar, and orange zest to a boil in a heavy-bottomed 2-quart saucepan. Stirring constantly, add the tapioca in a slow, steady stream. Reduce the heat to its lowest setting and cook the mixture, stirring frequently, for 20 to 25 minutes, or until the tapioca is soft and most of the liquid has been absorbed.

2. Add the boiled cream and coconut milk and, stirring constantly, cook over low heat for 3 minutes. Turn the tapioca out into a bowl, press a piece of plastic wrap against its surface, and cool to room temperature. When it is cool, wrap the tapioca airtight and refrigerate until thoroughly chilled, about 2 hours. *(The tapioca can be refrigerated for up to two days.)*

the fresh pineapple

- ¾ pineapple (the remainder of the pineapple, from above), peeled
- 2 tablespoons best-quality sweet orange marmalade
- Zest from 1½ limes — removed with a zester (see page 281)

Quarter the pineapple from top to bottom and cut away the core. Cut each quarter lengthwise into thin spears, then cut these long pieces crosswise into bite-sized spears. Blot the pineapple free of excess moisture with paper towels and put into a bowl. Add the marmalade and zest and toss until the mixture is well blended. Cover and chill for at least 1 hour or for as long as a day.

to assemble
- Red currants or pomegranate seeds, optional

For each serving, spoon about ½ cup of pineapple spears into a small cup or soufflé mold, pressing down on the mixture to pack it tightly. Unmold the fruit into the center of a soup plate (or a shallow bowl) and surround with about ⅓ cup of tapioca. Place a dried pineapple round on the fruit and garnish with currants or pomegranate seeds, if you're using them. Serve immediately.

51

Keeping
The dried pineapple can be made a few days ahead and stored in an air-tight tin, the tapioca can be refrigerated for up to 2 days, and the fresh pineapple can be prepared up to a day ahead, but once assembled, the dessert should be served immediately.

strawberry–rhubarb
SOUP

Cool, invigorating, and very beautiful, this rosy red soup, made by poaching rhubarb in a plastic bag filled with Strawberry Juice — a nifty process — is finished with dark red fruit, a scoop of pink strawberry ice cream, and a spoonful of pure white cream. Everything can be prepared ahead and stored for a few days, so you can put together the soup and its trimmings — the dessert equivalent of a thirst-quenching glass of pink lemonade — at a moment's notice.

《 *Strawberry and rhubarb are a remembrance of my childhood in Alsace, where the combination is very popular, particularly for jams. For this dessert, the combination is perfect because the fruit's acidity is its strong point — it makes the soup more refreshing.* 》 — P. H.

the soup

- 1 pound rhubarb (about 8 slender stalks without leaves)
- 2 cups (a double recipe) Strawberry Juice (page 35)
- ¼ cup sugar

1. Bring a large pot of water to a simmer.
2. Meanwhile, use a vegetable peeler to scrape the outer strings from the rhubarb (the way you would celery), and cut the stalks on the bias into slices about ½ inch thick. (If you want to have some longer stalks to finish each plate the way it's shown in the photograph on page 52, simply leave 12 to 18 pieces longer.) Pack the rhubarb into a large heavy-duty plastic bag, preferably a zipper-lock bag, add the strawberry juice and sugar, mix, and close the bag securely.

Makes 6 servings

3. Put the bag into the simmering water and poach the fruit for 20 minutes, never allowing the water to boil. Carefully lift the bag out of the water and, keeping the bag sealed, press a few pieces of rhubarb between your fingers. If the rhubarb is tender, it's ready; if it's not, give it a few more minutes. Transfer the bag to a rack and cool to room temperature, then chill overnight or for up to 3 days.

to assemble

- **1 pint strawberries, hulled and halved**
- **Sugar, if needed**
- **1 cup whipped cream, crème fraîche, homemade (see page 272) or store-bought, or sour cream**
- **Strawberry Ice Cream (page 87), optional**

Divide the pieces of poached rhubarb and the fresh strawberry halves among six soup plates. (If you do not have shallow soup plates, serve the soup in bowls.) Taste the soup and, if necessary, add sugar, then spoon it over the fruit. Finish each plate with a large scoop of cream and a smaller scoop (or quenelle) of strawberry ice cream, if you're using it. Serve immediately.

Keeping

The soup can be made up to 3 days ahead and kept refrigerated in its plastic poaching bag.

apricot PACKETS

You'll be amazed at what a heavenly dessert a couple of pounds of ripe apricots, a pinch of tea, ten minutes in the oven, and a whirred-in-the-blender sauce can produce. The apricots are tucked into aluminum foil or parchment packets — *papillotes* — with a few leaves of tea for aroma, a touch of pepper for spice, a sliver of butter for roundedness, and a spoonful of sugar to set the sweet-tart balance right, and then baked until the apricots soften, the juices bubble, and the scent of warm fruit fills the kitchen. Cut into a packet and the fragrance will make your head spin; add the ricotta sauce and you'll understand why people refer to apricots' "honey-sweetness"— the bit of honey in the creamy sauce is just enough to point up that quality in the fruit.

Be prepared: The sauce should be made as soon as the packets go into the oven.

«*Both the sauce and the method of cooking the fruit* en papillote *lend themselves to variation. The sauce is great over strawberries or any other fresh acidic fruit, and raspberries, peaches, and bananas are ideal for baking in a packet.* » — P.H.

the fruit
- 12 ripe apricots, pitted and cut into eighths
- 6 tablespoons freshly squeezed lemon juice, or to taste
- 6 tablespoons sugar
- 6 thin strands lemon zest — removed with a zester (see page 281)
- Earl Grey or apple tea

Makes 6 servings

- Freshly ground black pepper
- 2 tablespoons (1 ounce) unsalted butter

I. Center a rack in the oven and preheat the oven to 400°F. Cut six 12-inch squares of aluminum foil or parchment paper. (Parchment paper is pretty, but foil is easier to work with.)

2. Lay the squares out on a counter (if they're foil, they should be shiny side down). Place 16 apricot slices on each square, positioning the slices just below the center of the square. Sprinkle each packet's apricots with 1 tablespoon of the lemon juice (if the apricots are not dead-ripe and very sweet, use a little less lemon juice) and 1 tablespoon of the sugar and top with a strand of lemon zest. Sprinkle a pinch of tea and a pinch of pepper over each packet and finish each with 1 teaspoon of the butter. Fold the top of the foil or parchment over the packet until it almost meets the bottom and fold over the edges of the packet, then fold over the edges two or three times more — you need a tight seal that won't open under the pressure of the steam that develops when the package is heated. You should end up with packages roughly 5 by 7 inches — but precision isn't key here.

3. Place the packets on a baking sheet and bake for 10 to 12 minutes, or until they are puffed. Make the sauce while the packets are baking.

the sauce

- 1¼ cups ricotta (you can use part-skim)
- 1½ tablespoons honey
- 1½ tablespoons sugar
- 1 tablespoon orange flower water

Place all the ingredients in the container of a blender or food processor and whir until blended, about 30 to 45 seconds, scraping down the sides of the container as needed. The sauce should be velvety, thick, and smooth. Pour the sauce into a pitcher or sauceboat for serving.

to serve

You can serve the fruit in their packets — just place the packet on a plate and let each person slash his own — or you can transfer the fruit from each packet to a warm soup plate for serving. Pass the sauce and put everyone on guard — the fruit is tongue-searingly hot!

Keeping
Both the fruit and the sauce should be
served as soon as they're ready.

GOLDEN LEMON

FRUIT *LAYERS*

This dessert is a triple threat to the summertime blues: It's a bottom layer of fruit — corn niblets and cubes of pineapple and apple — both tart and sweet; a top layer of lemon cream lightened and enlivened with *fromage blanc* (or yogurt) and whipped cream; and a tropical coulis of strawberries and juice that will make you think of a frosty daiquiri. For an extra-special finish, top each serving with a paper-thin circle of white chocolate or a tuft of chocolate shavings.

« I had the idea to use corn in a dessert when I was in the United States and had the chance to taste different types of corn. It took me a long time to come up with the right dessert because I was searching for an interesting mix of tastes and textures. Finally, I hit on this dessert that matches corn's sweetness with the tangy flavors of lemon and pineapple and the crunch of apples. The lemon–fromage blanc cream and the fruit coulis continue the sweet-tart contrast. » — P.H.

the cream

- 1 teaspoon gelatin
- 2 tablespoons cold water
- $\frac{2}{3}$ cup *fromage blanc* or plain yogurt
- $2\frac{1}{2}$ tablespoons sugar
- 1 cup (packed) Lemon Cream (page 31)
- $\frac{2}{3}$ cup heavy cream, whipped to soft peaks

Makes 8 servings

1. Sprinkle the gelatin over the cold water and allow it to rest until softened. Heat the gelatin in the microwave oven for about 15 seconds, or cook over low heat, until the gelatin dissolves. Pour the gelatin into a bowl large enough to hold all the ingredients.

2. Stir a little of the *fromage blanc* or yogurt into the gelatin. Add the sugar and stir to blend, then mix in the rest of the *fromage blanc* or yogurt, followed by the lemon cream. Gently fold the whipped cream into the mixture. Cover and chill until set, about 1 hour. *(The cream can be made up to 1 day ahead and kept covered in the refrigerator.)*

the chocolate circles (optional)

- 6½ ounces best-quality white chocolate (preferably Valrhona Blanc Ivoire), finely chopped

1. To make the circles, the chocolate must first be tempered, then spread on a flat surface and cut to size. The best surface to use for spreading is a sheet of semistiff plastic or acetate, the kind used as report covers. It's available at stationery and artists' supply stores, and it's best to buy four sheets.

2. Melt 3½ ounces of the chocolate in a metal bowl over a small quantity of lightly simmering water (you want to melt this chocolate as gently as possible), making certain that the water doesn't touch the bottom of the bowl. When the chocolate is between 104°F and 114°F, as measured on an instant-read thermometer, stir in the remaining chocolate. As soon as the "new" chocolate is melted — this should take just seconds — remove the bowl from the saucepan of simmering water and allow the chocolate to cool to room temperature.

3. While the chocolate is cooling, set two sheets of plastic out on a counter (it's preferable to work with the chocolate on a "warm" surface — wood or plastic is better for this job than marble or stainless steel). Have a 4-inch round cutter — a dessert ring, biscuit cutter, or a cleaned-out tuna can (see facing page) — a long metal offset spatula, and the other two sheets of plastic ready.

4. Return the bowl of room-temperature chocolate to the saucepan of simmering water and heat the chocolate very gently until it reaches 86°F. Immediately remove the bowl from the heat, wipe the bottom of the bowl to avoid drips, and pour the chocolate out onto the two plastic sheets, quickly spreading it into a very thin, very even layer with the offset spatula. Again, working quickly, use the cutter to cut eight 4-inch circles from the chocolate — don't remove the circles or the excess chocolate, just cover the sheets of chocolate with the remaining sheets of plastic, carefully slide the set-ups onto one or two baking sheets, and chill the chocolate in the refrigerator until needed. *(The circles can be made up to 3 days ahead and kept covered in the refrigerator.)*

the coulis

- 1 pint strawberries, hulled
- ¼ cup sugar
- 3 tablespoons freshly squeezed lemon juice
- ¼ cup orange–passion fruit juice, optional
- ¼ cup guava nectar, optional
- Pinch of freshly ground black pepper

Put all the ingredients in the container of a blender or food processor and whir until puréed. (You can also purée the coulis with an immersion blender.) The purée will be very thin, especially if you've used the optional juices. Cover and chill until needed. *(You can keep the coulis in the refrigerator for about an hour; keep it longer, however, and it will lose its fresh, just-mixed flavor.)*

the fruit

- About ½ pineapple, peeled and cored
- 1 to 2 Granny Smith apples, peeled and cored
- 1½ cups canned or thawed frozen corn kernels

Cut the pineapple into cubes as small as you can make them. Measure out 1⅓ cups; reserve the remainder, if any, for another use. Cut the apple(s) into the same size cubes and measure out 1¾ cups; reserve the remainder, if any, for another use. Mix the fruits and corn together.

to assemble

- White chocolate circles (from above) or shavings, optional
- Whole strawberries, preferably with stems, optional

I. Set out eight dessert or soup plates and a 4-inch dessert ring. If you do not have a dessert ring, you can use a large (12-ounce) empty tuna fish can. Remove both ends of the can and wash and dry it thoroughly.

2. For each dessert, place the ring in the center of a soup plate and pack it about half-full with fruit cubes. Fill the ring with lemon cream, leveling the top with a spatula. Lift off the ring and, if you want, top the cream with a white chocolate circle or shavings and a strawberry. Surround the fruit and cream with the coulis and serve immediately. The coulis can be either drizzled sparingly or poured generously around the dessert.

Keeping
Each element of this dessert can be made ahead, but once assembled, the dessert should be served immediately.

61

CANDIED *citrus* PEEL

On its own, candied peel doesn't really make a dessert, but put it next to a cup of coffee or tea and the story changes. These are thick slices of citrus peel — choose grapefruit, orange, or lemon — that, after a leisurely simmer in a sweet, spiced syrup, are thoroughly candied and ready to be used in myriad ways. You can keep the peels in their syrup on hand to fold into applesauce, add to a cake batter, or finish a tart. Or you can dry them on a rack and toss them with sugar, the classic treatment for a classic treat. If you're feeling ambitious, dry the peels and dip them in tempered dark chocolate, preferably one that's not too bitter.

- 4 pink grapefruits, 5 oranges, or 6 lemons
- 4 cups water
- 2⅓ cups sugar
- ¼ cup freshly squeezed lemon juice
- 10 black peppercorns, bruised
- 1 star anise
- Pulp from 1 plump, moist vanilla bean (see page 281)
- Sugar for coating, optional

I. Put a large pot of water on to boil and have a colander ready. Working with a sharp knife, cut off a thin slice from the top and bottom of each fruit, then, cutting from top to bottom, cut wide bands of peel about 1 inch across, making certain that as you cut you include a sliver of

Makes about 12 servings

fruit as well with each one. Toss the slices of peel into the boiling water and allow them to boil for 2 minutes. Remove the peel from the water with a slotted spoon (don't pour out the water — you'll need it in a minute) and put it in the colander. Rinse the peel under cold running water for 2 minutes and then repeat the boiling and cooling process twice more. Set the peel aside for the moment.

2. Place all the remaining ingredients except the optional sugar for coating in a large casserole and bring to the boil. Add the peel, cover the pot, and adjust the heat so that the syrup simmers gently. Allow the peel to simmer, stirring occasionally, for 1½ hours, at which time the peel should be soft and completely candied. Remove the casserole from the heat and, with the cover still in place, allow the peel to macerate overnight.

3. The next day, pour the peel and its syrup into a canning jar and store it in the refrigerator, or lay the peel out on a rack to dry. Once the peel is dry, you can toss it in sugar to coat.

63

Keeping

The candied peel in its syrup can be kept in a tightly sealed jar in the refrigerator for 3 weeks. Dried peel tossed with sugar will keep in an airtight tin for about 4 days; chocolate-dipped peel should be eaten the day it is dipped.

FAUX *summer*

PUDDING

This is a somewhat more formal version of the Golden Lemon Fruit Layers (page 59), a not-quite-cricket play on a classic English summer pudding, and a winner no matter its lineage. From the bottom up what you'll relish is: a crunchy disk of sweet pastry dough; soft, sweet, citrus-spiked berries saturated with mint and vanilla syrup; a lightened rendition of Pierre's extraordinarily tangy-satiny-melty lemon cream; a crown of fresh berries; and, encircling it all, slices of toasted bread, the echo of summer pudding.

« A few years ago I had dinner with the chef of the Connaught in London. We ate in the kitchen and he served a summer pudding for dessert. I loved the pudding and it set me thinking about ways in which I could play around with its principles. The combination of sweet fruit and tart cream is untraditional for summer pudding, but it's a good one and it can stand alone — you can make this without the bread and/or the sweet pastry crust. Also, the size can be varied: This is as attractive as an individual plated dessert as it is made family-size. » — P.H.

the toast (optional)
- 10 slices soft white bread, crusts removed
- About 4 tablespoons (2 ounces) unsalted butter, melted

I. Center a rack in the oven and preheat the oven to 400°F. Brush the inside of an 8¾-inch/ 22-cm dessert ring with butter and place the ring on a large plate that has been covered with plastic wrap. You're going to put the syrupy fruit on the plate and it will drip, so it's best to choose a plate with a raised rim or to put the plate in a bowl or on a baking sheet.

Makes 8 servings

2. Trim the slices of bread so that they are just a little taller than the dessert ring and brush both sides of the bread with melted butter. Place the bread in a single layer on a baking sheet, preferably one with a nonstick finish, and bake just until the bread starts to take on some color — it shouldn't be too dark; turn and bake the other sides.

3. As soon as the bread comes out of the oven, press the slices against the inside of the dessert ring to create a circle of toast in which the edge of one slice of bread just touches the edge of its neighboring slice. Set aside until the fruit is ready.

the fruit

- 4 cups water
- 2 cups sugar
- $\frac{1}{4}$ cup freshly squeezed orange juice
- 1 plump, moist vanilla bean, split lengthwise and scraped (see page 281)
- 12 to 15 fresh mint leaves, stems removed
- $1\frac{1}{2}$ quarts mixed berries, primarily sliced hulled strawberries and whole raspberries, and a lesser amount of blueberries and blackberries

1. Bring the water, sugar, orange juice, and vanilla (pod and pulp) to a boil in a large saucepan, stirring the mixture to be certain the sugar dissolves. Remove the pan from the heat, add the mint leaves, cover the pan, and allow the syrup to infuse for 15 minutes. Strain the syrup and discard the mint leaves, then pour the syrup back into the saucepan and return it to the boil. Add the berries and boil for just 1 minute — you don't want to cook the berries and have them go mushy; you're aiming just to saturate them with syrup. Using a slotted spoon, transfer the berries to a strainer. (You can discard the syrup or save it for another maceration.)

2. When the berries are well drained, spoon them into the toast-lined dessert ring. Cover the ring with plastic wrap and refrigerate the setup for at least 6 hours, or, preferably, overnight.

the crust (optional)

- $\frac{1}{4}$ recipe Sweet Tart Dough (page 15), well chilled

1. Working on a well-floured surface, roll the dough into a round about $\frac{1}{8}$ inch thick. Trim the dough into a $9\frac{1}{2}$-inch circle and transfer it to a parchment-lined baking sheet. Prick the dough all over with the tines of a fork, cover with plastic wrap, and chill for at least 1 hour before baking.

2. Center a rack in the oven and preheat the oven to 350°F. Remove the plastic from the circle of dough and bake for about 18 to 20 minutes, until golden brown. Cool the crust to room

temperature and reserve until needed. *(The crust can be made ahead and kept at room temperature for up to 8 hours.)*

the cream

- 1 teaspoon gelatin
- 2 tablespoons cold water
- ⅔ cup *fromage blanc* or plain yogurt
- 2½ tablespoons sugar
- 1 cup (packed) Lemon Cream (page 31)
- ⅔ cup heavy cream, whipped to soft peaks

1. Sprinkle the gelatin over the cold water and allow it to rest until softened. Heat the gelatin in a microwave oven for about 15 seconds, or cook it over low heat, until it dissolves. Pour the gelatin into a bowl large enough to hold all the ingredients.
2. Stir a little of the *fromage blanc* or yogurt into the gelatin. Add the sugar and stir to blend, then mix in the rest of the *fromage blanc* or yogurt, followed by the lemon cream. Gently fold the whipped cream into the mixture. *(The cream can be made up to 1 day ahead and kept covered in the refrigerator.)*
3. Spoon the cream over the chilled fruit and spread the top smooth with an offset spatula. Cover the dessert ring loosely with plastic wrap and return it to the refrigerator for at least an hour to set the cream.

to assemble

- Mixed fresh berries

1. Remove the dessert from the refrigerator, tip the plate, and pour off any juices that may have accumulated.
2. Center the cooled pastry disk on a large serving plate. Now, working with courage and two large long metal spatulas, quickly lift the fruit-filled ring off its plate and onto the pastry disk. Once it's settled into place, carefully lift off the dessert ring (see page 272). Sometimes this can be messy, but if you don't get it just so, don't worry — the fruit is delightfully sticky and you can paste the dessert back together.
3. Finish the dessert with a topping of fresh berries. You can crown the entire top with a mass of berries or simply center a few berries on the lemon cream — the dessert will be both beautiful and delicious either way. Serve immediately.

Keeping

All of the dessert's components can (and most should) be made ahead, but once the fruit is placed on the pastry circle, it's best to *serve the dessert immediately or, at most, within an hour or two. If you're holding the assembled dessert, keep the dessert ring in place* *until serving time, and keep it in the refrigerator — this needs to be served well chilled.*

chocolate-caramel MOUSSE

with

CARAMEL PEARS

Chocolate and caramel, a celestial combination, are blended to cosmic perfection in this mousse. To get the just-right blend, make sure you cook the sugar to a deep color — one between dark amber and light mahogany. The caramel should not be bitter (as it would be if you let it get too dark), but it must be powerful enough to hold its own against the mousse's chocolate and whipped cream. Delicious as is, it is most special paired with slices of ripe, juicy pears cooked in a rich caramel sauce.

Once the sugar is caramelized for the mousse, it is blended with salted butter and whipped cream. I often add salt to caramel as well as to chocolate because it intensifies the best qualities of both flavors. And adding whipped cream rather than liquid cream is a truc *that keeps the caramelized sugar from bubbling over the pan.* — P. H.

the mousse

- 1½ cups heavy cream
- 3¾ ounces bittersweet chocolate (preferably Valrhona Noir Gastronomie), coarsely chopped
- 1 (scant) cup sugar
- 2½ tablespoons salted butter

I. Whip the cream until it holds soft-to-medium peaks. Spoon out a rounded ½ cup — you'll use this to liquefy the caramel — and keep both portions of whipped cream covered in the refrigerator until needed.

Makes 4 servings

2. Melt the chocolate in a microwave oven or in a bowl over simmering water. Set the chocolate aside to cool to 114°F, as measured on an instant-read thermometer.

3. Rinse a bowl with warm water, dry it well, and keep it in a warm place while you prepare the caramel. (You want the bowl to be warm so that when you pour in the caramel, it doesn't chill quickly and harden around the edges. Should it harden, it's not fatal — you can rewarm it over low heat.)

4. Working in a large heavy-bottomed skillet, preferably nonstick, caramelize the sugar bit by bit: Heat the pan over medium-high heat and then sprinkle about 2 tablespoons of the sugar into the center of the pan. Start stirring the sugar with a wooden spoon or spatula as soon as it begins to melt. When it is completely melted, bubbly, and caramelized, add 2 tablespoons more of the sugar, and cook, stirring constantly, until it, too, caramelizes. Repeat until all of the sugar has been caramelized and is a deep amber color; test the color by dropping a bit on a white plate. Reduce the heat to medium and, still stirring, add the butter and the reserved ½ cup whipped cream. Take care — even though you've whipped the cream, the mixture will still bubble. It also may seize and clump — just keep heating and stirring and it will even out. Bring the mixture to a boil again, then turn it into the warm bowl to cool to 114°F.

5. When the caramel and melted chocolate are both 114°F, delicately stir the chocolate into the caramel. Gradually and gently fold the remaining whipped cream into the mixture. (Start with about a quarter of the cream so its cold doesn't shock the caramel and chocolate.) Cover the bowl and refrigerate until the mousse is thoroughly chilled, about 2 hours. *(The mousse can be made up to 2 days ahead and kept covered and chilled.)*

the pears

- 4 ripe pears, cut into eighths and cored (peeling is optional)
- 1 tablespoon freshly squeezed lemon juice
- ¼ cup sugar
- 1½ tablespoons salted butter
- 2 tablespoons heavy cream
- Freshly ground black pepper

1. Toss the pears with the lemon juice to keep them from discoloring; reserve.

2. Working in a large heavy-bottomed skillet, preferably nonstick, caramelize the sugar bit by bit, as you did for the mousse. When the sugar is a deep amber, stir in the butter and then the cream. Let the caramel return to the boil before adding the pear slices. Cook the pears in the caramel for about 7 to 8 minutes, stirring frequently but gently, until the pears are caramel-coated and can be pierced with the tip of a knife. Remove the pan from the heat and pepper the pears lightly. The pears are ready to serve.

69

3. To serve, arrange eight slices of pear in a fan shape on each dessert plate and drizzle with caramel sauce, if any remains. Center three scoops of mousse on each plate and serve immediately. (You may have mousse left over.) If you want to shape the mousse into quenelles, dip two soup spoons into cold water, shake off the excess water, and dip one into the mousse to scoop up a generous spoonful; use the second spoon to smooth and round the top of the mousse in the first spoon and then to scrape it out of the spoon.

Keeping

The mousse can be kept covered in the refrigerator for about 2 days. While the caramelized pears are best served when they're just made, they can be prepared a day or two in advance, cooled to room temperature, covered, and refrigerated. When ready to serve, warm the pears and their sauce in a microwave oven at medium power. Take care not to overheat them — these are not meant to be served steaming hot.

prunes *in* SAUTERNES

With a bottle of prunes poached in Sauternes, a golden, honey-sweet wine, you'll never be without a dessert — or a gift — at the ready. Think of this when you're making your Christmas list or the next time you want to take something special to a friend.

« *This makes a good, homey dessert served in bowls with some crème anglaise poured over the prunes and their sauce. It's also delicious with ice cream — try spooning some over honey, caramel, or vanilla ice cream.* » — P.H.

- 1 bottle Sauternes
- 1/3 cup plus 2 tablespoons water
- 2 tablespoons plus 1 teaspoon honey
- 1½ tablespoons Cognac
- 2¼ pounds unpitted prunes

Pour the Sauternes, water, honey, and Cognac into a large casserole with a heavy bottom and bring to the boil. Add the prunes, lower the heat, and simmer, stirring frequently, for 5 minutes. Remove the casserole from the range and turn the prunes and sauce into a heatproof jar — a canning jar with a wide mouth would be good. Cool to room temperature, then cover and store in the refrigerator. The prunes and their sauce should be served well chilled.

Keeping
The prunes can be kept in a tightly sealed jar in the refrigerator for up to 3 weeks.

Makes 6 to 8 servings

71

TEA–FLAVORED

crème brûlée

Crème brûlée has captured America's culinary heart and held its affection so completely that, at times, it's hard to remember that it is, as its name declares, a French specialty. Part nursery treat, part top-of-the-trend sweet, crème brûlée is a simple baked custard, the crème, topped with a crackly coating of burnt sugar, the brûlée. This version is given a new twist — an infusion of tea, which lifts the rich, creamy dessert from the familiar to the fabulous — and an accompaniment of warm cooked-in-butter-and-sugar apricots. Although the crème is topped with light brown sugar and brûléed with a blowtorch (see page 267), this caramelization is optional.

The dessert should be made in small ovenproof *coupes,* gratins, ramekins, or soup plates that hold about three quarters of an inch of custard; thus, the number of servings you get from this recipe depends on the capacity of your ramekins.

« *It's a pleasure to have the creaminess of crème brûlée matched with the bitterness of the tea and the acidity — and aggressiveness — of the apricots. I use apple tea, but you can use Earl Grey and still retain the combination's intrigue.* **»** — P.H.

the custard
- 3¾ cups whole milk
- 1 tablespoon loose apple or Earl Grey tea
- 8 large egg yolks
- ⅔ cup sugar
- ⅔ cup heavy cream

Makes about 12 servings
(see recipe headnote)

1. Center a rack in the oven and preheat the oven to about 210°F.
2. Bring the milk to a boil in a medium saucepan or in a microwave oven. Stir in the loose tea, remove the milk from the heat, cover it, and allow it to infuse for 4 minutes. Strain the milk into a heatproof pitcher, and discard the tea leaves. In a mixing bowl, preferably one with a spout, whisk together the yolks, sugar, and heavy cream, beating to blend the ingredients but not to incorporate air. Whisking constantly, drizzle in about one quarter of the milk. When the yolks are acclimatized to the heat, add the rest of the milk in a steady stream.
3. Pour the custard into shallow ovenproof gratins, ramekins, or soup plates, making sure that the cream is not poured to a depth greater than ¾ inch; slip the dishes into the oven. (This is done most easily if you put the dishes on a baking sheet.) Bake the custards for about 45 minutes, or until a knife inserted in the center of the custard comes out clean. Transfer to a rack and cool to room temperature. Chill the custards for at least 2 hours before caramelizing the tops. (The custard can be made up to 2 days ahead and kept covered and chilled.)

the caramelization
- Light brown sugar, pushed through a strainer

1. Sprinkle a thin coating of light brown sugar over each chilled custard. (Do not use dark brown sugar — it burns before it caramelizes.) Using a blowtorch, caramelize the sugar a patch at a time. You should have a crispy, crackly topping. Once caramelized, the crème brûlée should be served quickly, so set to work on the apricots immediately.

the apricots
- 2 tablespoons (1 ounce) unsalted butter
- ¼ cup sugar
- 12 ripe apricots, pitted and cut into quarters
- Pulp from ½ plump, moist vanilla bean (see page 281)
- 2 tablespoons freshly squeezed lemon juice

1. Melt the butter in a large sauté pan, preferably one with a nonstick finish. Add the sugar, apricots, and vanilla bean and cook, stirring, over very high heat until the apricots are glazed with sugar and butter, about 3 to 4 minutes. Add the lemon juice and remove the pan from the heat. The apricots should be served immediately.
2. Spoon the hot sautéed apricots over the cold crème brûlée and serve.

Keeping

The crème brûlée, without its caramelized sugar topping, can be made up to 2 days ahead and kept tightly covered in the refrigerator.

Once caramelized, it should be served within a few minutes. The apricots should be served as soon as they're cooked.

salted, peppered, and sugared

PINEAPPLE CARPACCIO

with **lime sorbet**

This is a typical Hermé dessert — simple, surprising, and sublime. It is nothing more than thin slices of pineapple (think pineapple carpaccio) covered with a frothy pineapple purée that's sprinkled with the fruit's most complementary accents, salt, pepper, and sugar, and topped with a scoop of bracing lime sorbet. It's proof that the whole is greater — and in this case, more delectable — than the sum of its parts.

It was the foam on top of the just-puréed pineapple that gave me the idea of sprinkling it with sugar. Sprinkling the sugar over the foam changed the texture and so, in what seemed like a natural idea at the time, I added salt and pepper and it created a thin crust, which I find very pleasing. — P. H .

the sorbet
- $2/3$ cup water
- $2/3$ cup sugar
- $2/3$ cup freshly squeezed lime juice (from 5 to 6 limes)
- $2/3$ cup whole milk
- Finely grated zest of $1/2$ lime

I. If you want to be able to keep the sorbet in the freezer for a few days and have it maintain its smooth texture, stir the water and sugar together in a medium saucepan and bring the mixture just to the boil to make a simple syrup; remove from the heat and cool to room temper-

Makes 6 servings

ature. If you plan to use the sorbet within a day of making it, there's no need to boil the water and sugar into a syrup.

2. Whisk all the ingredients together, or whir them in a blender, and then transfer them to an ice cream maker; freeze, following the manufacturer's directions. Pack the sorbet into a freezer container and store in the freezer until needed. *(If you've used a sugar syrup, the sorbet will keep in the freezer for about a week. If you've just blended the ingredients, count on it keeping its texture for about 2 days.)*

the pineapple

- 1 pineapple, peeled
- 3 tablespoons unsweetened coconut milk
- Sugar, preferably crystal
- Salt, preferably fleur de sel or coarse salt crushed using a mortar and pestle
- Freshly ground black pepper, preferably Sarawak

1. Halve the pineapple from blossom to stem and remove the core. Cut one half of the pineapple into slices that are as thin as you can make them; if you have a meat slicer, put it to use slicing the fruit. Divide the slices among six large dinner plates, arranging them in a single layer on each plate. *(If you are not ready to serve the dessert immediately, you can press a piece of plastic wrap against the pineapple on each plate and chill the plates for up to 4 hours before serving.)*

2. At serving time, cut the remaining pineapple into chunks and place the chunks and the coconut milk in the container of a blender or food processor. (Alternatively, you can put the ingredients in a deep bowl or container and use an immersion blender.) Purée the mixture, blending until it is smooth and very bubbly. Quickly pour some of the purée over each of the "carpaccios." Sprinkle each plate with a couple of teaspoons of sugar, a pinch of salt, and a little black pepper. Place a scoop of lime sorbet in the center of each plate and serve immediately.

Keeping
Although the sorbet can be made ahead and, if necessary, the pineapple carpaccio can be plated a few hours in advance, the purée should be made at serving time and the whole dessert put together pronto.

grapefruit fans

and

FRESH MINT GRANITÉ

If refreshing had a taste, this would be it. It has the same effect on your palate that a splash of cool spring water has on your skin — it's a tonic. Simple to the point of spare, this dessert is made up of chilled slices of pink grapefruit drizzled with port and topped with a mouth-tingling mint granité.

Granité, or *granita* as it's called in Italy, is a frozen dessert, a cousin of sorbet and sherbet, although it has neither milk nor cream and doesn't need to be churned in an ice cream maker. For this granité, a minty sugar syrup is frozen to a slush, whisked, and then frozen again until solid. At serving time, it's scraped out of its pan with the point of a spoon, the scraping forming little grains of ice that, because they are so deeply infused with mint, pop with flavor as they melt in your mouth. You can think of this granité as the best snow cone you'll ever have.

« *The idea for this grew out of a grapefruit and mint salad I used to serve. I liked the flavors but wanted another texture and the ability to serve the dessert on a plate. The granité gave me the texture, and the change from grapefruit chunks to segments made it platable.* » — P.H.

the granité
- 3 cups water
- ⅔ cup sugar
- 1¼ cups (loosely packed) fresh mint leaves

Makes 6 servings

1. Bring the water and sugar to a boil in a 2-quart saucepan. Immediately remove the pan from the heat and add 1 cup of the mint leaves. Cover the pan and allow the syrup to infuse for 15 minutes. Strain the syrup (discard the leaves) and let it cool to room temperature.

2. Pour the mint syrup into a shallow metal pan — an 8 by 8-inch cake pan is fine — and freeze it for about 2 hours, or until it is thick and slushy. While the syrup is freezing, cut the remaining ¼ cup mint leaves into chiffonade, or thin strands.

3. When the syrup is slushy, remove the pan from the freezer and whisk the granité for a minute or so — it will become liquid again. Whisk in the cut mint and return the pan to the freezer until the granité is frozen solid. *(You can make the granité ahead and keep it covered in the freezer for up to 3 days.)*

the grapefruit
- 6 pink grapefruits

Using a sharp knife, peel the grapefruits down to the fruit, making sure to remove every trace of white cottony pith. Slice between the membranes to release the segments of fruit, then chill the segments until you're ready to serve them. This dessert is best if the fruit is very cold.

to serve
- ¼ cup (loosely packed) fresh mint leaves, cut into chiffonade
- Port

Divide the grapefruit segments among six plates, arranging them in a fan in the center of each plate. Strew the mint leaves over the fruit, and drizzle over a little port. When the plates are arranged, pull the granité out of the freezer and, using the tip of a spoon or the tines of a fork, scrape up enough granité to form a small scoop for each portion. Put the granité on top of the grapefruit and rush the plates to the table — granité, like snowflakes, melts quickly.

Keeping
The granité can be made ahead,
and the grapefruit, which needs to be
well chilled, can be cut ahead, but
once assembled, this dessert has to
be served immediately.

bittersweet CHOCOLATE *sorbet*

Just churned and chilled, this has a creaminess as rewarding as ice cream and a flavor as fulfilling as any "decadent" chocolate dessert.

Using chocolate, not cocoa powder, is the key to making a sorbet that has a true chocolate taste. If you want a special treat, serve the sorbet with warm sautéed raspberries. Melt 2 tablespoons of butter with 2 tablespoons of sugar in a skillet and when the mixture colors lightly, add the raspberries — just stir to warm the berries and coat them with the butter and sugar. — P. H.

- 7 ounces bittersweet chocolate (preferably Valrhona Guanaja), finely chopped
- 1 (scant) cup sugar
- 2 cups water

1. Fill a large bowl with ice cubes and set aside a small bowl that can hold the finished mixture and be placed in this ice bath.

2. Put all the ingredients in a heavy-bottomed 2-quart saucepan over low heat. Cook, stirring frequently, until the mixture reaches the boil — this can take 10 minutes or more. Then stir without stop and pay attention: This bubbles furiously. Keep the mixture at the boil for 2 minutes, then pour it into the smaller bowl. Set the bowl into the larger bowl and add cold water to the ice cubes. Allow the mixture to chill, stirring now and then.

3. Freeze in an ice cream maker, following the manufacturer's instructions. Serve the sorbet directly from the ice cream maker or pack it airtight and freeze until needed.

Keeping
While best eaten within a few hours of churning, if packed airtight, the sorbet will keep its smooth texture for up to a week in the freezer.

Makes a generous 1 pint

BASMATI RICE *and*
fruits-of-the-moment SALAD

This is a dessert for all seasons and any reason. As the name suggests, you can use whatever fruits are available in the market (or your refrigerator bin) and the dessert is as right after a light warm-weather lunch as it is following a hearty winter meal. Composed of equal parts cooked basmati rice and cubed fresh fruit, the salad is moistened with a sprightly syrup and strewn with a chiffonade of deep green basil leaves. If you're not accustomed to using herbs in desserts (it's not a new idea, but it is one that the French have embraced recently with great enthusiasm and élan), this is the place to take your first step. You'll love the boost the small amount of licoricey basil delivers — it acts like a cheering squad for the fruit.

The salad is best with imported basmati rice (the American basmati rice from Texas is not a good substitute, as it's too sticky), but if you cannot find it, don't deny yourself the pleasures of this dessert — make it with another long-grain rice.

« The choice of fruits is not important in this dessert — you can make a really good salad with almost any mix of fruits. What matters most is that you have equal amounts of rice and fruit. It's also important that the rice isn't overcooked, so that you maintain a nice contrast between it and the fruit. » — P. H.

the syrup
- 1½ cups water
- ½ cup sugar

Makes 6 servings

- Zest of ⅓ orange — removed with a peeler or knife and cut into broad strips
- Zest of ⅓ lemon — removed with a peeler or knife and cut into broad strips
- 3 quarter-sized pieces peeled fresh ginger
- ⅓ plump, moist vanilla bean, split lengthwise and scraped (see page 281)
- 3 fresh basil leaves
- ⅓ cup plus 1 tablespoon apricot nectar
- 3 tablespoons freshly squeezed lemon juice

Bring the water, sugar, zests, ginger, and vanilla bean (pulp and pod) to a boil in a 2-quart saucepan. Remove the pan from the heat, add the basil, cover, and let steep for 30 minutes. Strain the syrup into a jar (discard the solids) and stir in the apricot nectar and lemon juice. Cool the syrup to room temperature, then cover the jar and refrigerate until the syrup is thoroughly chilled. *(The syrup can be made up to 5 days ahead and kept refrigerated.)*

the rice

- 1¼ cups imported basmati rice
- 4¾ cups water
- 2½ tablespoons sugar
- ½ teaspoon salt

1. Place the rice in a colander or strainer and rinse it under cool running water until the water runs clear. (This washes away the excess starch in the rice and ensures that the grains will stay separate after cooking.)

2. Using a saucepan that has a capacity of at least 2 quarts, bring the water, sugar, and salt to a boil. Add the rice, stir to mix, and bring the mixture back to the boil. With the heat at medium so that the mixture boils lightly, cook the rice, uncovered, for 10 to 13 minutes, or until it is cooked through but still pleasantly firm under your teeth. Pour the rice into a colander or strainer and rinse it under cold water to cool it quickly. Drain the rice very well, then pack it into a covered container and chill for at least 2 hours, or until needed. *(The rice can be made up to 2 days ahead and kept covered airtight in the refrigerator.)*

the fruit

You need about 4 cups of fresh fruit cut into cubes or chunks about ¼ inch on a side. The following is just an example of a mix of fruits. Feel free to use your favorites or whatever happen to be the "fruits of the moment" chez-vous.

- 2 apricots, pitted and cubed
- 1 peach, peeled, pitted, and cubed
- 1 kiwi, peeled and cubed
- 1 green apple, peeled, cored, and cubed
- 1 chunk of pineapple, peeled, cored, and cubed
- ½ mango, peeled and cubed
- ½ papaya, peeled, seeded, and cubed
- 1 passion fruit, cut in half and its fruit scooped out
- 1 small banana, cubed and tossed with lemon juice
- Small berries or sliced berries

Place the fruit in a large serving bowl. (The fruit can be used now or kept covered in the refrigerator for up to 2 hours.)

to assemble

- Juice of 1 lemon
- About 2 tablespoons sugar
- Freshly ground black pepper, preferably Sarawak
- 4 fresh basil leaves, cut into thin strips (chiffonade)
- Berries for decoration, optional

Add the rice to the fruit and delicately fold the ingredients together. Gently stir in the lemon juice, sugar (as needed), pepper, and basil leaves. Pour the chilled syrup evenly over the salad and stir once or twice with a light hand. Decorate with the berries, if you're using them, and serve immediately, spooning individual servings into dessert *coupes* or bowls at the table. Alternatively, you can arrange the salad in individual *coupes* in the kitchen and decorate each portion before serving.

Keeping
You can make each element ahead, but once combined, the salad should be served as soon as possible.

83

crème brûlée
ice cream

Everything that's seductive about crème brûlée is frozen into this phenomenally rich, impossibly velvety ice cream. It's a dessert for which hyperbolic description can only be considered understatement.

The inspiration for this dessert is, obviously, the classic crème brûlée that's become a staple on restaurant menus here and abroad; it's the execution that's brilliant. The base of this ice cream is made like a classic crème brûlée: You bake a mixture of milk, cream, and eggs, infused with the perfume and flavor of vanilla, in a slow oven until it becomes a just-set custard. (It's made exactly the same way as the Tea Flavored Crème Brûlée on page 73.) And then — here's the brilliant part — you whir the cooled custard in a blender until it returns to its liquid state, strain it, and freeze it in an ice cream maker. The brûlée, a soft, pourable caramel, is swirled or layered into the ice cream once it's churned. You can serve the ice cream with a good cookie, but it stands on its own exceedingly well.

《 *Even if the composition of this ice cream is the same as that for vanilla ice cream — and it is — the taste for me is completely different. Because the custard that forms the base is baked in the oven (not cooked on the stovetop as it would be for a crème anglaise, the usual ice cream base), the taste is dramatically different.* 》 — P.H.

the custard
- 2¼ cups whole milk
- 2 cups heavy cream

Makes about 1½ quarts

- 5 plump, moist vanilla beans, split lengthwise and scraped (see page 281)
- 10 large egg yolks
- 1 cup plus 2 tablespoons sugar

1. Bring the milk, cream, and vanilla beans (pulp and pods) to a boil in a 2-quart saucepan. Remove the pan from the heat, cover, and set the mixture aside for 1 hour.

2. Center a rack in the oven and preheat the oven to 210°F, or as close to that temperature as you can get — 200°F or 225°F will still be fine. Set aside two 11 by 7 by 2-inch pans. (The pan size here is not crucial — what's important is to use a pan or pans in which, when you add the custard, the mixture will form a layer that's only ¾ inch thick.)

3. In a large mixing bowl, whisk the yolks and sugar together until the mixture thickens slightly. Slowly strain the vanilla-infused liquid over the yolks, whisking to blend the ingredients but taking care not to beat in lots of air. Discard the vanilla bean pods or wash, dry, and reserve them for another use (see page 281).

4. Pour the mixture into the pans and slide them into the oven. Bake for about 45 minutes, or until the custard is just set, at which point it will still shimmy when shifted but a knife inserted in it will come out clean. Transfer the pans to cooling racks and allow the custard to cool to room temperature, then refrigerate the custard for 2 hours, or until thoroughly chilled. (If you're in a hurry, you can proceed with the recipe when the custard reaches room temperature. You'll save chill time but need more churn time.)

the caramel

- ⅓ cup plus 1½ tablespoons sugar
- 4 teaspoons salted butter, softened
- ⅓ cup heavy cream

Working in a deep saucepan (such as a heavy-bottomed 2-quart saucepan), caramelize the sugar: Place the pan over medium heat. Sprinkle about 2 tablespoons of the sugar over the center of the pan and when the sugar starts to melt and color, stir it with a wooden spoon. When all the sugar is caramel colored, add another 2 tablespoons of sugar and cook and stir as before. Continue until all of the sugar is cooked and the caramel is a deep mahogany color — test the color by dropping a bit on a white plate. (For this recipe, you want to cook the sugar to the max, stopping just before it turns bitter.) Standing away from the pan, stir in the butter. Then, still standing back, add the heavy cream. Don't be alarmed if the caramel erupts in big bubbles — it's normal. (You can avoid this by whipping the cream before adding it to the hot sugar, but if your pan is deep enough and you stand away from it, the bubbling is harmless.) Stir the caramel until well blended and smooth. Remove the pan from the heat and pour the caramel into a heatproof container; a glass measuring cup with a spout is perfect. Set aside at room temperature until needed.

to finish

1. Pour the chilled custard into the container of a blender (or use a food processor or immersion blender) and whir until the cream is smooth and once again liquid. Freeze the mixture in an ice cream maker, following the manufacturer's directions. Remove the ice cream from the machine, pack it into a freezer container, and place it in the freezer for about 30 minutes to an hour before proceeding. (You can freeze the ice cream longer, but it's easier to mix with the caramel when it's still in the soft-freeze stage.)

2. To turn the crème into crème brûlée, you can add the caramel in one of two ways. The most elegant way to combine the two elements and prepare the ice cream for serving is to layer the ice cream and caramel in a terrine. (See Step 3 for the second way of adding the caramel to the ice cream.) If you have a metal terrine made especially for ice cream, one with a lid, use it; if not, a 9 by 5-inch loaf pan will be fine. Line the bottom of the terrine with a layer of ice cream — don't worry about getting a smooth layer — then drizzle a layer of caramel over the cream. Continue in this way until the terrine is filled; aim for about four layers of ice cream and three of caramel. Cover the terrine tightly with its lid or a double layer of plastic wrap and store in the freezer until set. To serve, you can either scoop or slice. If you decide to scoop the ice cream out of the terrine, dig into the terrine so that each scoop has both ice cream and caramel. If you're going to slice the terrine, it's best to unmold it first. Dip the terrine briefly into a basin of hot water, then turn it out onto a serving plate and cut into slices.

3. Alternatively, you can swirl the caramel into the ice cream in a large mixing bowl. Spoon about a quarter of the ice cream into the bowl, drizzle over about a third of the caramel, add more ice cream, and then add more caramel; continue in this fashion until all the ingredients are used. Now, using a large, sturdy rubber spatula or metal serving spoon, fold the caramel into the ice cream. Don't be too thorough — you want the ice cream to be swirled with caramel. (If you end up incorporating the caramel evenly throughout the ice cream, you'll produce the world's best caramel ice cream — not a hardship.) Pack the ice cream into a freezer container, seal tightly, and store in the freezer until set.

Keeping
The ice cream can be kept in the
freezer for about 1 week.

strawberry
ICE CREAM

Summer-fresh pink strawberry ice cream that's great on its own, super in a sundae, and ideal with Strawberry-Rhubarb Soup (page 53).

When I was growing up, sorbets were rare. We ate ice cream, and strawberry ice cream was something my father made regularly. I associate sorbets with coolness and ice cream with creaminess. This ice cream is certainly creamy and it has a good concentration of strawberry flavor. — P.H.

- 1 pint strawberries, hulled
- 1 cup Crème Anglaise (page 25)
- ½ cup strawberries left over from Strawberry Juice (page 35), coarsely chopped, optional

Purée the fresh strawberries in a blender or food processor and then, if the little seeds that remain aren't to your liking, press the purée through a strainer. Stir the purée and the crème anglaise together and freeze in an ice cream maker, following the manufacturer's directions. A minute or two before the ice cream is ready, add the chopped strawberries, if you're using them. You can serve the ice cream straight from the machine (it will be very soft but very delicious), or pack it into an airtight container and freeze it until needed.

Keeping
The ice cream can be packed airtight and frozen for a week. Allow it to soften slightly before serving.

Makes about 1 pint

LEMON *crêpes*

These may look like crêpes as you've known them, but there's nothing familiar about the bright addition of orange juice, rum, and Grand Marnier; the lemon cream filling, notably silky and tart, tart, tart; and the sauce, a blend of butter and honey, sweet orange, and sharp lemon in perfect equilibrium. And then there's the unexpected smattering of toasted hazelnuts, just the ticket for crunch. This is a thoroughly original — and winning — new reading of a classic.

The crêpe batter needs to rest in the refrigerator for several hours, or, preferably overnight, so keep this in mind when you're thinking about a game plan. You'd do well to make the crêpe batter, lemon cream, and toasted nuts a day ahead. You can even cook the crêpes and the sauce (a quick affair) ahead and reheat them at serving time.

《 *For a simpler dessert, you can replace the lemon cream filling with lemon marmalade. Brushed with jam, rolled, and sauced, these crêpes become a very traditional dessert.* 》 — P. H.

the crêpes

- 1⅓ cups whole milk (maybe a bit more), at room temperature
- 2 tablespoons sugar
- 2 large eggs, at room temperature
- 1 large egg yolk, at room temperature
- 2 teaspoons Grand Marnier
- 2 teaspoons rum

Makes 8 servings

- Grated zest of ⅓ orange
- 2 teaspoons freshly squeezed orange juice
- 3 tablespoons corn oil, plus oil for cooking crêpes
- 3 tablespoons brown butter (see page 267)
- ¾ cup plus 1½ tablespoons all-purpose flour, sifted
- Sugar for sprinkling

1. Put the milk, sugar, eggs, yolk, Grand Marnier, rum, orange zest, and juice in the container of a blender or food processor. Whir to blend well. Add the oil and then the butter, processing until blended. Finally, add the flour and process just until the flour is incorporated — don't overmix the batter. Pour the batter into a pitcher or other container with a pouring spout (a Pyrex measuring cup is ideal), cover, and chill overnight. *(The crêpe batter can be kept covered in the refrigerator for up to 1 day.)*

2. When you are ready to cook the crêpes, whisk the batter gently just to blend the ingredients. If the batter is too thick — it should pour easily and have a consistency a bit thicker than that of heavy cream — add a little more milk a drop at a time.

3. Rub a seasoned or nonstick 7½-inch crêpe pan with a thin film of oil (apply the oil with a crumpled paper towel), then place the pan over medium heat. As soon as the pan is hot, lift it from the heat and pour in about 3 tablespoons of batter; swirl the pan so that the batter spreads across it in an even, thin-as-possible layer. To get the most even layer, you'll probably find it easiest to pour in more batter than you need — that's fine. After swirling the pan, pour the excess batter back into the pitcher. (If you're new to crêpe making, it can take some practice to hit a rhythm and master the technique — keep at it even if you end up, as most people do, having to toss out your first few attempts.) When the batter has set, a matter of seconds, cut off the little tail that formed when you poured the excess back into the pitcher. Cook until the crêpe is set on top.

4. Run a blunt knife or small icing spatula around the edge of the crêpe to release it and then take a peek at the underside — if it's golden, flip the crêpe over (fingers work fine for this — just be careful) and cook until the other side is lightly browned. The second side will cook faster than the first but it will never be — and shouldn't be — as brown. Transfer the crêpe to a plate and sprinkle very lightly with sugar. Continue with the rest of the batch (you'll have enough batter for about 24 crêpes), oiling the crêpe pan as needed; be sure not to stack more than 10 crêpes on top of one another. *(The crêpes can be used now, or they can be wrapped airtight and refrigerated for a day or frozen for a month. To reheat, see* Keeping notes on page 90.)

the nuts
- 1 cup hazelnuts

Preheat the oven to 325°F. Place the nuts on a baking sheet and bake them for 10 to 15 minutes, or until they are thoroughly toasted. Cool the nuts and then wrap them in a kitchen towel and rub, rub, rub until the skins fall away. Coarsely chop the nuts and set them aside until needed. *(The nuts can be prepared ahead and kept covered at room temperature for 2 days or frozen for up to a month.)*

the sauce
- ⅓ cup honey
- ⅓ cup freshly squeezed orange juice
- ¼ cup freshly squeezed lemon juice
- 7 tablespoons (3½ ounces) unsalted butter, softened

You can make this sauce using a whisk, but it's particularly easy to make with an immersion blender. Melt the honey over low heat or in the microwave oven; allow it to cool for 5 minutes and then add the orange and lemon juices. Whisk or blend in the butter, adding it a tablespoon at a time. You should have a smooth, lightly thickened sauce. *(The sauce can be used now or kept refrigerated in an airtight container overnight. To reheat, see* Keeping *notes below.)*

to assemble
- ½ recipe Lemon Cream (page 31)

You can present the crêpes in rolls as pictured here or you can arrange them fan-style. *To make the rolls,* lay each crêpe out with its least golden side facing up. Spoon some lemon cream across the crêpe, just slightly off center, and roll the crêpe around the cream. *To create a fan shape,* lay the crêpe out in the same way and spoon some lemon cream into the upper right-hand quarter. Fold the crêpe in half from left to right and spoon some more cream into the upper right-hand sector. Now fold the crêpe up from the bottom, covering the cream and creating a fan shape. Repeat with the remaining crêpes. For each serving, place three crêpes on a large plate, pour sauce over and around the crêpes, and strew the plate with toasted nuts. (If you want to add a little crunch to the crêpes, you can crush the nuts and, instead of using them on the plates, add them to the crêpes with the lemon cream.)

90

Keeping
Although the components of this dessert can be made ahead, the assembled dessert should be served immediately. If you've made the crêpes ahead, the best way to reheat them is to wrap them in aluminum foil — no more than 5 to a packet — and heat them in a 350°F oven for about 5 minutes. If you've made the sauce ahead, you can reheat it in a microwave oven on low power or in a saucepan over the lowest heat possible.

RICE PUDDING *ice cream*

with

HOT SAUTÉED CHERRIES

I f you hear "Rice Pudding Ice Cream" and think vanilla ice cream and rice, you're thinking all wrong. Sure, you start with a vanilla crème anglaise, the base of many ice creams, but the cooked milk flavor that you get from blending rice pudding into that rich base transforms it. You get the taste of rice pudding, but because it's frozen, it has the sensation of being an entirely different dessert. The dessert becomes even more unusual when you spread a layer of ice cream in a soup plate and top it with piping-hot cherries sautéed in butter, sugar, and a bit of balsamic vinegar. It's a great combination — hot and cold, creamy and firm, delicious and more delicious.

« *Since I love rice pudding, I'm always looking for new ways to use it. I was in the process of making crème brûlée ice cream when it occurred to me that if I could use crème brûlée as a base, surely rice pudding would be fine too.* **»** — P. H .

the rice
- 3 tablespoons Arborio (or other short-grain) rice
- 2½ cups whole milk
- 3 tablespoons sugar
- Pinch of salt

I. Bring 2 cups of water to the boil in a saucepan, add the rice, and boil for 1 minute. Drain the rice and rinse it under cold water. Repeat the boiling-and-rinsing procedure twice more.

Makes about 1 quart ice cream; 8 servings

2. Bring the milk, sugar, and salt to a boil in a heavy-bottomed 2-quart saucepan. Add the rice, stir to mix, and cook over medium-low heat, keeping the mixture at a low simmer and stirring frequently, until much of the liquid has evaporated, about 40 to 50 minutes. When it's properly cooked, you'll have a creamy rice pudding that's about one third the volume of the original; each grain of very soft rice will be encapsulated by sweet cooked milk and there'll be a thin layer of milk over the grains. Set the rice aside to cool to room temperature.

the ice cream

- 1 cup whole milk
- ½ cup heavy cream
- 1 plump, moist vanilla bean, split lengthwise and scraped (see page 281)
- 4 large egg yolks
- ½ cup (slightly rounded) sugar

1. Bring the milk, cream, and vanilla bean (pulp and pod) to a boil in a saucepan over direct heat or in a microwave oven. Remove from the heat, cover, and set the mixture aside for 10 minutes to infuse. Meanwhile, fill a large bowl with ice cubes and set out a smaller metal bowl that can hold all of the ingredients and fit inside the larger bowl to make an ice bath. Set aside a fine-mesh strainer too.

2. In a heavy-bottomed 2-quart saucepan, whisk the yolks and sugar together until the mixture pales and thickens. Whisking constantly, slowly strain about a quarter of the vanilla-infused liquid over the yolks. When the yolks are acclimatized to the heat, add the remainder of the liquid in a steadier stream. Discard the vanilla bean pod, or wash, dry, and reserve it for another use (see page 281).

3. Place the saucepan over medium-high heat and, stirring energetically and constantly with a wooden spoon or spatula, cook the cream until it thickens slightly, lightens in color, and, most important, reaches 180°F, as measured on an instant-read thermometer — which will take less than 5 minutes. (Alternatively, you can stir the crème anglaise, and then draw your finger down the spatula or bowl of the wooden spoon — if the cream doesn't run into the track you've created, it's done.) Remove the saucepan from the heat.

4. Allow the cream to rest, or "poach," for a few minutes until it reaches 182°F, then strain it into the small metal bowl. Place the bowl over the ice cubes (you can add water to the cubes now) and, stirring frequently, let the crème anglaise cool to room temperature.

5. Stir the rice into the crème anglaise and pour the mixture into the ice cream maker; freeze according to the manufacturer's directions. The ice cream can be used as soon as it is churned, or it can be packed airtight and stored in the freezer.

the cherries

- 2 tablespoons (1 ounce) unsalted butter
- 3 tablespoons sugar, or more to taste
- 1 pound Bing or other sweet cherries, stemmed
- 3 tablespoons balsamic vinegar
- Juice of $\frac{1}{2}$ to 1 lemon
- Pinch of freshly ground black pepper

I. Melt the butter in a large skillet, preferably one with a nonstick finish, over high heat. Add the sugar and cherries and cook, stirring constantly, until the cherries are coated with butter and sugar. Add the balsamic vinegar and cook until the vinegar boils down to a glaze, about 1 to 2 minutes. Add a splash of lemon juice and then taste the sauce — you may want to add more lemon juice or more sugar. Remove the pan from the heat and stir in the black pepper.

2. To serve, spread a portion of ice cream over the bottom of each shallow soup or dessert plate. Top with the hot cherries and serve immediately so that everyone can enjoy the warm cherries against the cold — but quickly melting — ice cream. You can serve the ice cream more traditionally in scoops with the cherries on top, but you'll miss a lot of the melt and therefore much of the pleasure of this out-of-the-ordinary combination.

Keeping

The ice cream can be packed airtight and kept in the freezer for about a week. The cherries are meant to be made à la minute and served right out of the pan.

BRETON *sand* cookies

These belong to a family of French cookies called *sablé,* for their appealingly sandy texture (*sablé* means sandy). Buttery, crumbly, rich, and addictive, these cookies are made like icebox cookies (they're shaped into logs, sliced, and baked), but they most closely resemble shortbread, and are uncommonly good with tea.

You may be surprised to find these not only sandy, but slightly salty — that's just the way they're supposed to be.

- 2⅓ cups all-purpose flour
- 1 tablespoon double-acting baking powder
- 2 sticks (8 ounces) unsalted butter, softened
- ¾ cup plus 2 tablespoons sugar
- 1 teaspoon salt
- 5 large egg yolks, lightly beaten

I. Sift the flour and baking powder together and set aside for the moment. Working in a mixer fitted with the paddle attachment, cream the butter until it is soft and smooth. Add the sugar in a slow, steady stream, followed by the salt, and continue to beat, scraping the bowl as needed, for about 3 minutes, or until the mixture is light, pale, and fluffy. Add the yolks and beat to incorporate. At this point, the mixture should be light, creamy, and satiny. Remove the bowl from the mixer and, working with a large rubber spatula, fold in the sifted dry ingredients, taking special care not to overwork the dough.

Makes about 32 cookies

2. Divide the dough in half and, working on a smooth surface, such as marble, mold each half into a log with a diameter of about $1\frac{1}{2}$ inches and a length about 8 inches. The dough is going to be baked inside muffin tins, so you might have to adjust the thickness of the logs to the size of the tins; the logs should be about $\frac{1}{4}$ to $\frac{1}{2}$ inch slimmer than the muffin cups. (The thickness of the log is more important than its length — get the diameter right and the length will come along for the roll.) Wrap each log in a double thickness of plastic wrap and chill for at least 4 hours. *(The dough can be made ahead and kept refrigerated for 2 days or frozen for up to a month.)*

to bake

1. Center a rack in the oven and preheat the oven to 325°F. Set out one or two muffin tins.

2. Unwrap one log and, using a sturdy chef's knife, slice the log into $\frac{1}{3}$- to $\frac{1}{2}$-inch-thick cookies. Put one slice of dough in each cup of the muffin tins. Bake the cookies for 12 to 15 minutes, or until they are just firm. (Frozen cookies may take a minute or two longer.) These cookies are meant to be pale — don't let them brown; it's okay if the bottoms are lightly browned, but the tops should remain uncolored. Transfer the cookies to a rack to cool. Repeat with the remaining dough.

Keeping

The dough can be made ahead, wrapped airtight, and kept refrigerated for 2 days or frozen for a month. The baked cookies can be packed in an airtight tin and kept for 3 to 4 days at room temperature.

COCONUT
domes

Soft, chewy, bet-you-can't-eat-just-one treats for every coconut lover, these petite domes, child's play to make, could quickly become your house specialty. The dough is mixed in a minute, chilled overnight, and then rolled between your palms. Once shaped, the cookies can be baked immediately (they need less than ten minutes in the oven) or wrapped airtight and kept in the freezer until unexpected company or an irrepressible urge for coconut turns up. Of course, you can always double the recipe and have now-and-later cookies: a batch of domes to enjoy now, another to bake later.

These are my adaptation of the classic rochers congolais, *coconut cookies that were traditionally shaped like pyramids. Here, I've changed the form.* — P. H.

- ⅓ cup plus 2 tablespoons whole milk
- 1½ cups plus 1 tablespoon (5¼ ounces) unsweetened finely grated dried coconut (see page 271)
- ⅓ cup plus 2 tablespoons sugar
- 2 large eggs, lightly beaten

I. Warm the milk in a microwave oven or over direct heat until it is 85°F, as measured on an instant-read thermometer. (This isn't very hot at all; so you may overshoot the mark and have to let the milk cool to the right temperature.)

Makes about 24 cookies

2. Toss the coconut and sugar together in a mixing bowl. Stir in the warm milk and then the lightly beaten eggs, and continue to stir until all the ingredients are blended. Press a piece of plastic wrap against the dough to seal it airtight, and refrigerate the dough for 24 hours.

to bake

1. Line a baking sheet with parchment paper and set it close to you on the counter. Using 1 level tablespoon of dough for each cookie, shape the dough into balls between your palms, and place the cookies, 1 inch apart, on the parchment-lined sheet. When all the dough is shaped, place the baking sheet in the freezer while you preheat the oven. *(The cookies can be made ahead to this point; when they are frozen, remove them from the parchment and pack airtight for long-term storage. Properly packed, the cookies can be frozen for a month; they should not be defrosted before baking.)*

2. Center a rack in the oven and preheat the oven to 475°F.

3. Remove the baking sheet from the freezer, slide another baking sheet under it (or transfer the cookies and parchment to an insulated baking sheet), and bake the cookies for 7 to 11 minutes. The outside of the cookies should be just set and the tops should take on just a little color — that's all. The centers of the domes should remain soft, moist, and chewy. Transfer the cookies to a rack and allow them to cool before serving.

4. Depending on the absorbency of your coconut, you may find that during baking the domes seep a little liquid. Once the cookies have cooled, you can cut this extra little skirt of dough away with a pair of scissors. However, if you always buy the same coconut and always have the same problem, use a little less milk when you make the cookies.

99

Keeping

The cooled cookies can be kept for 2 to 3 days wrapped in plastic, but they're at their best freshly made, *a condition easily achieved since the dough can be molded and stored in the freezer for up to 1 month.*

ORANGE *tuiles*

A tuile is a type of dainty French cookie that is often molded over a rolling pin or wine bottle to give it a graceful shape and make it true to its namesake, a curved roof tile. These orange cookies are dainty (in fact, fragile) and graceful, but, while you can certainly mold them into a curve, Pierre often serves them flat, the better to appreciate the ridges and plains that form as the cookie dough bubbles under the oven's heat. Tuiles are often served alongside fruit desserts and sorbets since they're high in crunch, but these tuiles are so full of caramely orange flavor that they make a lovely lone accompaniment to tea or espresso.

The dough needs to chill overnight and it can be kept in the refrigerator for a week. With the dough at the ready, it's just minutes between baking and serving.

« *Tuiles can be made in any size. In fact, if you make one the size of a cake or tart, you can use it as a topping. Spread the batter out on the baking sheet, bake, and then, as soon as the cookie comes out of the oven, cut it to size using the right-sized tart or dessert ring as a guide. You can also use large shards of tuile to decorate a cake or tart.* » — P. H .

- Grated zest of 1 orange
- ½ cup (slightly rounded) sugar
- 2 tablespoons all-purpose flour
- 2½ tablespoons freshly squeezed orange juice
- 7 tablespoons (3½ ounces) unsalted butter, melted

Makes about 40 cookies

Put the orange zest and sugar in a medium bowl and rub them together between your fingers until the sugar is moist, grainy, and very aromatic (signs that the orange zest has released its essential oils and the sugar has absorbed them). Add the remaining ingredients one by one, mixing them into the dough with a rubber spatula. Cover the bowl with plastic wrap, pressing the plastic against the dough, and refrigerate overnight before baking. *(Wrapped airtight, the dough can be kept in the refrigerator for up to a week.)*

to bake

1. Center a rack in the oven and preheat the oven to 300°F. Have at the ready one or two non-stick or parchment-lined baking sheets and a large sheet of parchment paper to hold the cookies after they've baked.

2. To shape perfectly round cookies, you need to create a template. From a large plastic top, such as the type that comes with yogurt, cottage cheese, or ice cream, cut out an interior circle that's 2¾ to 3 inches in diameter; leave the rim intact. (You can make attractive tuiles without this template, but you won't be guaranteed that each cookie will be of uniform thickness and therefore that they will bake evenly.)

3. For each tuile, drop ½ teaspoon of dough onto the baking sheet(s), leaving about 4 inches of space between each dollop. (You'll probably be able to put 9 cookies on each sheet.) If you're using a template to shape the tuiles, position the template flat against the baking sheet so that the dollop of dough is in the center of the circle and, using a small metal icing spatula (an offset spatula is best), spread the dough across the template; lift off the template. Scrape whatever dough remains on the template back into the bowl and continue until all the cookies on the sheet have been shaped. If you are not using a template, just place the dollops of dough on the baking sheet — they'll spread and flatten more as they bake. It's best to bake one sheet at a time, so if you've spread dough on two sheets, keep one sheet in the refrigerator while you bake the other.

4. Bake the cookies for 14 to 16 minutes, during which time the batter will spread and bubble, forming a honeycomb pattern. The cookies are done when they are golden brown, and they need to be removed from the baking sheet immediately. Using a large metal spatula (a pancake turner is ideal), carefully work the blade under each cookie and, taking care not to let the cookie crumple on itself, lift it onto the piece of parchment paper to cool — the cookies will cool almost instantly. (If you put these cookies on a rack, they'll stick to the rack.) If you want the cookies to be curved, instead of putting them on parchment, drape them over a wine bottle or rolling pin. Repeat with the second baking sheet and then the remaining dough, always remembering to put the dough on a cool baking sheet.

Keeping

The dough will keep covered airtight in the refrigerator for 1 week, while the baked cookies can be kept in a cool, dry place for about 2 days. (As you can imagine, humidity is a tuile's worst enemy.) It's a good idea to place sheets of parchment or wax paper between the layers of baked cookies.

coconut TUILES

Not as fragile as Orange Tuiles (page 101) but every bit as alluring, these coconut cookies are a welcome mate to just about any fruit or chocolate dessert — if they're not snatched off the cooling rack and eaten out of hand. To get the tuiles paper-thin, the way they're meant to be, you have to pulverize the coconut and sugar in a food processor or blender before mixing the dough. This done, you've got two options when it comes to spreading the dough on the baking sheet: For a very professional look, you can cut a template from the top of a plastic container and spread a skim-coat of the dough inside it; or you can use a more artisanal method and thump the dough into a round with the heel of your hand. Either way, the baked cookies can be served flat or molded into the traditional tuile shape.

This dough, which takes just minutes to make, needs to rest in the refrigerator for several hours or overnight, so plan accordingly.

- 1¼ cups unsweetened finely grated dried coconut (see page 271)
- ½ cup (slightly rounded) sugar
- 2 large eggs, at room temperature, lightly beaten
- 1 tablespoon unsalted butter (1½ ounce), melted and still hot

Put the coconut and sugar in the work bowl of a food processor (or use a blender) and pulse and process until the coconut is powder-fine. Scrape the mixture into a small mixing bowl and, working with a rubber spatula, stir in the eggs and then the melted butter, stirring just

Makes about 40 cookies

until the ingredients are incorporated. Cover the bowl with plastic wrap, pressing the plastic against the dough, and refrigerate for several hours or overnight before baking. *(Wrapped airtight, the dough can be kept in the refrigerator for up to 1 week.)*

to bake

1. Have at the ready a plastic pastry scraper or an offset metal spatula (a pancake turner is fine) and one or two nonstick baking sheets. If you don't have nonstick sheets, cut parchment paper to line regular baking sheets.

2. To shape perfectly round cookies, you need to create a template. From a large plastic top, such as the type that comes with yogurt, cottage cheese, or ice cream, cut out an interior circle that's 2¾ to 3 inches in diameter; leave the rim intact.

3. Stir the dough gently with a rubber spatula to blend the ingredients (there is likely to be some liquid that's seeped out of the mixture). For each tuile, drop ½ teaspoon of dough onto the baking sheet(s), leaving about 2½ inches of space between each dollop. (You'll probably be able to put 9 cookies on each sheet.) Place the baking sheets in the refrigerator and chill for 15 minutes.

4. Center a rack in the oven and preheat the oven to 300°F.

5. Remove one baking sheet from the refrigerator. If you're using a template to shape the tuiles, position the template flat against the baking sheet so that the dollop of dough is in the center of the circle and, using a small metal icing spatula (an offset spatula is best), spread the dough across the template; lift off the template. Scrape whatever dough remains on the template back into the bowl and continue until all the cookies on the sheet have been shaped. If you are not using a template, run the heel of your hand under cool water, shake off the excess water, and tap the cookies into shape. (Their shape won't be perfect, but their taste and texture will be.) No matter which method you use, it's important that the dough be spread (or flattened) very thin and that the thinness be uniform.

6. Bake only one sheet of cookies at a time. Bake for 15 to 18 minutes, or until the cookies are evenly browned. Check the tuiles at the 8-minute mark — if the tuiles on one part of the baking sheet are coloring faster than the others, rotate the sheet as necessary. The cookies need to be removed from the baking sheet as soon as they come from the oven, so, working quickly and carefully, gently slide the plastic pastry scraper (or, in a pinch, a metal spatula) under each tuile and lift the cookie from the baking sheet to a cooling rack. If the cookies are difficult to remove, it may be because they've cooled too much — return the baking sheet to the oven for a minute and then try again. To mold the cookies into traditional tuiles, instead of placing them on a rack, press them over a rolling pin or a wine bottle; they'll mold and cool almost instantly. Repeat with the remaining dough, always using a cool baking sheet.

Keeping
The dough will keep covered airtight in the refrigerator for 1 week. The baked cookies can be kept in a cool, dry place for 2 days — they'll go limp if they're exposed to humidity. These are best packed between sheets of parchment or wax paper.

dainty
ALMOND CUPS

If you're not in the habit of serving elegant little cookies with afternoon tea or alongside small cups of steaming espresso, these might inspire you to start. The batter for these cookies — they're really more petit fours than cookies as we think of them in America — is made in minutes in a food processor and then stored in the fridge until teatime, when you just put small knobs of it in fluted paper petit four or candy cups (a.k.a. the tiniest cupcake liners), top with a little of anything you like from pine nuts to pineapple, bake, and serve. These could make you feel very European.

- 9 ounces (1¼ logs) almond paste (see page 266)
- 2 large eggs, at room temperature, lightly beaten
- 5 tablespoons (2½ ounces) unsalted butter, melted and cooled

Break up the almond paste and put it in the work bowl of a food processor fitted with the metal blade. Pulse several times to start reducing the almond paste to small pieces. With the machine running, or working in pulse mode, gradually add the beaten eggs, mixing until the almond paste is very smooth. (Don't hurry this — add the eggs little by little.) Still working with the machine running or pulsing, gradually add the melted and cooled butter. You'll have a batter that's thick, silky, and very smooth. Pour it into a refrigerator container, cover with a sheet of plastic, pressing the plastic against the batter to create a seal, and chill overnight before baking. *(The dough can be made up to a week ahead and kept covered airtight in the refrigerator.)*

Makes about 30 cups

toppings

Think of these as suggestions — you can top each little cookie with a bit of anything that appeals to you.

- Walnut halves
- Pine nuts
- Pistachios
- Hazelnuts, skinned (see page 90)
- Small pieces of fresh pineapple
- Raisins macerated in rum (see page 121)

1. When you are ready to bake, center a rack in the oven and preheat the oven to 350°F.
2. Fill each paper cup with a rounded teaspoon of batter and finish with the topping of your choice. After you slide the baking sheet into the oven, insert the handle of a wooden spoon into the oven to keep the door slightly ajar. Bake the cookies for about 10 to 12 minutes, or until they puff and spring back when touched; they won't take on much color. Cool before serving.

Keeping

The batter can be kept covered in the refrigerator for 1 week. Once baked, the cookies will keep at room temperature for 2 days wrapped loosely in plastic.

linzer cookies

with

HOMEMADE RASPBERRY JAM

There's a reason linzer cookies have survived the centuries: The combination of cinnamon-almond pastry and just-on-the-edge-of-sweet raspberry jam is timelessly appealing. This linzer's base is the cinnamon pastry Pierre uses for his Melody and Mozart cakes. Freshly made, when they're best, the cookies are as flaky as puff pastry — break one and you'll have a shower of crumbs and several strata of pastry. Fresh is also when the contrast between the flaky cookies and the thick jam is most pronounced. That said, leftovers, soft and even soggy, have never been left over for long.

Of course, you can use store-bought jam to sandwich the cookies — a premium-quality raspberry jam makes an admirable filler — but the homemade jam, its tiny seeds like little palate-ticklers, is fun to cook and you can make it with fresh or frozen berries. The full recipe yields about a quart — enough for a batch of cookies and lots of breakfast toast — halve it if you want.

the jam
- 2¼ pounds fresh or thawed frozen unsweetened raspberries
- 2¾ cups sugar
- About ¼ cup freshly squeezed lemon juice

I. Before you start cooking the jam, you need to purée the raspberries for a long time in a blender or food processor. Pierre purées his for a full 10 minutes with his heavy-duty immersion blender, in order to break up the seeds and release their pectin. However, most

Makes about 50 cookies

food processors and blenders made for home use cannot withstand 10 minutes of nonstop whirring. To get the best results at home, put the berries in the blender or processor (or in a bowl in which you can use an immersion blender) and whir for only 1 minute, then turn the machine off and let it rest for about 2 minutes before giving the berries another 1-minute whir. (Depending on your machine, you may have to adjust the timing for the on-and-off intervals.) Process the berries for a total of 5 minutes.

2. Scrape the berries into a large heavy-bottomed casserole and stir in the sugar. Bring the mixture to a full rollicking boil, stirring occasionally and taking care that nothing sticks to the bottom of the pot, and boil for 10 to 15 minutes, or until the jam thickens slightly and the bubbles look clear. (Since the jam will thicken as it cools, the best way to get a preview of its viscosity is to drop a small amount of it onto a cool plate.) Stir in 3 tablespoons of the lemon juice and then scrape the jam into a heatproof jar or bowl. Allow the jam to cool to room temperature, then taste it and add more lemon juice if you think it needs it. Once cool, the jam can be packed airtight and stored in the refrigerator. *(The jam can be kept in the refrigerator for about 1 month.)*

the cookies

- 1 recipe Cinnamon Dough (page 18), chilled
- Egg Wash (page 40)

1. Line two baking sheets with parchment paper and keep them close at hand. Have ready two cookie or biscuit cutters, one a fluted round cutter about 2¼ inches across, and the other a straight-sided round cutter with a 1¼-inch diameter. (You can use other size cutters if you want, and they can be either straight-sided or fluted. Just try to find one cutter that's about half the size of the other; you will be using the smaller one to cut an opening for the jam.) If the dough has been divided into thirds, work with a third at a time; if not, cut the dough in half and work with one piece at a time. Since this dough softens so quickly at room temperature, make sure you keep whatever dough you're not working with in the refrigerator.

2. Dust a work surface (marble would be ideal for this) with flour, dust the top of a piece of dough with flour, and roll the dough to a thickness of about ⅛ inch. Using the larger cutter, cut out as many cookies as you can from the rolled-out dough; gather the scraps and chill them — they'll be fine for more cookies. Using an offset spatula, lift the cookies onto a parchment-lined baking sheet. Pop the sheet into the refrigerator while you roll out and cut the remaining dough. If at any time while you're working with the dough it gets too soft to roll and cut easily, chill it immediately. Chill the second sheet of cookies too while you preheat the oven.

3. Position the racks to divide the oven into thirds and preheat the oven to 350°F.

4. Brush half the cookies lightly with cold water. Now, using the smaller cookie cutter, cut out the centers of the other (not-moistened) cookies. (Gather the cut-out centers and add them to your scrap dough. When the scraps are well chilled, roll them out to make more cookies.) Lift the cut-out rings onto the full cookies and brush all of the sandwiches with a little egg wash. Bake the cookies for 15 to 18 minutes, or until they're golden and firm to the touch, rotating the pans top to bottom and front to back midway through the baking period. Remove the cookies from the oven and transfer them carefully to racks to cool.

5. When the cookies are absolutely cool, fill their centers with raspberry jam. You can spoon the jam into the centers or pipe it through a pastry bag; either way, it's nice to give the jam a slightly domed top. If your jam is too runny, you can either boil it for a few minutes over direct heat or pour as much as you need into a large microwave-safe container — a Pyrex measuring cup is perfect for this job — and boil the jam in the microwave oven until it thickens sufficiently.

Keeping

The cookies are best served as close to freshly baked as possible. However, the jam can (and should) be made ahead and, if you'd like, you can roll out and sandwich the cookies and then store them, packed airtight, in the freezer for a month. There's no need to thaw frozen cookies before baking.

sweet GRISSINI

Grissini is the Italian word for bread sticks. Here, Pierre has taken the name and the form of these crunchy nibbles and made sweet, twisty-turny sticks out of light, airy puff pastry. Great with coffee or ice cream, these are fun to make. The recipe is given for a half-pound of puff pastry, but you can use more or less and make the grissini taller or shorter, slimmer or stouter — these are whimsical cookies with very few rules.

- ½ pound puff pastry, homemade (page 21) or store-bought
- Egg Wash (page 40)
- Sugar

I. Working on a floured surface, roll the puff pastry out to a thickness of about ⅛ inch, more or less. (The shape of the rolled-out pastry is unimportant — it can be a rectangle or square — it's the thickness that counts.) Brush the top of the dough with some egg wash and then sprinkle the surface generously with sugar. Run your rolling pin very (very) lightly across the dough to press in the sugar and help it to adhere. Turn the dough over and give the other side the same egg, sugar, and rolling pin treatment. Transfer the dough to a baking sheet, cover it loosely with plastic, and chill it while you preheat the oven. The rolled-out dough should chill for at least 15 minutes, but you can keep it in the refrigerator for a few hours, if that's more convenient.

Makes about 20 grissini

III

2. Position a rack in the center of the oven and preheat the oven to 350°F. Have a baking sheet or two, preferably with a nonstick finish, close at hand.

3. Using a sharp knife or a pizza cutter, cut the dough into strips about 8 inches long and ½ inch wide. Again, precision is not important. Lift each strip and gently twist it to form a corkscrew. It's best if the twists aren't too tight, but tight or loose, the grissini will be fine. Place the twists on one baking sheet, leaving puffing room, about an inch, between each one, and, using your finger, press each end of each twist down firmly against the baking sheet. If you've cut and twisted more than can fit on one baking sheet, start another sheet, but keep it in the refrigerator while you bake the first sheet. Slide the baking sheet into the oven and bake the grissini for about 15 minutes, or until they are puffed and their sugar coating has caramelized. Transfer the cookies to a rack to cool and, if necessary, bake the second sheet.

Keeping
Like all sweets made with puff pastry, these are best eaten as soon after they're baked as possible. Certainly they should be served the day they are made.

TARTS
AND
TARTLETS

LEMON
tart

Lemon tarts sparkle from every Paris pastry shop window, but tarts with sparkle that's more than glaze-deep are rare. Here's that rarity, a glorious lemon tart with fearlessly intense fruit flavor and a texture that's smooth, sensuous, and silken. It is a model of simplicity, composed merely of a sweet crust and Pierre's impeccable lemon cream, the one that's easy to make, hard to resist, and impossible to improve upon. The tart is an ideal do-ahead dessert; a good finisher for dinners plain or fancy, hearty or light; and a good sport — you can play around with it, changing its size or adding fruits to its base. For variety, try lining the crust with colorful fresh berries.

If you're new to tart making, start here. Not only is success guaranteed, but everyone, amateur or pro, finishes with a tart that looks shop-window perfect.

If you'd like, this tart can be topped with an Italian meringue [see the mousse recipe on page 190]. Pipe rosettes of meringue over the surface of the tart, making sure to cover all of the lemon cream, dust with confectioner's sugar, and caramelize with a blowtorch. Or put the tart under a broiler or in a 475°F oven for a few minutes, just until it's nicely browned. — P. H.

the crust

- 1 fully baked 10¼-inch/26-cm tart shell made from Sweet Tart Dough (page 15), cooled to room temperature

Keep the cooled crust, in its ring, on the baking sheet or transfer it to a cardboard cake round. *(You can make the crust up to 8 hours ahead and keep it in its ring at room temperature.)*

Makes 8 to 10 servings

to assemble

- 1½ cups Lemon Cream (page 31)
- Transparent Glaze (page 38) or lemon jelly or apple jelly
- Lemon slice, blueberries, and/or strawberries, optional

I. Spoon the lemon cream into the crust and use a long metal offset spatula to smooth the top. If the cream is hot, put the tart in the freezer for half an hour to cool it; if not, proceed with the glazing.

2. Warm the glaze if necessary, or, if you're using jelly, heat the jelly in a microwave oven or a small saucepan over low heat until it liquefies. Pour or spoon the glaze evenly over the top of the tart, reserving a little of the glaze if you'd like to finish the tart with a slice of lemon or a small cluster of berries. Brush the fruit with a little hot glaze or jelly to give it a shine. The tart can be chilled until needed or served immediately.

3. At serving time, slide the tart onto a decorative platter and remove the tart ring.

Keeping
The tart is meant to be served cold and can be kept loosely covered in the refrigerator for about 2 days.

tropical TART

The filling for this glazed fruit tart may remind you of nothing so much as a Mounds bar, reworked to tempt grown-ups with discriminating palates. It's richer and less sweet than the candy bar, and the almond flavor is truer and more pronounced, but the full coconut taste is here, front and center. Pierre tops this tart with a mix of mango, papaya, and kiwi, a colorful combination with ample acidity to balance the richness of the creamy, rummy filling. But it's a tart that invites variation. If mango, papaya, and kiwi are not available — or not to your taste — use red berries or pineapple, sliced, cubed, or whole.

The filling, which is put together very quickly, can be used as soon as it is made, but if you have the time, it benefits from an overnight rest in the refrigerator. Chilling and resting the filling takes the air out of it so that it doesn't rise and fall in the oven. — P. H .

- 1 unbaked 10½-inch/26-cm tart shell made from Sweet Tart Dough (page 15)

Center a rack in the oven and preheat the oven to 350°F. If the crust is not already on a parchment-lined baking sheet, transfer it to a lined sheet now.

the filling
- 1 stick plus 3 tablespoons (5½ ounces) unsalted butter, softened
- 1½ cups confectioner's sugar

Makes 8 to 10 servings

- ¾ cup finely ground blanched almonds (see page 277)
- 1 (slightly rounded) cup unsweetened finely grated dried coconut (see page 271)
- 1 tablespoon cornstarch
- 2 tablespoons dark rum
- 2 large eggs, lightly beaten
- ½ cup (very full) heavy cream

1. Working in a large bowl with a flexible rubber spatula, mix the filling ingredients together, one by one, in the order in which they are listed. Your aim is to blend the ingredients without beating or whipping them, so save your energy. If you whip too much air into the filling, it will rise in the oven and then sink — not tragic, but not attractive. *(The filling can be used now or covered and refrigerated overnight.)*

2. Spoon the filling into the tart shell and bake for 38 to 42 minutes, or until the filling is golden and the bottom of the crust is very brown. (You can check the bottom of the crust by lifting the tart gently with a wide metal spatula and taking a peek. Don't worry about testing the filling — the filling will never be baked before the crust.) Transfer the tart, still in its ring, to a rack to cool to room temperature.

118

the topping

- 1 ripe mango
- 1 ripe papaya
- 3 to 4 kiwis
- ½ cup Transparent Glaze (page 38) or quince or apple jelly

1. Peel the mango and papaya and cut into small cubes. Place the cubes in the center of the tart; leave a border bare for the kiwis. Peel the kiwis and cut them in half the long way. Place each half cut side down on a board and cut crosswise into very thin slices. Arrange the kiwi slices in a circle around the mango and papaya cubes, slightly overlapping the slices.

2. Warm the glaze and pour or spoon it over the fruit to cover the top of the tart evenly. (If you're using jelly, warm it in the microwave oven to liquefy it and then brush it over the tart.) Refrigerate the tart for a few hours, or until it is thoroughly chilled. At serving time, slide the tart onto a decorative platter and remove the tart ring.

Keeping

This is best eaten the day it is made.

WARM
chocolate and banana
TART

Nothing could be simpler than the made-in-minutes warm chocolate ganache that fills this tart: It's sleek, sexy, and a suave companion to the golden raisins and caramelized bananas that are tucked into the crust. And the tart is just as lush (and faster to prepare) with raspberries (see the variation on page 122).

Pierre serves this tart as soon as it comes from the oven — one taste and you'll know why: Minutes from the heat, the ganache offers a progression of textures from the set-like-chocolate-pudding periphery to the on-the-verge-of-setting-but-still-molten center. But you'll find it also wins fans at room temperature or even the next day, when the ganache has a lovely levelness — everything is seductively soft and creamy except the still-snappy crust.

《 *The ganache that forms the tart's filling is unusual. It's not a classic ganache made with heavy cream — that would separate if it were baked — but one made with eggs. It's the eggs that bind the ganache and allow it to hold up in the oven. This ganache is a little heavier than the classic but, at the same time, I find it seems less rich.* 》 — P.H.

the crust

- 1 fully baked 8¾-inch/22-cm tart shell made from Sweet Tart Dough (page 15), cooled to room temperature

Keep the cooled crust, with the tart ring still in place, on the parchment-lined baking sheet. *(You can make the crust up to 8 hours ahead and keep it in its ring at room temperature.)*

Makes 6 to 8 servings

the raisins
- ½ cup golden raisins
- 3 tablespoons dark rum
- 3 tablespoons water

Place all the ingredients in a small saucepan over low heat and cook, stirring, just until the raisins are soft and plump, about 2 minutes. Remove the pan from the heat and allow the raisins to macerate for at least 2 hours, or for up to a day.

the banana
- 1 ripe but firm banana
- 1 tablespoon freshly squeezed lemon juice
- 1½ tablespoons (¾ ounce) unsalted butter
- Sliver of habanero pepper, optional
- 3½ tablespoons sugar
- Pinch of freshly ground black pepper (about 2 turns of the peppermill)

1. Line a baking sheet with parchment paper and set it close to your range.
2. Peel the banana and cut it on the bias into slices about ⅛ inch thick. Toss the banana slices with the lemon juice to keep them from discoloring.
3. Melt the butter in a large heavy skillet, preferably nonstick, over high heat. If you are using the habanero pepper, add it to the pan along with the butter, then remove it when the butter starts to bubble. Add the bananas and turn to coat them with the bubbling butter. Sprinkle the sugar over the bananas and cook, still on high heat, turning the bananas, until they are golden and caramel-coated. (You need to work over high heat so that the bananas caramelize rather than melt.) Add the black pepper, stir, and cook for 1 minute more; the bananas will be soft inside and caramel-crisp outside. Transfer the bananas to the parchment-lined baking sheet and pat them gently on both sides with paper towels to remove any excess butter; cool to room temperature. *(The bananas can be caramelized a couple of hours ahead of time and kept at room temperature.)*

the ganache
- 4¾ ounces bittersweet chocolate (preferably Valrhona Noir Gastronomie), finely chopped
- 1 stick (4 ounces) unsalted butter, cut into 8 pieces
- 1 large egg, at room temperature
- 3 large egg yolks, at room temperature
- 2 tablespoons sugar

1. Center a rack in the oven and preheat the oven to 375°F. fill the crust, still on its parchment-lined baking sheet, with the raisins and all but a few slices of the banana. (You'll use the reserved slices to top the tart.)

2. Melt the chocolate and the butter in separate bowls and cool each to 104°F, as measured on an instant-read thermometer. (It's crucial to the creamy texture of the ganache that both the chocolate and the butter be 104°F.)

3. In a medium mixing bowl, gently stir together the egg, yolks, and sugar with a small whisk; whisk just until the sugar is blended into the eggs, taking care not to beat air into the mixture. Switch to a rubber spatula and, little by little, gently stir in the melted chocolate; stir in concentric circles, starting with a small circle in the center of the bowl and working your way out into larger circles. Add the butter in the same manner — you'll have a glossy, perfectly smooth mixture; by incorporating the chocolate and butter slowly, you are creating an emulsion not unlike mayonnaise. Once mixed, the ganache must be used immediately, so quickly pour it into the crust.

to bake

Bake the tart for exactly 11 minutes — no longer — at which point the top will look a little dry around the edges but the center will still be shiny and a little jiggly. Remove the tart from the oven and top with the reserved slices of caramelized bananas. The tart is ready to eat as soon as it comes from the oven.

to serve (optional)

- Cremè Anglaise (page 25)

Transfer the tart to a serving platter, remove the tart ring, and serve with chilled crème anglaise, if desired. Don't worry if the center is runny when you cut into the tart — that's just the way it's supposed to be.

VARIATION

WARM CHOCOLATE AND RASPBERRY TART

By omitting the rum-soaked raisins and caramelized bananas, and scattering about ½ cup of fresh red raspberries over the ganache before baking, you'll produce a dessert with a flavor surprisingly different from the original.

Keeping

The crust can be made ahead, as can the caramelized bananas and rum-soaked raisins, but once the ganache is made, it must be baked immedi-ately. While meant to be eaten as soon as it comes from the oven, the tart can be kept overnight in the refrigerator and brought to room temperature before being eaten the next day, when the filling will have firmed and become a different kind of delicious.

coconut – dried cherry
FLAN

You'll fall in love with this tart even before you taste it — it's the aroma that grabs you. The fragrance of pungent cherries, sweet vanilla, and warm coconut that fills the kitchen as this bakes is thoroughly enticing, promising what it delivers: a great play between tart and sweet. Baked in a large pâte brisée shell, the filling is a remarkable cherry-studded coconut pastry cream made (untraditionally) with whole eggs and equal parts milk and water. As refined as the flavor is, that's how rustically charming the look is. Since the pastry cream puffs as it bakes and shrinks as it cools, the top of the tart resembles an aerial view of the Alps. For a change of taste, substitute dried apricots for the cherries.

« Inspiration can come from anywhere at any time, there are no rules — you just have to have an open mind. The idea for this tart came to me when I was shopping in a New York City supermarket. I hadn't seen dried cherries before — France doesn't have the variety of dried fruits you find in America — and after tasting them, I couldn't wait to pair their acidity and intense flavor with a creamy coconut flan. » — P. H.

the filling
- 1 cup whole milk
- 1 cup water
- ½ plump, moist vanilla bean, split lengthwise and scraped (see page 281)
- 4 large eggs
- ½ cup sugar

Makes 8 to 10 servings

- ½ cup cornstarch
- ½ cup unsweetened finely grated dried coconut (see page 271)

1. Fill a large bowl with ice cubes and set aside a smaller bowl that can hold the finished cream and be placed in this ice bath.

2. In a small saucepan, bring the milk, water, and vanilla bean (pulp and pod) to a boil over medium heat (or do this in the microwave oven). Cover the pan, turn off the heat, and allow the mixture to rest for 10 minutes, time enough for the liquids to be infused with the warm flavor of vanilla.

3. Whisk the eggs and sugar together in a heavy-bottomed 2-quart saucepan; whisk in the cornstarch. Whisking all the while, very slowly drizzle a quarter of the hot liquid into the eggs. Still whisking, pour the rest of the liquid in a steady stream over the tempered eggs. Remove and discard the vanilla pod (or save it for another use — see page 281) and stir in the coconut.

4. Place the saucepan over medium-high heat and, whisking vigorously and without stop, bring the mixture to the boil. Keep the mixture at the boil, whisking energetically, for a minute or two then remove the pan from the heat and turn the cream into the reserved small bowl. Set the bowl in the ice bath (you can add some cold water to the cubes now) and, stirring frequently, allow the cream to cool completely, about 10 minutes. *(The pastry cream can be made ahead, covered tightly with plastic wrap — press the wrap against the cream's surface — and refrigerated for up to a day.)*

to assemble

- 1 unbaked 10¼-inch/26-cm tart shell made from Perfect Tart Dough (page 12)
- 1 (rounded) cup plump, moist dried cherries (or chopped dried apricots)

1. Center a rack in the oven and preheat the oven to 350°F. If the crust is not already on a parchment-lined baking sheet, transfer it to one now.

2. Spread the cherries evenly over the bottom of the crust and spoon in the cooled pastry cream. Smooth the top with an offset spatula and slip the tart into the oven to bake for 45 to 50 minutes, or until the filling is dark brown and puffed and the crust beautifully golden. If the filling browns too quickly, cover it loosely with a foil tent and continue to bake until the crust is golden. (To make certain the crust is done, lift the tart gently with an offset spatula and take a peek at the bottom.) Transfer the tart to a rack to cool to room temperature.

3. At serving time, slide the tart onto a decorative platter and remove the tart ring.

Keeping
The filling and the unbaked tart shell can be made a day ahead if necessary, and the finished tart, while best at room temperature, can be wrapped airtight and refrigerated for up to 2 days.

125

apple GALETTE

A galette is a flat pastry, and this galette, two rounds of puff pastry encasing a few cups of caramely sweet Twenty-Hour Apples, gives the entire genre a good name. It's simple and satisfying, and the ideal finish for fall and winter dinners, casual or posh. Store-bought puff pastry, usually found in the frozen foods section, is fine here. Look for a brand that's made with butter.

This galette can be made with many other fillings. I particularly like it with the roasted fig and raspberry mixture that I use in the Caramelized Cinnamon Tart [page 137]. — P. H.

the pastry
- About 1 pound puff pastry, homemade (page 21) or store-bought, chilled

1. Line two baking sheets with parchment. Moisten one of the pieces of parchment with water and keep both sheets close at hand.
2. If necessary, cut the dough into two pieces, each about ½ pound. Work with one piece of dough at a time and keep the remaining pastry refrigerated. Fold the corners of one piece of the dough into the center, and, cupping your hands, turn the dough around on the work surface to round it a bit. Dust the work surface and the dough lightly with flour and roll the dough into a 12-inch circle. (Don't worry about being exact — you're going to trim the circle later.) Brush off the excess flour and lift the circle onto the baking sheet with the dry parchment paper; cover with plastic wrap and chill for 30 minutes. Repeat with the second piece of dough; place it on the baking sheet with the moistened parchment.

Makes 6 to 8 servings

to assemble

- Egg Wash (page 40)
- 2 ⅓ cups (about ½ recipe) Twenty-Hour Apples (page 33)

1. Remove the baking sheet with the moistened parchment from the refrigerator. Using a small sharp knife or a pizza cutter, cut the dough into an 11-inch circle. Brush a 1-inch border of the dough with a little egg wash.

2. Spread the apples evenly over the circle of puff pastry, leaving a 2-inch border. Top with the second circle of pastry, trim the edge with a knife to make it even with the bottom circle, and then press the edges with your fingertips to seal the two sheets of pastry. Cover the galette with plastic wrap and chill for 30 minutes.

3. To decorate and further seal the edge of the galette, use the back of a table knife and, pushing against the edges of the dough on the diagonal, make an ⅛-inch-deep incision into the circle every ¾ inch.

4. Paint the galette with an even coating of egg wash and, using the point of a small sharp knife, incise a decorative pattern across the top of the dessert, taking care not to cut all the way through the pastry. Traditional designs include a simple crosshatch or closely spaced double lines that give the galette a lattice-topped look. Chill the galette, uncovered, for 1 hour.

to bake

- 2 tablespoons light corn syrup

1. Center a rack in the oven and preheat the oven to 425°F. Place the galette in the oven and immediately reduce the temperature to 375°F. (If you are using store-bought puff pastry, check the package for baking instructions. Commercial puff pastry is often best baked at 350°F.) Bake the galette for 40 to 45 minutes, or until puffed and well browned.

2. Remove the baking sheet from the oven and brush the tart with the corn syrup. Slip the galette back into the oven and bake for another 2 to 3 minutes, just until the top is glazed and shiny. Immediately transfer the galette to a cooling rack. Let the galette cool slightly, about 15 to 20 minutes, before sliding it onto a platter and serving — it should not be eaten piping hot.

Keeping

The galette is best eaten the day it is made, but it can be kept covered in the refrigerator overnight and re-heated for 15 minutes in a 350°F oven; cool for about 10 minutes before cutting and serving.

poached pear

and W A L N U T *tart*

Crowned with beautifully rosy pears and nuggets of walnuts, this tart captures the goodness of autumn and the holiday season. The pears, poached in a spiced wine syrup, make a tempting dessert on their own, but matched with a walnut pastry cream and a buttery crust, they're beyond the limits of resistibility.

If, like so many of us, you can't stand to see a good thing go to waste, you'll want to find a use for the flavorful liquid that's left over once the pears are poached. Pierre often boils it down to a half cup, adds about three quarters of a cup of raspberry purée (you can make the purée from fresh or frozen berries, sweetened or not), and sugar to taste, and heats the mix just to blend the flavors. This makes a sauce that's terrific spooned over the pears (if you're offering them solo) or served alongside the tart.

If the pears are red all the way through, the wine taste will be very prominent. Some people like this, but I'm happier when the pears are red around the rim and white in the center, then the wine flavor is less strong and the look is prettier. — P . H .

the pears
- 1 bottle strong red wine (Pierre prefers Cahors)
- ½ cup sugar
- ½ cinnamon stick
- Zest of ½ orange — removed in broad strips with a peeler or knife
- Zest of ½ lemon — removed in broad strips with a peeler or knife
- 4 ripe but firm medium pears

Makes 8 to 10 servings

1. Place all of the ingredients except the pears in a large casserole. Bring the mixture to the boil, stirring to dissolve the sugar, and allow the syrup to boil gently for a minute or two. Meanwhile, peel the pears. Lower the pears into the boiling syrup, return the syrup to the boil, and remove from heat.

2. Transfer the pears and syrup to a bowl that holds them snugly and lay a sheet of plastic wrap over the pears. Place a plate on top of the plastic to weight down the pears and keep them submerged in the syrup, then cover the setup with another piece of plastic wrap. Allow the syrup and pears to cool to room temperature, then refrigerate them overnight. (If you can't find just the right size bowl, submerge the pears as best you can and remember to turn them in the syrup from time to time while they're in the refrigerator.)

the crust

- 1 fully baked 10¼-inch/26-cm tart shell made from Perfect Tart Dough (page 12), cooled to room temperature

Keep the crust, tart ring in place, on the baking sheet or transfer it to a cardboard cake round. *(You can make the crust up to 8 hours ahead and keep it in its ring at room temperature.)*

130

the cream

- 1 cup Vanilla Pastry Cream (page 27)
- ⅓ cup finely chopped walnuts
  (don't chop the nuts into a powder; it's nice to have a few large pieces)
- 1 tablespoon walnut liqueur
- ¼ cup heavy cream, lightly whipped

Whisk the pastry cream to loosen it and then gently stir in the walnuts and the liqueur. Fold in the whipped cream with a rubber spatula. *(The filling can be made a day ahead and kept covered, airtight, in the refrigerator.)*

to finish

- Walnut halves
- ½ cup Transparent Glaze (page 38) or apple jelly

1. Spoon the cream into the baked tart crust and smooth the top with a spatula.

2. Remove the pears from the poaching syrup and dry them gently between paper towels. Cut each pear in half from blossom to stem end and remove the core with a melon baller. Working with the pears cut side down, cut each half lengthwise into thin slices, between 1/16 and

⅛ inch thick. Starting at the edge of the tart, arrange the pears in concentric circles so that each slice slightly overlaps its neighbor; it's nice to arrange the slices so that the red edge is on the outside and the whiter part of the pear is just peeking out (see photo on page 128). Use the largest pieces to make the circles and the small end pieces as tuck-ins to even out the circles. Strew walnut halves sparingly over the top of the tart.

3. Warm the glaze and pour or spoon it over the fruit to cover the top of the tart evenly. (If you're using jelly, warm it in a microwave oven to liquefy it and then brush it over the tart.) Refrigerate the tart for a few hours, or until it is thoroughly chilled. At serving time, slide the tart onto a decorative platter and lift off the tart ring.

131

Keeping
The tart is best eaten the day it is made.

RICE TART
IMPÉRATRICE

Whenever you see the word *impératrice*, you can be sure you're in for a royal treat: The name is given to dishes inspired by empresses. This dessert takes its inspiration from *riz impératrice*, a fruited rice custard created for Empress Eugénie, but neither the name nor the tart's appearance tells the full story. What you see at first glance is an elegant tart topped with sliced strawberries and strands of mint, but what's really here is a bundle of surprises. You've got texture upon texture — the crunch of the crust, the nursery-smoothness of the rice pudding filling, the chewiness of the plump raisins that are added to it, and the softness of the strawberries that top it. And you've got taste upon taste — the crust is buttery, the pudding rich, the mint fresh, and the berries sweet, bright, and slightly acidic. Everything is set off by the totally unexpected heat provided by a few turns of the peppermill — don't leave them out.

» *To get a creamy texture that has some variety, you need to use a rice that will still be toothsome after forty minutes of cooking. Thai rice is recommended. If you can't find it, try an Arborio rice, the kind used to make risotto. Above all, take care not to overcook it.* » — P. H.

the filling
- 2½ cups whole milk
- ¼ cup Thai jasmine or Arborio rice
- 2½ tablespoons sugar
- Pinch of salt

Makes 6 to 8 servings

- 2 large egg yolks
- 2 tablespoons (1 ounce) unsalted butter
- ½ cup (loosely packed) plump golden raisins

1. Put the milk, rice, sugar, and salt in a heavy-bottomed 2-quart saucepan over medium heat. Bring the mixture to the boil, stirring occasionally, then reduce the heat to low. (Keep an eye on the pot — milk has a tendency to bubble up and then boil over quickly.) Cook, stirring frequently, until about three quarters of the liquid has evaporated; the mixture will thicken slightly and, as you stir, your spoon will leave tracks on the bottom of the pan. At this point, which may take 35 to 40 minutes to reach, you'll be able to see individual grains of rice beneath a thin top layer of milk. Whatever you do, don't cook this until all of the liquid has evaporated. Remove the pan from the heat.

2. Place the yolks in a small bowl and, stirring constantly, gradually add two tablespoons of the rice mixture. Stir in another spoonful of rice. Add the yolks, butter, and raisins to the pan and return the pan to medium heat. Stir vigorously and cook just until one or two bubbles pop on the surface — don't bring the pudding to a boil again, or it will curdle. Quickly scrape the creamy pudding into a clean bowl.

3. Press plastic wrap against the surface of the pudding and allow the pudding to cool to room temperature. *(The pudding can be made a day ahead and kept covered in the refrigerator.)*

the crust

- 1 fully baked 8¾-inch/22-cm tart shell made from Perfect Tart Dough (page 12), cooled to room temperature

Keep the cooled crust, with the tart ring still in place, on the parchment-lined baking sheet. *(You can make the crust up to 8 hours ahead and keep it in its ring at room temperature.)*

to bake

1. Center a rack in the oven and preheat the oven to 350°F.

2. Turn the cooled rice pudding into the tart shell, and use a flexible rubber spatula or a metal offset spatula to get the pudding into the crevices and to spread the top even. Bake for 8 minutes (or for about 15 minutes, if the pudding has been chilled), then transfer the tart to a rack to cool to room temperature.

133

to finish

- About ¾ cup best-quality red currant jelly
- 1 to 2 tablespoons chopped fresh mint
- About 3 cups strawberries (or a mixture of fresh berries, such as strawberries, raspberries, blueberries, and currants)
- Freshly ground black pepper, preferably Sarawak

1. Place the tart on a cardboard cake round or a serving platter. Warm the jelly in a small pan over low heat or in the microwave oven. Using a feather brush or fine pastry brush, paint the top of the tart with a light coat of warm jelly. Sprinkle about two thirds of the chopped mint over the tart (reserve a few strands of mint for the strawberries) and, using little dabbing touches, give the tart a second coat of jelly.

2. The tart can be topped with berries now or right before serving. If you think you'll have time to arrange the berries close to serving time, choose this option — fresh-cut berries and mint and a last-second dash of black pepper are a special treat. In either case, cut the strawberries lengthwise into thin slices and arrange them in concentric circles over the top of the tart. (If you're using mixed berries, arrange the berries in an attractive pattern over the top of the tart.) Give the berries a light coat of warm jelly glaze and finish the tart with a dusting of freshly ground black pepper (about 3 turns of the mill should do it) and a shower of the remaining mint strands. If you aren't doing this *à la minute,* you can refrigerate the tart for up to 6 hours before serving, but serve the tart at cool room temperature. At serving time, transfer the tart to a platter if necessary, and lift off the tart ring.

134

Keeping

Although the rice pudding and crust can be made ahead, the assembled tart is best served the day it is made.

CARAMELIZED
cinnamon tart

If this tart were in the American repertoire, it would belong to the chiffon family, that group of open-faced pies (usually made with crumb crusts) filled with marshmallowy-light creams that are melt-on-your-tongue evanescent. The seemingly weightless cinnamon cream that's spread over roasted figs and fresh berries in this totally French tart is a modern play on a *crème chibouste*. Essentially a pastry cream lightened with meringue and stabilized with a touch of gelatin, the filling gets its unusually deep flavor from a double whammy of caramel and cinnamon, a combination dreamy on its own, spectacular with fruit. Figs are the perfect choice here, but their season is short and their availability iffy, so think about using roasted apples or sautéed pears during non-fig months (see page 140 for variations).

Pierre finishes this tart by sprinkling the *chibouste* with sugar and caramelizing it to a gloss with a blowtorch (see page 267). This gives the tart a very professional look, but if you don't have a blowtorch, don't let it stop you — this is a standout with or without the caramelized finish.

《 *To keep a fully baked crust crisp when it has to hold a moist, juicy filling like this one, line it sparingly with crumbs from stale génoise, ladyfingers, or butter cookies. It's a good trick that's also useful with American-style fruit pies.* 》 — P.H.

Makes 8 servings

the crust

- 1 fully baked 8¾-inch/22-cm tart shell made from Perfect Tart Dough (page 12)

The crust should be cooled to room temperature with its tart ring still in place. *(You can make the crust up to 8 hours ahead and keep it in its ring at room temperature.)*

the figs

- 8 fresh purple figs
- 1 tablespoon sugar
- 1 tablespoon unsalted butter

1. Center a rack in the oven and preheat the oven to 475°F.
2. Cut each fig into 6 segments by cutting it in half from blossom to stem end and then cutting each half lengthwise into thirds. Toss the figs with the sugar and place them in a small baking pan — it's best if the figs fit snugly in the pan. Cut the butter into small pieces and scatter over the figs. Bake for 4 to 5 minutes, or until the butter and sugar are melted and the figs are warm; transfer the pan to a cooling rack and allow the fruit to cool to room temperature. *(The figs can be made up to 1 day ahead and kept covered in the refrigerator.)*

138

the cream topping

- ¾ cup whole milk
- 2 cinnamon sticks, each broken into 3 pieces
- 7 tablespoons sugar
- 3 large egg yolks
- 1 tablespoon cornstarch
- 1½ teaspoons gelatin
- 1½ tablespoons cold water
- 4 large egg whites

1. Bring the milk to the boil (you can do this in a microwave oven) and set it aside.
2. Put the cinnamon sticks in a medium skillet, preferably one with a nonstick finish, and turn the heat to medium-high. Measure out 2 tablespoons of the sugar, and set the remainder aside. Sprinkle 1½ teaspoons of sugar over a small portion of the center of the pan and, as soon as it starts to melt and color, stir with a wooden spoon until it caramelizes. Make sure to stir the cinnamon with the sugar so that you're both caramelizing the sugar and infusing it with cinnamon flavor. Continue cooking and stirring the 2 tablespoons sugar, 1½ teaspoons at a time, until it turns a medium-brown color, about 2 minutes. Still stirring, add the warm

milk slowly and steadily, then raise the heat to high and bring the mixture to the boil. Don't worry if the caramel seizes and clumps; stirring and heating it will smooth it out. Remove the pan from the heat and strain the caramel sauce into a mixing bowl; discard the cinnamon sticks (or wash and dry them for another use) as well as any solids that remain in the strainer.

3. Whisk the yolks, cornstarch, and 2 tablespoons of the remaining sugar together in a heavy-bottomed 2-quart saucepan until thick and pale. Still whisking, add about one third of the hot caramel sauce, a little at a time, to acclimatize the yolks to the heat; whisk in the rest of the sauce. Place the saucepan over medium heat and, whisking vigorously and without stop, cook until the mixture thickens, lightens in color, and comes to the boil. Keep the mixture at the boil, whisking energetically, for a minute, then remove the pan from the heat. Strain the cream into a bowl large enough to handle an immersion blender, or transfer it to the container of a blender or food processor.

4. Sprinkle the gelatin over the cold water and allow it to soften. Dissolve the gelatin by placing it in the microwave oven for 15 seconds or heating it over gentle heat. If you're working with an immersion blender, turn it on and add the gelatin to the pastry cream; if you're using a blender or processor, add the gelatin while the machine is whirring. In any case, process only until the mixture is blended. If necessary, turn the pastry cream into a bowl.

5. In an impeccably clean, dry mixing bowl, whip the egg whites until they hold soft peaks. Still beating, gradually whip in the remaining 3 tablespoons sugar and beat until the whites form a meringue with firm, glossy peaks. With a whisk, stir one third of the meringue into the hot pastry cream and then, with the whisk or a large rubber spatula, gently fold the pastry cream into the remaining meringue to make a *chibouste*. Once blended, the cream should be used immediately.

to assemble

- About 2 tablespoons cake, ladyfinger, or cookie crumbs
- ½ cup fresh or thawed frozen raspberries

1. This tart can be finished in two ways: Either you can mound the *chibouste* over the fruit, in which case the tart should be placed on a cardboard cake circle and the tart ring removed, or you can give the tart a flat top. In order to do that, you need to put the tart on a cardboard cake round, keeping the tart ring in place, and stack another tart ring on the original to give you a ring with a height of 1½ to 1¾ inches. In either case, scatter the cake crumbs evenly over the bottom of the crust. Place the figs in the crust, arranging them in an even layer, and then sprinkle the raspberries over. Scrape the cream into the crust and, using an offset spatula, mound or smooth the top of the cream, as you please.

2. Place the tart in the freezer for 20 to 30 minutes to set the cream and chill it enough to withstand the heat of the blowtorch in the next step. (Even if you're not going to caramelize the cream, you should chill the tart — either for 20 minutes in the freezer or 40 minutes in the fridge — to set the cream.)

to finish

- Sugar for caramelizing the top, optional
- 1 fig, for decoration
- 1 raspberry, for decoration

1. You'll need a blowtorch to caramelize the top of the tart, an optional but sensational way to finish this dessert — the crackle of the caramel on the cream is a great textural counterpoint to the airy *chibouste*. Working on one patch of tart at a time, sprinkle with some sugar and apply the flame. When the sugar melts and caramelizes, move on to another patch. Try to work as quickly as possible to avoid melting the cream.
2. Set the fig on the cutting board pointed end up. With a small sharp knife, cut the fig into 8 segments from blossom to stem end, taking care not to cut all the way through the bottom. Gently spread the segments apart to form a flower. Place the raspberry in the center of the fig and place the fig in the center of the tart; refrigerate until serving time.
3. When you're ready to serve the tart, slide it carefully onto a decorative platter and, if you haven't already done so, remove the tart rings.

VARIATIONS

Instead of the figs and raspberries, the tart can be filled with either one of the following.

sautéed pears

- 3 tablespoons (1½ ounces) unsalted butter
- 3 tablespoons sugar
- Pulp of ½ plump, moist vanilla bean (see page 281)
- 3 medium dead-ripe pears, peeled, cored, and cut into sixths
- For optional decoration: ½ pear and Simple Syrup (page 39)

1. Melt the butter in a large heavy skillet, preferably nonstick. Add the sugar and vanilla bean pulp and cook, stirring, over medium-high heat until the sugar just starts to caramelize. Add the pear sections and sauté until the pears are caramelized and cooked through; the tip of a small knife should pierce the pears easily. Cool the pears to room temperature.

2. For the optional decoration, poach the pear half in some sugar syrup for a few minutes — just until it is soft enough to pierce easily with the tip of a small knife; let it cool in the syrup. At serving time, drain and dry the pear, cut it into thin slices, and arrange the slices attractively on top of the tart.

roasted apples

- 3 medium apples, preferably Granny Smith or Fuji, peeled, cored, and cut into sixths
- 3 tablespoons sugar
- 3 tablespoons ($1\frac{1}{2}$ ounces) unsalted butter

1. Center a rack in the oven and preheat the oven to 475°F.
2. Toss the apples with the sugar and place them in a baking pan. Cut the butter into small pieces, scatter over the apples, and bake for 10 to 15 minutes, or until the apples are golden brown and soft enough to be pierced easily with the tip of a small knife. Cool the apples to room temperature.

Keeping
*While the crust and figs can be
made ahead, the* chibouste *must
be used as soon as it is made
and the tart should be served the
day it is made.*

CHESTNUT *and* **pear** *tart*

This tart, soothing and mild, is a great alternative to traditional pumpkin and sweet potato pies. Here, the pears and chestnuts complement one another in surprising ways: The pears give the chestnuts bounce, and the chestnuts give the pears creaminess — a fair and delicious exchange, especially when you throw in the chestnut-whisky clafoutis that serves as the tart's filling. (A clafoutis is a custard, in this case a quickly mixed blend that includes chestnut purée and crème fraîche.) The tart is finished with a triple layer of caramelized phyllo, a shiny, whimsical, crinkly crown that transforms this homey tart into company fare.

Both chestnut purée and whole cooked chestnuts are featured here. Unsweetened chestnut purée comes in cans (usually imported from France) and dry-cooked chestnuts in bottles. These ingredients are often available year-round but are readily available in the fall, so, since each has a long shelf life, you might want to buy more than you'll need for this one tart. (You'll also use the purée in the Christmas Log on page 211.)

《《 *Pears and chestnuts have linear flavors and similar textures, similarities that are not always immediately apparent but that become clear in this tart.* **》》** — P. H.

the crust

- One unbaked 10¼-inch/26-cm tart shell made from Perfect Tart Dough (page 12)

I. Center a rack in the oven and preheat the oven to 350°F.

2. Place the crust on a parchment-lined jelly-roll pan or baking sheet. (For this tart, whose fill-

Makes 8 to 10 servings

ing can bubble over, it's good to use a pan with raised sides.) Line the tart with parchment paper (cut the paper large enough to extend over the side of the tart), fill with beans or rice and bake it for just 15 minutes. Transfer the pan to a rack and allow the crust, still in its ring, to cool to room temperature. *(You can make the crust up to 8 hours ahead and keep it, still in its ring, at room temperature.)*

the filling

- 2 to 3 very ripe medium pears (Comice or Bartlett pears are good here)
- Juice of ½ lemon
- 3 tablespoons chestnut purée (stir before measuring)
- ⅔ cup whole milk
- ⅓ cup crème fraîche, homemade (see page 272) or store-bought
- 1½ teaspoons Scotch whisky
- ¼ cup sugar
- 2 large eggs
- ⅔ cup bottled dry-cooked chestnuts

144

1. Center a rack in the oven and preheat the oven to 350°F.

2. Cut the cored, unpeeled pears into small (about ⅓-inch) cubes; you should have about 2½ cups of fruit. Toss the pears in a bowl with the lemon juice to keep them from darkening and set aside. (Pierre likes the extra flavor and texture he gets by keeping the skin on the pears. If the skin on your pears is thick, or if keeping the skin on doesn't appeal to you, by all means, peel the pears.)

3. Scrape the chestnut purée into a medium bowl and, using a whisk, stir the purée to loosen it, then blend in the milk and crème fraîche. One by one, add the whisky, sugar, and eggs, stirring until the mixture is smooth. There's no reason to be overzealous — you're aiming to make sure the filling is smooth, not airy. With your fingers, break the chestnuts into small pieces and scatter them over the bottom of the crust. Turn the pears into the crust, spreading them evenly over the chestnuts, and then pour in the filling (you might find this easier to do if you put the baking sheet with the tart shell into the oven before you pour in the filling); depending on how much or how little your crust shrank during baking, you may have some filling left over. Bake the tart for 35 to 40 minutes, or until a slender knife inserted into the custard comes out clean. Remove the tart from the oven and, keeping it on the baking pan and in its ring, set it on a rack to cool. (You can make the phyllo topping while the tart cools or do it later, at your convenience.)

to finish
- 3 sheets phyllo
- Confectioner's sugar

1. Center a rack in the oven and preheat the oven to 450°F.

2. Place a 10¼-inch/26-cm tart or dessert ring on a baking sheet. Working with 1 piece of phyllo at a time, and keeping the other pieces under a damp cloth, scrunch the phyllo to fit inside the tart ring. Neatness doesn't count here, so just get the phyllo, with all its hills and valleys, into the ring and then pat it down lightly. Repeat with the 2 remaining sheets, piling the sheets on one another. Dust the top of the phyllo crown evenly but not too heavily with confectioner's sugar and slide the baking sheet into the oven. Bake the phyllo for 5 to 7 minutes, or just until the top sheet is shiny and caramelized. Remove the baking sheet from the oven and let the phyllo crown cool to room temperature.

3. To serve, transfer the tart to a serving platter, remove the ring, and top with the phyllo.

145

Keeping
The tart should be served at room temperature — it's really best kept out of the refrigerator — and eaten the day it is made.

mirliton–citrus
TART

Mirliton is a specialty of Normandy, where the name is often given to small almond-filled puff pastries and tarts. Similar to frangipane, a classic almond filling, the mirliton is subtler — the almond flavor is less defined, the texture smoother, and the overall sensation lighter. In this tart, the soft, warmly buttery and roundly sweet mirliton custard covers spirals of fresh orange and grapefruit sections. Before the citrus sections are laid in the crust, they're pressed between layers of paper towels for several hours until, still juicy, their texture takes on a little spring — a delightful contrast to the soft, just-set custard. The tart, with its bits of glistening fruit peeking out from beneath the custard's light sugar coating, has a plain, unassuming, and unfailingly appealing look.

the fruit

- **2 navel oranges**
- **1 grapefruit, preferably pink**

Using a small sharp knife, peel the oranges and grapefruit down to the fruit. Slice between connective membranes to release the fruit, and discard the membranes. Place the segments between triple layers of paper towels and set aside for at least 4 hours, preferably overnight, until the fruit is almost dry. If it's convenient, change the paper towels halfway through the drying time.

Makes 8 servings

the crust

- 1 fully baked 10¼-inch/26-cm tart shell made from Perfect Tart Dough (page 12), cooled to room temperature

Keep the cooled crust, with its ring still in place, on the parchment-lined baking sheet. *(You can make the crust up to 8 hours ahead and keep it in its ring at room temperature.)*

the filling

- 2 large eggs, at room temperature
- ¾ cup sugar
- ⅓ cup (packed) finely ground almonds (see page 277)
- ⅓ cup heavy cream, at room temperature
- ⅓ cup whole milk, at room temperature
- 2 tablespoons (1 ounce) brown butter (see page 267), cooled

1. Center a rack in the oven and preheat the oven to 350°F.
2. Arrange the fruit in concentric circles in the bottom of the crust. You can alternate orange and grapefruit sections, but you needn't be concerned about a decorative pattern.
3. Whisk the eggs and sugar together in a medium bowl. Add the remaining ingredients one by one, whisking just until each ingredient is incorporated — mix gently; the mirliton shouldn't be foamy. Pour the mixture over the fruit and slip the tart into the oven to bake for 20 to 25 minutes, or until the custard is set — the filling shouldn't jiggle when you shake the pan gently. Transfer the tart to a rack to cool completely.
4. At serving time, slide the tart onto a platter and lift off the tart ring.

Keeping

The fruit must be drained ahead and the crust can be made in advance, but the tart should be eaten the day it is made.

CARIBBEAN
tartlets

What makes these tartlets Caribbean is the mix of sweet, juicy pineapple and lime; what makes them such charmers is their simplicity. The tartlets, made in one-and-a-half-inch tins, shimmer with apricot glaze and sparkle with pomegranate seeds. If you cut the pineapple early in the day and make the tartlet shells ahead, all you'll have to do at serving time is fill the shells and pass the Caribbean coffee — or some good island rum.

the pineapple
- ½ ripe pineapple

Peel the pineapple and, using a large serrated knife, slice it into rounds about ¼ inch thick. Remove the core — easily done with a small cookie or biscuit cutter — and slice the pieces of pineapple into very thin sticks. Lay the sticks out in a single layer on a triple thickness of paper towels, cover with another three layers of paper towel, and let the pineapple drain for about 2 hours, changing the paper once or twice during this period if possible.

the shells
- ⅓ recipe Sweet Tart Dough (page 15), cut in half, covered, and chilled

1. To mold the tartlets, butter and set aside twenty 1½-inch tartlet tins, fluted or plain (or other small tins). You can use mini-muffin tins, if it's convenient. Also set aside a 2-inch round bis-

Makes about 20 tartlets
(depending on the size of the tins)

cuit or cookie cutter, preferably fluted (or a cutter that is about ½ inch larger than the diameter of the tartlet tins you're using), as many 3- to 4-inch square pieces of aluminum foil as you have tins, and some dried pea beans or rice. (You'll use the foil and beans to weight the dough while you bake the shells.)

2. Working on a floured surface with one piece of dough at a time (keep the other piece in the refrigerator), roll the dough to a thickness of about ⅛ inch. Use the biscuit cutter to cut out as many circles of dough as you can from the rolled-out sheet. Clear away the excess dough and set it aside for the moment. Fit each round of dough into a buttered tin. To get a good fit without roughing up the dough, use a small ball of excess dough to push the dough into the bottom and up the sides of the tin. Place the tins on a jelly-roll pan and refrigerate them while you roll out, cut, and mold the second piece of dough. Place the second set of shells on the jelly-roll pan and chill the tins for at least 30 minutes. If you'd like, the scraps can be rolled and cut to make additional tartlets; gather the scraps from both pieces of dough, form them into a disk, and cover and chill them for at least an hour before rolling out.

to bake

Center a rack in the oven and preheat the oven to 350°F. Remove the pan with the tartlet tins from the refrigerator and gently press a square of aluminum foil into each tin. (The foil should cover the tart shell and extend above the rim.) Put a few beans or a spoonful of rice into each tin — just enough to keep the foil in place — and bake the tartlets for about 15 minutes. Remove the foil and beans and bake the shells for another 2 minutes or so, just until they are lightly colored. Transfer the pan to a rack and allow the shells to cool to room temperature. *(The tartlet shells can be made up to 8 hours ahead and kept at room temperature.)*

to assemble

- 1 cup apricot preserves
- Zest of 1 to 2 limes — removed with a zester (see page 281)
- Pomegranate seeds, optional

1. Bring the apricot preserves to a boil in a small saucepan. As soon as the preserves come to the boil, remove the saucepan from the heat and press the preserves through a strainer into a bowl. (The strained preserves will be used as the glaze.)

2. Remove the tartlet shells from their tins and fill each shell with a mound of pineapple spears. Lay two or three strands of lime zest over each tartlet. To finish, brush the tartlets with a thin coat of apricot glaze and decorate with a few pomegranate seeds, if you're using them. The tartlets can be served now or kept at cool room temperature or in the refrigerator; they should be served just cool.

Keeping

The tartlet shells can be made up to 8 hours ahead, and the pineapple should drain for a few hours, but once assembled, the tartlets should be served on the day they are made.

orange TARTLETS

The filling for these tartlets is simple yet startling. Thin slices of orange are chopped, mixed with marmalade, tossed with ribbons of fresh mint, and, in the process, transformed. It's the chopping that does it. It turns oranges into what few would expect them to be — comfort food. While the filling's flavor is bright and refreshing, shining with the orange's liveliest and most winning characteristics, its texture, soft and slithery, is decidedly un-orange-like and, indeed, comforting.

You have some leeway in the size of the tartlets. Pierre likes to make these bite-size, using tartlet tins that are a mere one and a half inches across, but you can change the size depending on your whim or the size of the tins you have on hand. Don't, however, make these too large; they are meant to be petit fours, with the emphasis on *petit*. Keep in mind that if you change the size of the tartlets, you might have to make accordingly more or less filling.

the oranges

- 4 large oranges
- $2\frac{2}{3}$ cups water
- 2 tablespoons sugar

Peel the oranges down to the fruit, making sure to remove any traces of white, cottony pith. Slice the oranges crosswise into very thin rounds — cut them as thin as you possibly can — and put the slices in a large glass pan or stainless steel bowl. Bring the water and sugar just to the boil (you can do this in a saucepan over direct heat or in the microwave oven), and

Makes about 20 tartlets
(depending on the size of the tins)

immediately pour the hot liquid over the oranges. Cover the pan or bowl with plastic wrap and allow the mixture to cool to room temperature, then transfer it to the refrigerator. The oranges should macerate overnight. *(You can make the oranges ahead and keep them covered in the refrigerator for up to 2 days.)*

the shells

- ⅓ recipe Sweet Tart Dough (page 15), cut in half, covered, and chilled

1. To mold the tartlets, butter and set aside twenty 1½-inch tartlet tins, fluted or plain (or other small tins). You can use mini-muffin tins, if it's convenient. Also set aside a 2-inch round biscuit or cookie cutter, preferably fluted (or a cutter that is about ½ inch larger than the diameter of the tartlet tins you're using), as many 3- to 4-inch-square pieces of aluminum foil as you have tins, and some dried pea beans or rice. (You'll use the foil and beans to weight the dough while you bake the shells.)

2. Working on a floured surface with one piece of dough at a time (keep the other piece in the refrigerator), roll the dough to a thickness of about ⅛ inch. Use the biscuit cutter to cut out as many circles of dough as you can from the rolled-out sheet. Clear away the excess dough and set it aside for the moment. Fit each round of dough into a buttered tin. To get a good fit without roughing up the dough, use a small ball of excess dough to push the dough into the bottom and up the sides of the tin. Place the tins on a jelly-roll pan and refrigerate them while you roll out, cut, and mold the second piece of dough. Place the second set of shells on the jelly-roll pan and chill the tins for at least 30 minutes. If you'd like, the dough scraps can be rolled and cut to make additional tartlets; gather the scraps from both pieces of dough, form them into a disk, and cover and chill them for at least an hour before rolling out.

to bake

Center a rack in the oven and preheat the oven to 350°F. Remove the pan with the tartlet tins from the refrigerator and gently press a square of aluminum foil into each tin. (The foil should cover the tart shell and extend above the rim.) Put a few beans or a spoonful of rice into each tin — just enough to keep the foil in place — and bake the tartlets for about 15 minutes. Remove the foil and beans and bake the shells for another 2 minutes or so, just until they are lightly colored. Transfer the pan to a rack and allow the shells to cool to room temperature. *(The tartlet shells can be made up to 8 hours ahead and kept at room temperature.)*

to assemble

- ½ cup sweet orange marmalade
- 20 fresh mint leaves, very finely sliced (chiffonade) or chopped,
  plus 20 small fresh mint leaves (or as many as you have tartlets), for garnish

1. Drain the orange slices well, pressing out as much liquid as you can, and then blot the slices as dry as possible between layers of paper towels. Chop the oranges — don't make the chop too fine or too regular — and transfer the pieces to a mixing bowl. Add the marmalade and the sliced mint and toss lightly to mix evenly.

2. Remove the tartlet shells from their tins. Using a small spoon, fill each shell with the chopped orange mixture, mounding the filling slightly and using the spoon to pat it into a dome. Top each tartlet with a small mint leaf and serve.

155

Keeping

The oranges should be macerated at least a day ahead and the tart dough should be prepared ahead, but once assembled, the tartlets are best served quickly. If necessary, the tartlets can be kept at room temperature for a few hours. However, they should be eaten the day they're made.

passionately chocolate

TARTLETS

This is one of Pierre's dangerous desserts — dangerous because it seems so cool and refreshing you forget that it's really a high-octane mix of chocolate and cream, a ganache that is, as it should be, richly rich. The illusion of lightness is the result of the completely unexpected addition of passion fruit, its bright acidic flavor a quirky counterpoint to the chocolate. Tucked into each tartlet, and topping it too, are cubes of lemon-drenched dried apricots, another riff in the sweet-tart refrain.

I created these because I adore the combination of chocolate and passion fruit, but it's neither an obvious combination nor one that's easy to put together. To get the right balance, you've got to use a chocolate that's not too bitter. — P.H.

the apricots

- 10 moist, plump, dried apricots (Turkish apricots are good here), cut into small cubes
- ½ cup water
- 3 tablespoons freshly squeezed lemon juice
- 1 teaspoon honey
- Pinch of freshly ground black pepper

Place all of the ingredients in a heavy-bottomed 2-quart saucepan over medium heat and bring to the boil. Reduce the heat to its lowest setting and simmer for about 8 to 10 minutes, or until the apricots are soft and puffy. Remove the pan from the heat, cover, and allow the apricots to steep in the liquid for 3 to 4 hours. When you're ready to use the apricots, drain

157

Makes about 24 tartlets
(depending on the size of the tins)

them and pat dry between paper towels. *(The apricots can be prepared a day ahead and kept covered, in their liquid, at room temperature.)*

the crust

- ⅓ recipe Sweet Tart Dough (page 15), cut in half, covered, and chilled

1. To mold the tartlets, butter and set aside twenty-four 1½-inch tartlet tins, fluted or plain (or other small tins). You can use mini-muffin tins, if it's convenient. Also set aside a 2-inch round biscuit or cookie cutter, preferably fluted (or a cutter that is about ½ inch larger than the diameter of the tartlet tins you're using), as many 3- to 4-inch-square pieces of aluminum foil as you have tins, and some dried pea beans or rice. (You'll use the foil and beans to weight the dough while you bake the shells.)

2. Working on a floured surface with one piece of dough at a time (keep the other piece in the refrigerator), roll the dough to a thickness of about ⅛ inch. Use the biscuit cutter to cut out as many circles of dough as you can from the rolled-out sheet. Clear away the excess dough and set it aside for the moment. Fit each round of dough into a buttered tin. To get a good fit without roughing up the dough, use a small ball of excess dough to push the dough into the bottom and up the sides of the tin. Place the tins on a jelly-roll pan and refrigerate them while you roll out, cut, and mold the second piece of dough. Place the second set of shells on the jelly-roll pan and chill the tins for at least 30 minutes. If you'd like, the scraps can be rolled and cut to make additional tartlets; gather the scraps from both pieces of dough, form them into a disk, and cover and chill for at least an hour before rolling out.

to bake

Center a rack in the oven and preheat the oven to 350°F. Remove the pan with the tartlet tins from the refrigerator and gently press a square of aluminum foil into each tin. (The foil should cover the tart shell and extend above the rim.) Put a few beans or a spoonful of rice into each tin — just enough to keep the foil in place — and bake the tartlets for about 15 minutes. Remove the foil and beans and bake the shells for another 2 minutes or so, just until they are lightly colored. Transfer the pan to a rack and allow the shells to cool to room temperature. *(The tartlet shells can be made up to 8 hours ahead and kept at room temperature.)*

the ganache

- 5¾ ounces bittersweet chocolate (preferably Valrhona Noir Gastronomie), very finely chopped
- ⅓ cup heavy cream
- ⅓ cup freshly pressed or bottled passion fruit juice
- 3 tablespoons (1½ ounces) unsalted butter, at room temperature

1. Place the chocolate in a large heatproof bowl. Bring the heavy cream to a boil in a small saucepan; in another saucepan, bring the passion fruit juice to a boil. (Both the cream and the juice can be heated in a microwave oven.)

2. Pour half of the boiling cream over the chopped chocolate and stir gently, starting in the center of the bowl, with a rubber spatula. Using a very light touch and taking care not to overmix, stir in increasingly larger concentric circles until the cream is incorporated. Repeat with the remaining cream and then, in the same manner, stir in the warm passion fruit juice. Cut the butter into pieces and add it to the ganache, stirring gently to combine. If the ganache has cooled so much that the butter is not melting into it, place the bowl over a pan of simmering water and warm the chocolate gently. Once the butter is blended, the ganache will need a few minutes in the refrigerator to set up. Chill it for 10 minutes, then take a look. Chill for another 5 minutes if needed. (If you warmed the ganache to incorporate the butter, it will need a longer chilling — just keep an eye on it.) You want the ganache to remain smooth, shiny, and of a consistency that is easy to pipe. *(You can make the ganache a day ahead and keep it covered overnight in the refrigerator. Be certain to allow it to come to room temperature before piping it into the tartlets.)*

to assemble

Put a few small cubes of steeped (and patted dry) apricots into the bottom of each tartlet shell, making sure to set aside a dozen or so cubes for topping. Spoon the ganache into a pastry bag fitted with a ½-inch star tip and pipe a swirl of ganache into each shell. (If the ganache is very soft after piping, pop the tartlets into the fridge for a couple of minutes.) Put a cube of apricot on the top of each tartlet and serve. These are meant to be served at room temperature when the ganache is soft, smooth, shiny, and at its most chocolaty.

Keeping
Although the components of this dessert can be made ahead, once the tartlets are filled, they're best served soon.

CAKES

LEMON
loaf cakes

These loaves are reminiscent of fine-crumbed pound cake (although made by a method more commonly used for sponge cakes), each morsel offering up a bit of sweet, buttery flavor and the puckery punch of lemon and crème fraîche. The batter is put together by hand in five minutes (it's an ideal beginner's cake) and yields two loaves that are good keepers, inviting end-of-the-run toasting — slices of the cake are great straight from the toaster, topped with jam. Appealing as is, the loaves can be given a shiny finish with a brush of melted lemon marmalade.

If you want even more lemon flavor, soak the hot cakes with a lemon syrup. When the cakes go into the oven, heat ⅓ cup water and 3½ tablespoons sugar just until the sugar dissolves. When the syrup cools, add 2 tablespoons freshly squeezed lemon juice. Then, as soon as the cakes are baked, place them on a rack and brush on the syrup. — P. H.

- 2⅔ cups cake flour
- ¾ teaspoon double-acting baking powder
- Zest of 3 lemons — removed with a zester (see page 281) and very finely chopped
- 2 cups sugar
- 6 large eggs, at room temperature
- ¾ cup crème fraîche, homemade (see page 272) or store-bought, at room temperature, or heavy cream
- 3½ tablespoons rum

Makes 2 cakes, each serves 6 to 8

- Pinch of salt
- 1 stick plus 1 tablespoon ($4\frac{1}{2}$ ounces) unsalted butter, melted and cooled
- About 1 cup lemon marmalade, for glaze, optional

1. Center a rack in the oven and preheat the oven to 350°F. Butter and flour two $7\frac{1}{2}$ by $3\frac{1}{2}$ by $2\frac{1}{2}$-inch loaf pans, dust the interiors with flour, and tap out the excess; set aside. (These are the perfect size pans for these cakes, but they're not always easily found. If you don't have them, use two $8\frac{1}{2}$ by $4\frac{1}{2}$ by $2\frac{1}{2}$-inch loaf pans. Your cakes won't be as tall, but they'll be every bit as flavorful.) Prepare an insulating layer for the cakes by stacking two baking sheets, one on top of the other, or use an insulated (air-cushioned) baking sheet.

2. Sift the flour and baking powder together and reserve.

3. Place the chopped zest and sugar in a large mixing bowl and rub them together between your fingers until the sugar is moist, grainy, and very aromatic. Add the eggs and, using a whisk, beat until the eggs are foamy and pale. One by one, add the crème fraîche (or heavy cream), rum, and salt and whisk until the ingredients are incorporated. Using the whisk or a large rubber spatula, gently stir the flour mixture into the batter in four additions; you'll have a smooth, thick batter. Finally, fold in the cooled melted butter in two to three additions.

4. Immediately pour the batter into the prepared loaf pans, place them on the baking sheet(s), and slip them into the oven. Bake for 55 to 65 minutes, or until the cakes are crowned, split down the center, and golden. A long thin knife inserted into the center of each cake should come out dry and crumb-free. (Check the cakes at the 40-minute mark. If they are browning too quickly, cover them loosely with foil tents for the remainder of the baking period.) Remove the cakes from the oven and turn them out of the pans onto a cooling rack; invert them so they're right side up. Allow the cakes to cool to room temperature before glazing or serving. (If you want to use Pierre's soaking syrup [see page 163], you should brush on the syrup before you glaze the cakes.)

5. If you want to glaze the cakes, place the marmalade in a small saucepan and bring to the boil over low heat (or heat it in the microwave oven); strain the marmalade. Use a broad pastry brush to paint every surface (except the bottoms) of the cakes with a thin coat of glaze. Allow the glaze to dry at room temperature before serving (or wrapping).

VARIATION

VANILLA BEAN LOAVES

Replace the lemon zest with the fragrant pulp scraped from the insides of 2 plump, moist vanilla beans (see page 281).

Keeping

Wrapped tightly in plastic, the cakes will keep at room temperature for about a week. If you haven't glazed the cakes, you can wrap them airtight and freeze them for up to a month.

Slices of stale cake can be lightly toasted in a toaster or brushed with melted butter and browned under the broiler.

coconut *LOAF CAKE*

Yes, this is a plain-looking loaf cake, big and golden brown, crowned and cracked down the middle, homey and wholesome, but it packs a jolt: a couple of tablespoons of ground coriander — just enough to both puzzle and please. Barely discernible as coriander, however, it plays the part of an intensifier, pushing the taste of the coconut and adding its own elusive but appreciated extra layer of flavor.

The cake is made in the traditional cream-the-butter-and-sugar-together method, the simplest in the baker's bag of tricks and the one guaranteed to give you the right texture. If you'd like it even moister, soak it with rum syrup (page 167) when it comes out of the oven.

«*I had the idea for a coconut cake in my head for a long time before I created this cake. I'd been looking for a spice to pair with coconut and then one evening I was eating a savory dish with coriander and voilà! There it was and I knew it was right. This cake can be served at any temperature, but I think it's most interesting when it's toasted. I even toast it when it's fresh, and I love to serve it with the Gourmandise [page 49].* » — P. H.

- 1½ cups unsweetened finely grated dried coconut, plus optional additional coconut for the cake pan (see page 271)
- 1¼ cups sugar
- 1½ cups all-purpose flour
- 2 tablespoons coriander
- 1 teaspoon double-acting baking powder

Makes 8 to 10 servings

- 1 stick plus 1 tablespoon (4½ ounces) unsalted butter, softened
- 3 large eggs, at room temperature
- ¼ cup powdered milk
- ¾ cup whole milk, at room temperature

1. This cake has the best texture when you use coconut that is almost as powdery as ground nuts. To get the coconut to this consistency, place it in the container of a food processor or blender with 1 tablespoon of the sugar and process until the coconut is pulverized. But take care not to process the coconut into a paste — it should be powdery and dry.

2. Center a rack in the oven and preheat the oven to 350°F. Butter an 8½ by 4½ by 2½-inch loaf pan, dust the interior with the optional finely grated coconut, and tap out the excess; set aside. (You can omit the coconut, in which case the pan should be dusted with flour.) Prepare an insulating layer for the cake by stacking two baking sheets, one on top of the other, or use an insulated (air-cushioned) baking sheet.

3. Sift the flour, coriander, and baking powder together and reserve.

4. Working at medium-high speed in a mixer fitted with the paddle attachment, beat the butter until it is creamy. Add the remaining 1 cup plus 3 tablespoons sugar and continue to beat, scraping down the sides of the bowl as needed, until the mixture is pale, thick, and fluffy, about 2 minutes. Beat in the eggs one by one, beating well after each addition and scraping the bowl as necessary. Decrease the mixer speed to low and, one by one, add the coconut, powdered milk, and whole milk, beating only until each addition is incorporated. (The batter may look soupy and curdled — don't worry, it will come together when you add the dry ingredients.) Remove the bowl from the mixer and, working by hand with a large rubber spatula, fold the flour mixture gently into the batter in two or three additions; you'll have a smooth, thick batter.

5. Immediately spoon the batter into the prepared pan — it will just about fill the pan — place it on the baking sheet, and slip it into the oven. Bake for about 70 to 80 minutes, or until the cake is crowned, split down the center, and golden. A long thin knife inserted into the center of the cake should come out dry and crumb-free. (This cake has a tendency to brown quickly, so it's a good idea to cover it loosely with a foil tent after it's been in the oven for 30 minutes.) Remove the cake from the oven and turn it out onto a cooling rack; invert it so that it is right side up. If you want to soak the cake with rum syrup, do it now while the cake is still hot (see facing page). Allow the cake to cool to room temperature before wrapping for storage (see "Keeping" notes, opposite).

rum syrup (optional)

- ¼ cup Simple Syrup (page 39)
- ¼ cup water
- ¼ cup white rum

Stir the syrup, water, and rum together. Place the cake on its cooling rack over a piece of wax paper and, working with a pastry brush, brush the syrup over the top and sides of the cake.

167

Keeping

Of course you can enjoy this cake as soon as it cools, but it is really better — the flavors are more powerful — after a day's rest. To "ripen" the cake, wrap it airtight in plastic and keep it at room temperature for a day before serving. Wrapped airtight, the cake will keep for 5 to 7 days at room temperature, or for 1 month in the freezer.

hazelnut–carrot

LOAF CAKES

Whether these should be called Hazelnut-Carrot or Carrot-Hazelnut Loaf Cakes is up for grabs (they're so well balanced it's hard to know which ingredient takes precedence), but it's certain you won't mistake them for anything typically American. While an American carrot cake is substantial, very moist, and often very sweet, these loaves are light, soft, and spongy, just moist enough, and hardly sweet at all. Served plain or with crème anglaise or whipped cream, they are good with tea.

« *My father brought this recipe home from his training in Switzerland, and it's one he continues to make at his pâtisserie in Colmar. When he makes it, he grates all of the carrots, but when I started making it, I decided to purée some of them to give the cake a little more aroma. Even with the change, the cake always brings back memories of my childhood.* » — P.H.

- 8 medium carrots, peeled
- 1½ cups ground hazelnuts (see page 277), plus ⅓ cup hazelnuts, toasted, skinned (see page 90), and finely chopped
- 1½ cups ground almonds (see page 277)
- ¾ cup all-purpose flour
- 1 teaspoon double-acting baking powder
- Pinch of salt
- 10 large egg whites
- ¾ cup plus 2 tablespoons sugar

Makes 2 cakes, each serving 8 to 10

- **5 large egg yolks**
- **Zest of 1 orange** — removed with a zester (see page 281) and very finely chopped

1. Finely grate 5 of the carrots using the shredding blade of a food processor or a box grater. You should have about 2 loosely packed cups carrots (don't push them into the measuring cup). Spread the carrots out on a triple thickness of paper towels, cover with another triple layer of towels, and set aside for an hour.

2. Coarsely chop the remaining carrots and steam them until they are very tender and can be pierced easily with the tip of a knife. (Alternatively, you can cook the carrots in the microwave oven.) While the carrots are still hot, purée them in a food mill, food processor, or blender. You should have ½ cup firmly packed purée. Set the purée aside to cool to room temperature.

3. Center a rack in the oven and preheat the oven to 350°F. Butter two 9 by 5 by 3-inch loaf pans, dust them with flour, and tap out the excess; set aside.

4. Whisk together the ground nuts (hazelnuts and almonds) and the chopped hazelnuts, and set aside. Sift together the flour, baking powder, and salt, and set this mixture aside for the moment too.

5. In an impeccably clean, dry bowl, whip the egg whites until they start to mound. Still whipping, add half of the sugar little by little, and continue to beat until the whites form glossy peaks; reserve.

6. Working in a bowl large enough to hold all the ingredients, whisk the egg yolks and the remaining sugar together until the sugar dissolves. Stir in the nut mixture with a rubber spatula. Still working with the spatula, stir in the grated carrots and the carrot purée. Next, gently stir in the flour mixture, followed by the orange zest. Stir about one quarter of the glossy egg whites into the mixture to lighten it and then delicately fold in the remaining whites.

7. Divide the batter evenly between the two pans. Slide the pans into the oven and bake for 40 to 45 minutes, or until the cakes are honey brown and pull away from the sides of the pans. A long thin knife inserted into the center of the cakes should come out clean. Transfer the loaves to a rack and immediately turn them out of the pans; invert them so they're right side up. Allow the cakes to cool to room temperature before serving or wrapping for storage.

Keeping
Wrapped airtight in plastic, the
cakes will keep at room temperature
for about 4 days or in the freezer
for a month.

FRUIT and SPICE
loaf cake

Here's a loaf cake made in the style of old-fashioned *pain d'épices,* or French spice cake. Not a typical gingerbread, but not quite American spice cake either, *pain d'épices,* a specialty of Dijon, is a hearty sweet. In this rendition, the spices — cinnamon, ginger, coriander, cardamom, pepper, nutmeg, and star anise — are joined by nuts, zest, and cubes of fruit to produce a deeply flavorful teatime sweet that falls somewhere between quick bread and cake, between a spicy fruit cake and fruity nut cake. Like its ancestors, this cake benefits from a rest before tasting, making it a perfect do-ahead offering.

- ¾ cup plus 2 tablespoons water
- 10 pieces star anise
- ⅓ cup honey (Pierre uses pine honey)
- 5½ tablespoons (2¾ ounces) unsalted butter, melted
- 2¼ cups all-purpose flour
- ¼ cup rye flour
- 2½ teaspoons double-acting baking powder
- 1 tablespoon cinnamon
- 1 teaspoon ginger
- 1 teaspoon freshly ground black pepper, preferably Sarawak
- ½ teaspoon coriander
- ½ teaspoon cardamom

Makes 16 to 20 servings

- ½ teaspoon freshly grated nutmeg
- ⅔ cup coarsely chopped walnuts
- ⅓ cup sliced blanched almonds, toasted (see page 277)
- 5¼ ounces pitted, moist prunes (about 13), cut into ¼-inch cubes
- 4¼ ounces moist, plump dried apricots (about 13), cut into ¼-inch cubes
- Zest of 1 lemon — removed with a zester (see page 281) and finely chopped
- Zest of 1 orange — removed with a zester (see page 281) and finely chopped

1. Place the water and star anise in a saucepan over high heat, or in a microwave-safe container in the microwave oven, and bring to the boil. Remove from the heat, cover, and infuse for 1 hour.

2. Center a rack in the oven and preheat the oven to 300°F. Very lightly spray an 8 by 4 by 2½-inch loaf pan with vegetable oil spray and then line the pan with parchment paper; set aside until needed. Prepare an insulating layer for the cake by stacking two baking sheets, one on top of the other, or use an insulated (air-cushioned) baking sheet.

3. Stir the honey and melted butter together in a medium bowl, then strain the star anise–infused water into the bowl. Stir to blend and then set the bowl aside.

4. Sift the all-purpose flour, rye flour, baking powder, and spices together into a large bowl. In another bowl, stir together the nuts, dried fruits, and zests. Add 1 tablespoon of the dry ingredients to the nuts and fruits and toss to coat the ingredients lightly with the flour.

5. Pour the honey mixture into the bowl with the flour and spices and stir gently with a wooden spoon or large rubber spatula. Treat this batter as you would a quick bread or muffin mixture — stir it only until the dry ingredients are moistened. Add the nuts and fruits and lightly stir them into the batter — thoroughness isn't important here. (The batter will be very thick, more like a quick bread dough than a cake batter.)

6. Spoon the batter into the pan and bake for 65 to 75 minutes, or until a thin knife inserted deeply into the cake comes out clean. Transfer the cake to a cooling rack and unmold it, then invert it to cool to room temperature right side up. When the cake is absolutely cool — this can take a couple of hours since the fruits and nuts retain the heat — wrap the cake in a double thickness of plastic wrap and allow it to "ripen" for a day before slicing and serving in very thin slices. (Of course, you can eat it now if you want to.)

172

Keeping

Wrapped airtight in plastic, the cake will keep at room temperature for about 4 days or in the freezer for a month. It should be served in thin slices and is wonderful with hot tea or cider.

chocolate–nut
LOAF

Like so many of Pierre's loaf cakes, this one's a fooler. It looks like a plain, grandmotherly chocolate loaf, but when you cut into it, you discover it's moist, dense, completely chocolaty, and chockful of chewables: chunks of bittersweet chocolate and lots of large pieces of almonds, hazelnuts, and pistachios. With a base of almond paste and a finish of melted butter, it's a good keeper — you could nibble on this from Monday to Friday. In fact, you'll find that a day under wraps will give the flavors a chance to blend.

« *When I wanted to create a chocolate loaf cake, I wanted a* vrai *chocolate cake, a true chocolate cake made with true chocolate, not just cocoa powder. I put the large pieces of chocolate into the batter to underscore the cake's deep chocolate flavor.* » — P. H .

- 1⅓ cups all-purpose flour
- 7 tablespoons Dutch-processed cocoa powder
- ½ teaspoon double-acting baking powder
- ⅔ cup sugar
- 5 ounces almond paste (see page 266)
- 4 large eggs, at room temperature
- ⅔ cup whole milk
- ½ cup hazelnuts, toasted (see page 277), skinned (see page 90), and coarsely chopped
- ⅓ cup blanched almonds, toasted (see page 277) and coarsely chopped

Makes 8 to 10 servings

- $\frac{1}{3}$ cup skinned pistachios, coarsely chopped
- 3 ounces bittersweet chocolate (preferably Valrhona Manjari), cut into small chunks
- 1 stick plus 5 tablespoons ($6\frac{1}{2}$ ounces) unsalted butter, melted and cooled to room temperature

1. Center a rack in the oven and preheat the oven to 350°F. Prepare an insulating layer for the cake by stacking two baking sheets, one on top of the other, or use an insulated (air-cushioned) baking sheet. Butter a 9 by 5-inch loaf pan and set it aside.

2. Sift together the flour, cocoa, and baking powder and set this mixture aside.

3. Put the sugar and almond paste in a mixer fitted with the paddle attachment and beat on medium speed until the almond paste breaks up and blends with the sugar; the mixture will look sandy. Add the eggs one at time, beating for about 2 minutes after each addition. Replace the paddle with the whisk attachment, increase the mixer speed to high, and beat for 8 to 10 minutes, until the ingredients have formed an emulsion — the batter will look like mayonnaise and the whisk will leave tracks as it spins.

4. Reduce the mixer speed to low and add the milk, mixing until combined, then add the sifted dry ingredients. Continue beating on low until the mixture is homogenous.

5. Working with a large rubber spatula, fold in the hazelnuts, followed by the almonds, pistachios, and chocolate. Gently fold in the melted butter.

6. Turn the batter into the prepared pan and level the top. Bake for 60 to 70 minutes, or until a slender knife inserted in the center of the cake comes out clean. (The cake will crack as it bakes. If you want to help it crack more evenly than it might by chance, wait until the cake just starts to develop a crust, at about the 20-minute mark, then run a pastry scraper dipped in melted butter lengthwise down the center of the cake.) Remove the cake from the oven and let it cool on a rack for 10 minutes before unmolding. Invert the cake so that it's right side up and cool to room temperature on the rack. The cake can be served now, although it's best to wrap it in a double thickness of plastic wrap and allow it to "ripen" for a day before cutting it into very thin slices and serving.

174

Keeping
Wrapped in plastic and stored at room temperature, the cake will remain moist for at least 5 days; wrapped airtight, it will keep in the freezer for a month.

PLAIN OR FANCY

LIGURIAN
lemon cake

Moist, lemony, and dotted with raspberries, this simple round cake gets much of its depth of flavor from the unexpected addition of extra-virgin olive oil. While mild Ligurian olive oil is Pierre's oil of choice, any fine-quality olive oil that's not too assertive will give you what you're looking for — a cake with a rich aroma, a light olive taste, and a soft texture. Serve the cake plain, just out of the pan, or fancy, spread with meringue, browned in the oven, and finished with fresh berries.

«*In addition to the distinctive taste you get from using olive oil in this cake, you'll notice that it makes the texture unusually smooth and supple too.* » — P.H.

the cake
- 1¾ cups all-purpose flour
- 1½ teaspoons double-acting baking powder
- 1 cup sugar
- Zest of 2 lemons — removed with a zester (see page 281) and very finely chopped
- 4 large eggs, at room temperature
- 3 tablespoons whole milk, at room temperature
- 1 tablespoon freshly squeezed lemon juice
- 7 tablespoons (3½ ounces) unsalted butter, melted and still warm
- ⅔ cup mild extra-virgin olive oil
- About 1 pint fresh raspberries

Makes 10 to 12 servings

1. Center a rack in the oven and preheat the oven to 350°F. Butter a 10-inch round cake or springform pan, dust the interior with flour, and tap out the excess.
2. Sift the flour and baking powder together and reserve.
3. Place the sugar and chopped zest in the bowl of a mixer and rub the ingredients together between your fingers until the sugar is moist, grainy, and very aromatic. Fit the bowl into the mixer with the whisk attachment in place, add the eggs, and beat on medium-high speed until the mixture is pale and thick, about 3 minutes.
4. Set the mixer to its lowest speed and beat in the milk. Add the sifted dry ingredients, beating only until they are incorporated, and then add the lemon juice, warm melted butter, and olive oil, again beating only until blended.
5. Pour about one third of the batter into the prepared pan — it should be just enough to form a thin, even layer. Top with enough raspberries to cover the batter, then pour on the rest of the batter, using a rubber spatula to gently spread the batter so that it runs down between the berries and just covers them. You'll have a very thin top layer of batter, and that's the way it's supposed to be.
6. Bake the cake for 30 to 33 minutes, or until it is golden and pulls away from the sides of the pan; a knife inserted into the center of the cake should come out clean. Remove the cake from the oven and immediately unmold it onto a cooling rack; invert so that the cake is right side up and allow it cool to room temperature. Once cooled, the cake is ready to serve or to decorate with meringue.

the meringue (optional)

- 1 large egg white
- ¼ cup sugar
- Confectioner's sugar
- Fresh raspberries or a mixture of raspberries, strawberries, and blueberries, optional

1. Center a rack in the oven and preheat the oven to 475°F. Place the cake on a parchment-lined baking sheet.
2. Working in an impeccably clean, dry mixing bowl, beat the egg white until it holds soft peaks. Add the sugar in a slow, steady stream and continue to beat until the mixture forms firm, glossy peaks. Immediately spread the meringue over the top of the cake, using a metal icing spatula or a spoon. Dust the meringue with confectioner's sugar and bake for 4 to 6 minutes, or until lightly browned. (Alternatively, you can brown the meringue using a blowtorch.) Top the cake with berries, if you're using them.

Keeping

"Unmeringued," the cake can be wrapped in plastic and kept at room temperature for at least 4 days or frozen for up to a month. However,

once the cake is topped with meringue, it should be served or stored in the refrigerator and eaten the day it is made.

melody

This is the stuff of standing ovations. Composed of a cake, a crust, and two fillings, this complex Melody — really more a symphony — is a mix of wildly contrasting textures. The cake, a downy génoise, is sandwiched between two disks of crunchy, crumbly, butter-and-cinnamon pastry, and together the cake and crust cradle a layer of Twenty-Hour Apples and a cushion of exceptionally light caramelized-cinnamon Bavarian cream. (A Bavarian cream is a classic preparation based on crème anglaise and stabilized with both gelatin and whipped cream.) The flavors blend seamlessly; the apple-cinnamon cream mix is, indeed, melodic, and the cake, while unlike anything Yankee, appeals absolutely to every apple-loving American.

With the exception of the Bavarian cream, which must be used as soon as it is mixed, each of the Melody's elements can be — in fact, must be — made ahead, and the whole cake, minus the pastry, can be frozen. But once it's fully assembled, the cake should be served the day it is made.

>> *Apples and cinnamon marry easily, but here there are other elements, like orange and almonds, that make this dessert at once classic and original. If you don't want to make the whole cake, you can make a simpler plated dessert with just the Twenty-Hour Apples and the Bavarian cream: Spread a portion of the apples on a plate, cover with the cream, and serve.* >> — P. H.

the apples
- 1¼ cups (about ¼ recipe) Twenty-Hour Apples (page 33)

Makes 8 to 10 servings

179

At least 2 days before assembling the cake, prepare the apples, making certain they have the chance to chill for at least 10 hours. Keep the apples refrigerated until needed.

the crust

- 1 recipe Cinnamon Dough (page 18), chilled

I. For the Melody, the cinnamon crust should be slightly thicker than usual. Cut the dough into thirds and reserve one piece for another use. Working with one piece of dough at a time, and keeping the work surface and the dough well floured, roll the dough to a thickness of ⅛ inch. Cut an 8¾-inch/22-cm circle from each piece (use a dessert or tart ring to get the size right) and carefully transfer the dough to one or two parchment-lined baking sheets. The dough is very fragile and is transferred most easily — and safely — by slipping the removable bottom of a metal tart pan under it. If necessary, dust the metal round with flour for extra insurance. Prick both pieces of dough all over with the tines of a fork. Cover with sheets of plastic wrap and chill for at least 30 minutes. *(The dough can be kept, well covered, in the refrigerator for several hours.)*

2. Center a rack in the oven and preheat the oven to 350°F. Remove the sheets of plastic and bake the disks for about 18 to 20 minutes, or until they are honey brown. (If you are baking on two sheets, rotate the sheets front to back and top to bottom halfway through the baking period.) Transfer the pastry, parchment paper and all, to a rack to cool to room temperature. *(The pastry can be kept at room temperature for up to 8 hours, but it should be used the day it is baked.)*

the cake

- One 9-inch Génoise (page 2), cooled

Cut two very thin layers from the génoise, each between ¼ and ½ inch thick. Wrap the cut layers in plastic and set them aside. (Wrap the leftover cake airtight and store it in the freezer — génoise crumbs are good in the base of fruit tarts; see page 137.)

the cream

- 1 cup heavy cream
- ⅓ cup sugar
- 1 cup whole milk
- 1 cinnamon stick, broken into 3 pieces
- 2 teaspoons gelatin

- **2 tablespoons cold water**
- **4 large egg yolks**

1. In a medium bowl, whip the heavy cream until it holds medium-firm peaks. Cover the bowl with plastic wrap and refrigerate until needed.

2. Spoon out 2 tablespoons of the sugar and set it aside to use with the yolks. Bring the milk to the boil (you can do this in the microwave oven); set aside until needed.

3. Put the pieces of cinnamon in the center of a medium skillet, preferably one with a nonstick finish, and turn the heat to medium. Sprinkle 1 tablespoon of the remaining sugar over a small portion of the center of the pan and, as soon as it starts to melt and take on color, stir the sugar with a wooden spoon or spatula until it caramelizes. (Make sure to stir the cinnamon with the sugar so that you're both caramelizing the sugar and infusing it with cinnamon flavor.) Continue cooking and stirring the sugar, adding it a tablespoon at a time, until it is a deep amber color. (You want a strong caramel flavor, but you don't want to burn the sugar, so take care and, if needed, lower the heat.) Still stirring, add the warm milk, then raise the heat to high and bring the mixture to the boil. Don't worry if the caramel seizes and clumps; stirring and heating it will smooth it out in no time. Remove the pan from the heat and strain the caramel sauce into a container; discard the cinnamon sticks (or wash, dry, and reserve them for another use).

4. Sprinkle the gelatin over the cold water and allow it to soften. Dissolve the gelatin by placing it in the microwave oven for 15 seconds or heating it over gentle heat.

5. Whisk the yolks and the reserved 2 tablespoons sugar together in a 2-quart saucepan until thick and pale. Still whisking, add about one third of the hot caramel sauce, a little at a time, to acclimatize the yolks to the heat; whisk in the rest of the sauce. Place the pan over medium heat and, stirring constantly with a wooden spatula or spoon, cook until the mixture thickens slightly, lightens in color, and, most important, reaches 180°F, as measured on an instant-read thermometer — which will take less than 5 minutes. (Alternatively, you can stir the cream and then draw your finger down the spatula or the bowl of the wooden spoon — if the cream doesn't run into the track you've created, it's done.) You now have a caramel crème anglaise. Immediately remove the saucepan from the heat and allow the crème anglaise to rest, or "poach," for about 2 minutes. While the crème anglaise is resting, fill a large bowl with ice cubes and set aside another bowl that can hold the finished cream and be placed in this ice bath.

6. Strain the crème anglaise into the reserved small bowl and stir in the dissolved gelatin. Place the bowl in the ice-filled bowl, add some cold water to the bottom bowl to make an ice bath, and, keeping the mixture over ice, stir constantly until it is cool and mounds gently when stirred, about 2 to 3 minutes. Immediately remove the mixture from the ice bath and deli-

181

cately fold in the reserved whipped cream. The Bavarian cream is ready and must be used immediately.

to assemble

1. Center an 8¾-inch/22-cm dessert ring on a cardboard cake round. Place one piece of génoise, cut side up, in the ring. Spread the apples over the cake, using an offset spatula to get an even layer. Next, pour the Bavarian cream into the ring, smoothing the top with the offset spatula. Top the cream with the second layer of génoise, gently jiggling the cake to settle it on the cream.

2. To set the cake, chill it for 2 hours in the refrigerator or freeze it for an hour. *(Once frozen, the cake can be wrapped airtight and kept in the freezer for up to 2 weeks.)*

to finish

- 2 red apples
- 1 tablespoon freshly squeezed lemon juice
- 3 tablespoons apple jelly or strained apricot jam

1. Slip the removable metal bottom of a tart pan under a disk of cinnamon pastry and then slide the pastry onto the center of a serving platter. Remove the dessert ring (see page 272), slip two spatulas under the cake, and lift it off its cardboard round and onto the cinnamon pastry. Use the tart pan bottom to slide the remaining disk of pastry onto the top of the cake.

2. Cut the apples in half from stem to blossom end and remove the cores. Place the apples cut side down on a cutting board and cut them crosswise into very thin slices. Toss the apples gently with the lemon juice and, starting at the edge of the cake, lay them on top of the cake in concentric circles, each circle slightly overlapping the preceding circle. Brush the apples with the jelly or jam.

3. If the cake is still frozen, place it in the refrigerator to defrost. The cake should be served when the Bavarian cream has returned to its original texture and is just cool.

Keeping

The assembled cake, minus the cinnamon pastry, can be frozen for up to 2 weeks. However, once the pastry is put in place and the cake is decorated, it must be served within 8 hours, preferably sooner.

PEAR *and* FIG *charlotte*

Built as a charlotte — there are two ladyfinger disks sandwiching a cream filling, a band of ladyfingers around the edge, and a top-knot of fruit — this classy cake, like so many of Pierre's, holds a surprise. Working your way down, you get the still-slightly-firm-to-the-bite pears, the light, chewy cake, and the soft Poire William cream, and then, all of a sudden, there's the surprise — the crunch of tiny seeds, the centers of sweet dried figs.

Don't think twice about using the canned pears that are specified in this recipe, and don't think about using anything else. By the time you "refresh" the canned pears with an overnight dunk in a sweet lemon and vanilla syrup, you'll wonder why they're not used in more recipes.

« This cake uses two delicately perfumed fruits from the end of summer that go very well together because one is not stronger than the other. While I often create cakes with flavors in opposition, this one is unusual for its harmony. » — P.H.

the pears
- Two 29-ounce cans pear halves packed in syrup
- 2 cups water
- 1 cup sugar
- 2 tablespoons freshly squeezed lemon juice
- Pulp of 1 plump, moist vanilla bean (see page 287)

Makes 10 to 12 servings

1. Drain the pears and place them in a large bowl (a deep bowl is best); set aside.

2. Bring the water, sugar, lemon juice, and vanilla bean pulp to a boil in a medium saucepan or the microwave. Remove the syrup from the heat and pour it over the pears. Press a piece of wax paper against the pears and, if the paper alone isn't enough to submerge the pears in the syrup, place a plate on top of the wax paper. Cover the setup with plastic wrap and refrigerate overnight. *(The pears can be made up to 3 days ahead and kept covered in the refrigerator.)*

the figs

- 8 dried soft, moist Calimyrna figs

Cut the figs into small cubes (about ¼ inch on a side) and put them in a small saucepan. Cover with water and bring the water just to the boil. Transfer the figs and water to a container, cover, and refrigerate overnight.

the soaking syrup

- 6 tablespoons water
- ⅓ cup sugar
- 4½ tablespoons Poire William (pear *eau-de-vie*)

Bring the water and sugar to a boil in a small saucepan or the microwave oven. Remove from heat and, when the syrup is cool, stir in the Poire William. *(The syrup can be made up to a week ahead and kept in an airtight container in the refrigerator.)*

the cake

- 1 recipe Ladyfinger Batter (page 7), or store-bought ladyfinger biscuits

If using the Ladyfinger Batter, following the recipe, pipe the batter into two 9-inch disks and two 8-inch-long bands of 4-inch-high ladyfingers; bake, cool, and reserve. *(The ladyfinger disks and bands can be made ahead, wrapped airtight, and kept at room temperature for 2 days or frozen for a month.)*

the poire william cream

- 7 ounces (about 4) pear halves (from above)
- ¾ cup plus 2 tablespoons whole milk
- ½ cup (slightly rounded) sugar

- 4 large egg yolks
- 2 tablespoons Poire William (pear *eau-de-vie*)
- 2½ teaspoons (1 packet) gelatin
- ¼ cup cold water
- 1 cup heavy cream

1. Drain the pears and whir them to a purée in a blender or food processor; set aside. Fill a large bowl with ice cubes and have at the ready a smaller bowl and a fine-mesh strainer.

2. Bring the milk to a boil. Meanwhile, whisk the sugar and yolks together in a heavy-bottomed 2-quart saucepan. Whisking without stop, drizzle in about one third of the boiling liquid. Once the yolks are acclimated to the heat, whisk in the rest of the milk in a slow, steady stream. Place the saucepan over medium heat and, stirring constantly with a wooden spatula or spoon, cook the cream until it reaches 180°F, as measured on an instant-read thermometer — this will take less than 5 minutes. (Alternatively, you can stir the cream, and then draw your finger down the spatula or the bowl of the wooden spoon — if the cream doesn't run into the track you've created, it's done.) The cream will not thicken much. Immediately remove the saucepan from the heat and allow the cream to rest for 2 minutes. Strain the crème anglaise into the small reserved bowl and stir in the Poire William.

3. Sprinkle the gelatin over the water and allow it to rest until softened. Heat in the microwave oven for about 15 seconds, or cook over low heat, until the gelatin dissolves. Stir the gelatin into the crème anglaise and then gently stir in the reserved puréed pears. Set the bowl in the ice bath, adding cold water to the ice cubes, and, stirring from time to time, cool the crème anglaise to about 70°F.

4. To finish the filling, whip the heavy cream until it holds medium-firm peaks and fold it gently into the crème anglaise with a rubber spatula. The filling is now ready and should be used immediately.

to assemble

1. Remove and drain 3 of the remaining pears, pat them dry between paper towels, and cut them into cubes, about ½ inch on a side. Drain and pat dry the cubed figs. Mix the fruits together.

2. Place a piece of parchment paper on a cardboard cake round and center an 8¾-inch/22-cm dessert ring on it; butter the inside of the ring. Cut the bands of ladyfingers lengthwise in half and fit the halves around the interior of the ring, making certain that the biscuits' flat side faces in; you'll have a piece of band left over. Fit a ladyfinger disk into the bottom to form a base. (If you are using store-bought ladyfingers, cut the biscuits as necessary to form a band

and base.) Brush the ladyfinger disk and band with the soaking syrup, using enough syrup to thoroughly moisten the cake.

3. Spoon enough filling into the biscuit-lined ring to form a layer that comes about halfway up the ladyfinger band, and spread it even with a spatula. Cover with the cubed fruit and then cover the fruit with another layer of filling, this time coming almost to the top of the ring, and again using the spatula to get an even layer. Top this with the second ladyfinger disk and moisten this layer with some syrup. (You may have syrup left over.) Cover the disk with a thin layer of filling (you may have filling left over — it makes a fine dessert on its own or served with cookies) and set the cake into the refrigerator to chill for 2 hours. *(The cake can be made to this point and, when chilled, covered airtight and frozen for up to 2 weeks.)*

to finish
- Fresh figs, optional

1. Remove the dessert ring (see page 272), but keep the cake on the cardboard round for maneuverability.

2. Slice the remaining pears from blossom to stem end and arrange the slices in overlapping concentric circles over the top of the cake. If fresh figs are available, slice them from blossom to stem end and slip them into the arrangement as Pierre did for the photo on page 184. If not, a purely pear topping is just fine. Serve the cake now or keep it in the refrigerator, loosely covered, until ready to serve.

Keeping
While the pears and figs must be made ahead and the syrup and cake disks can be made ahead, once the cream is prepared, you must assemble the cake immediately. Once *assembled, the cake can be kept undecorated in the freezer for up to 2 weeks or decorated in the refrigerator for 1 day.*

MASCARPONE *and* *blueberry* CAKE

Imagine the supreme shortcake, light, creamy, rich, beautiful, berry-bedecked, and beyond delicious — and now imagine it even better. If you've got a great imagination, then you've got an idea of how appealing this cake is. Not really a shortcake as we know it to be, but rather two soft golden ladyfinger layers sandwiching plump poached blueberries and a feather-light mousse of mascarpone, Italy's finest triple-cream cheese (a cross between America's cream cheese and any country's best whipped cream). The cake is wreathed in Italian meringue, encased in a band of ladyfingers (like a charlotte), and topped with a circle of jammy blueberries. It is a glorious confection.

The blueberries, lemon syrup, and ladyfinger layers and band should be made ahead so that on construction day you can concentrate on the mousse and assembly, straightforward operations that will take you a while only because you'll have to stop a couple of times for quick chills in the freezer.

the blueberries

- 2 cups water
- 1 cup sugar
- 1 pint blueberries

Bring the water and sugar to the boil in a medium saucepan and stir to dissolve the sugar. Add the blueberries and immediately remove the pan from the heat. Cool to room temperature and refrigerate until needed. *(The berries are best made a day ahead and kept tightly covered in the refrigerator.)*

Makes 8 to 10 servings

the lemon syrup

- ¼ cup water
- 2½ tablespoons sugar
- Zest of ¼ lemon — removed with a zester (see page 281)
- 3 tablespoons freshly squeezed lemon juice

Mix the water, sugar, and zest together in a small saucepan and bring to the boil, stirring to dissolve the sugar; boil for 1 minute. Remove the pan from the heat, stir in the lemon juice, and strain the syrup into a bowl or jar. Cool, cover, and chill until needed. *(Kept in a tightly sealed container, the syrup can be refrigerated for 1 week.)*

the cake layers

- 1 recipe Ladyfinger Batter (page 7), or store-bought ladyfinger biscuits

If using the Ladyfinger Batter, following the recipe, pipe the batter into two 9-inch disks and two 8-inch-long, 4-inch-high bands of ladyfingers; bake, cool, and reserve. *(Cooled freshly baked layers can be wrapped airtight and kept at room temperature for 2 days or frozen for a month.)*

the mousse

- 3 large egg whites
- 1 cup sugar
- ½ cup cold water
- 1 cup heavy cream
- 1 cup (packed) mascarpone
- 1½ tablespoons cold milk
- 2 teaspoons gelatin

1. This mousse is based on an Italian meringue: To make the meringue, put the egg whites in an impeccably clean, dry mixing bowl, preferably the bowl of a mixer fitted with the whisk attachment, and beat until they hold firm peaks. Set aside while you make the syrup.

2. In a small saucepan, bring the sugar and ¼ cup of the water to the boil, stirring occasionally and washing down splatters along the sides of the pan with a pastry brush dipped in cold water. Boil the syrup, without stirring, until it reaches 247°F, as measured on a candy thermometer. Immediately remove from the heat.

3. With the mixer set at its lowest speed, beat the egg whites for a few seconds and then very slowly add the syrup in a thin, steady stream. To avoid splatters, try to pour the syrup down

the side of the bowl, not into the spinning whisk. (Inevitably, some will splatter, but don't attempt to scrape the hardened syrup into the meringue — you'll get lumps.) Increase the speed to medium and continue to beat the meringue until it is absolutely cool, about 10 minutes; it will be smooth, shiny, and marshmallowy.

4. Spoon out 1 cup of meringue to finish the mousse and set aside; cover the remainder (which will be the frosting) with plastic wrap and hold at room temperature. (If you need your mixing bowl to whip the cream, transfer the meringue to another bowl before proceeding.)

5. Beat the heavy cream until it holds soft peaks; cover with plastic and refrigerate until needed. Scrape the mascarpone into a large mixing bowl and stir in the cold milk to loosen the cheese a bit; set this aside too.

6. To dissolve the gelatin, sprinkle it over the remaining ¼ cup cold water and allow it to rest until softened. Heat in the microwave oven for about 15 seconds, or cook over low heat, until the gelatin dissolves.

7. Using a whisk, stir the dissolved gelatin into the mascarpone. Switch to a large flexible rubber spatula and fold the reserved 1 cup of meringue into the mixture. Don't worry about being too thorough at this point. Now, very gently fold in the reserved whipped cream. (Because the quantities are small, this process can be messy and a bit fussy until you fold in the whipped cream — just keep at it.)

to assemble

1. Drain the blueberries and discard the syrup.

2. Place a piece of parchment paper on a cardboard cake round and center an 8¾-inch/22-cm dessert ring on it; butter the inside of the ring. Cut the bands of ladyfingers lengthwise in half and fit the halves around the interior of the ring, making certain that the biscuits' flat side faces in; you'll have a piece of band left over. Fit a ladyfinger disk into the bottom to form a base. (If you are using store-bought ladyfingers, cut the biscuits as necessary to form a band and base.) Brush the ladyfinger disk and band with the lemon syrup, using enough syrup to thoroughly moisten the cake.

3. Spread half the mousse over the cake and top with an even layer of blueberries. (You may have some blueberries left over.) Now, cover the berries with enough mousse to come almost to the top of the dessert ring. (Depending on how plump your ladyfingers are and/or how deflated they became after absorbing the syrup, you may have some mousse left over — it's great with cookies.) Brush the flat side of the remaining cake disk with lemon syrup and place it, moistened side down, over the mousse. (You may have some syrup left over.) Jiggle the cake layer to settle it evenly.

3. Place plastic wrap over the assembly and freeze the cake for 1 hour to set the mousse.

to frost

With the dessert ring still in place, create a decorative layer on the top of the cake with the reserved Italian meringue. You can either spread all of the meringue over the top of the cake and use a spoon to pull the meringue into points, leaving a smooth center circle of 3 to 5 inches in diameter, or you can give the cake a more polished look: Start by spreading an even layer of meringue across the top of the cake. Put the remaining meringue into a pastry bag fitted with a star tip. Leaving a center circle of 3 to 5 inches in diameter, pipe the rest of the top with whatever design you want: shells, stars, squiggles, no matter. You'll have lots of meringue to play with, so have fun. Return the cake to the freezer for 1 hour. (The purpose of this deep chill is to ready the cake to withstand the blast of heat it will get when the meringue is browned in the oven. Alternatively, you can remove the dessert ring [see page 272], pipe on the meringue decoration, and brown the meringue with a blowtorch.)

to finish

- 1½ cups blueberries
- 2 tablespoons blueberry jam

1. Center a rack in the oven and preheat the oven to 475°F.

2. Place the cake, on its cardboard and still in its ring, on a baking sheet and set it into the hot oven to color lightly — about 3 to 5 minutes should be all that's needed to set the meringue and give it a touch of color here and there. Remove the cake from the oven and quickly return it to the freezer for 15 minutes (or longer — at this point you can freeze it for up to 2 weeks; thaw the cake before proceeding).

3. For the final touch, mix the berries and jam together, keeping 3 or 4 berries to the side for decoration. Remove the cake from the freezer and spoon the blueberry topping onto the cake, spreading it evenly within the flat circle of meringue. Place the reserved berries in the center. Remove the dessert ring (see page 272) and serve, or chill until needed. (The cake can be kept in the refrigerator for up to 12 hours.)

192

Keeping

The ladyfinger disks and band can be made 2 days ahead and kept at room temperature or frozen for a month; the lemon syrup can be made up to a week in advance; and the

poached blueberries are best made a day ahead. The meringue-covered cake — minus the blueberry jam decoration — can be frozen for 2 weeks; just make certain the mousse

is fully defrosted before serving. With cakes like this, it's always a good idea to give them a day in the refrigerator to defrost.

philadelphia ALMOND
CAKE

Cream cheese, the star of American cheesecakes, rarely makes even a cameo appearance in French bakers' spectaculars, and when it does, it's billed as "Philadelphia," a name derived from Kraft's well-known Philadelphia Brand Cream Cheese. In this recipe, Pierre, who's always looking for new foods or ways to make familiar foods seem new, uses the "Philadelphia" in a most un-American but dazzlingly delicious way — it forms a thick layer of extra-creamy mousse interlaced with griottes, small, tart cherries. The mousse is smoothed across a soft, chewy, brown sugar–sweetened almond cake and topped with a crunchy almond streusel so good it deserves a "best-of-class" blue ribbon. The cake is not formal, but it is very chic, and as right for a dinner party as for a midafternoon nibble. ("Breakfast too," says Pierre.) You can even vary it: Try it with a layer of Twenty-Hour Apples or some fresh raspberries standing in for the griottes (see page 199 for instructions).

Once the griottes are macerated (best done a day ahead), you can make this cake in one fell swoop, but you don't have to. If you get all the components prepared ahead, you'll have only the mousse as an *à la minute* must-do.

« *This cake is full of sensations: It's smooth, creamy, and moist, but there's also a little crunch from the streusel. I love it when a cake has these kinds of contrasts.* » — P. H.

Makes 8 to 10 servings

the griottes

- 2 cups drained bottled or thawed frozen griottes (available in specialty stores; or see Variations, page 199)
- ¾ cup water
- ¾ cup sugar

I. Turn the griottes into a medium bowl or refrigerator container; set aside. Bring the water and sugar to a boil in a medium saucepan. Pour this syrup over the griottes, stir to moisten all of the cherries, and cool to room temperature. When the mixture is cool, cover and refrigerate 24 hours. *(The cherries can be kept under refrigeration for 1 week.)*

2. Two hours before you need them, put the cherries in a colander to drain. Gently pat off any excess moisture before layering them with the mousse.

the cake

- ⅔ cup ground blanched almonds (see page 278), plus 1 tablespoon blanched almonds, toasted (see page 277) and coarsely chopped
- ½ cup confectioner's sugar, sifted
- 2½ tablespoons all-purpose flour
- 3 large egg whites
- ¼ cup (packed) light brown sugar, pushed through a strainer

I. Center a rack in the oven and preheat the oven to 350°F. Line a baking sheet with parchment paper and place an 8¾-inch/22-cm dessert ring on the sheet; set aside.

2. In a medium mixing bowl, stir the ground almonds, chopped almonds, confectioner's sugar, and flour together just to combine. Place the egg whites in an impeccably clean, dry mixing bowl, preferably the bowl of a mixer fitted with the whisk attachment, and beat on medium-high speed just until the whites form soft peaks. Mixing all the while, add the brown sugar a little at a time. Increase the speed to high and beat until the whites form firm, glossy peaks.

3. Working with a large flexible rubber spatula, gently fold the almond mixture into the meringue in three additions, taking care to maintain as much of the meringue's volume as possible. Turn the mixture into the dessert ring and use the spatula to smooth the top.

4. Slip the baking sheet into the oven and, as you're closing the oven door, insert the handle of a wooden spoon into the oven so that the door remains slightly ajar. Bake the cake for 24 to 26 minutes, or until the top, which will look dry, is springy to the touch and honey brown. Transfer the baking sheet to a cooling rack and allow the cake to cool to room temperature. When the cake is absolutely cool, run a thin knife between it and the ring and lift off the ring.

(Don't be concerned if, after you remove the ring, the cake shrinks a little — it's inevitable.) Wash and dry the ring — you'll need it to construct the finished cake. *(Wrapped airtight in plastic, the cake can be kept at room temperature for 4 days or frozen for a month.)*

the mousse

The mousse needs to be molded as soon as it is made, so, before you begin preparation, make certain to drain the griottes and check that the cake layer is cool.

- 1 cup heavy cream
- 6 ounces cream cheese
- 1 tablespoon confectioner's sugar
- 3 large egg yolks
- $4\frac{1}{2}$ tablespoons sugar
- 3 tablespoons cold water
- $1\frac{1}{2}$ teaspoons gelatin

1. In a medium bowl, whip the heavy cream until it holds medium-firm peaks. Cover the bowl with plastic wrap and refrigerate until needed.
2. Place the cream cheese in a metal bowl over a pan of simmering water and heat to melt, stirring occasionally with a rubber spatula. Whisk in the confectioner's sugar and continue to whisk until the mixture is smooth. Remove the bowl from the saucepan and set the cream cheese aside to cool while you prepare the rest of the ingredients for the mousse.
3. Bring a couple of inches of water to a simmer in a saucepan. Put the yolks in a metal bowl that can fit into the saucepan and serve as the top of a double boiler; reserve. Bring the sugar and 1 tablespoon of the water to the boil in a small saucepan or a microwave oven. Whisking the yolks constantly, scrape the sugar syrup onto the yolks and whisk to blend. Set the bowl over the pan of simmering water and heat, whisking lightly, until the mixture is very foamy and slightly thickened, about 5 to 7 minutes. Remove the bowl to a counter and allow the yolks to cool, stirring occasionally, until they reach 77°F, as measured on an instant-read thermometer. (The yolks will continue to thicken as they cool.)
4. While the yolks are cooling, sprinkle the gelatin over the remaining 2 tablespoons cold water and allow it to rest until softened. Heat the gelatin in the microwave oven for about 15 seconds, or cook over low heat, until the gelatin dissolves.
5. Working with a large rubber spatula, stir the gelatin into the cream cheese mixture. Fold in the cooled yolks and, finally, the reserved whipped cream.

to assemble

Center the 8¾-inch/22-cm dessert ring on a cardboard cake round and set the almond cake in the ring. Spoon about one third of the mousse over the cake, smoothing the layer with an offset spatula. Cover the mousse with a single, even layer of the well-drained griottes, then spoon on the rest of the mousse and smooth the top. Freeze the cake for at least 2 hours to set the mousse. *(Once frozen, the cake can be wrapped airtight, still in the dessert ring, and frozen for up to 2 weeks.)*

the streusel

- 3 tablespoons plus 1 teaspoon unsalted butter, softened
- 3½ tablespoons sugar
- 6 tablespoons ground blanched almonds (see page 277)
- Pinch of salt
- 6 tablespoons all-purpose flour

1. Working in a medium bowl, beat the butter with a large rubber spatula until creamy. Add the remaining ingredients one by one, blending each ingredient into the mixture before adding the next. Cover the bowl and refrigerate the mixture until it is thoroughly chilled, about 45 minutes.

2. Center a rack in the oven and preheat the oven to 325°F. Line a baking sheet with parchment paper and set it aside.

3. Remove the bowl from the refrigerator and, using your fingers, break the streusel into clumps of varying sizes (the unevenness of the pieces will add textural interest to the finished cake). Spread the streusel out on the lined baking sheet and bake for 10 minutes. Using a metal spatula, break up any streusel that may have formed large pieces, stir and turn the streusel, and continue to bake until well browned, another 5 to 10 minutes. Transfer the streusel, still on the parchment paper, from the pan to a rack and cool to room temperature. *(The streusel can be made a day or two ahead and kept at room temperature in an airtight container.)*

to finish

- Confectioner's sugar

1. Thirty minutes to an hour before serving, remove the cake from the freezer. Transfer the cake to a serving platter and remove the dessert ring (see page 272). Allow the cake to defrost at room temperature. (If your cake has been in the freezer long enough for it to freeze solid,

you'll need more than an hour to defrost it. Long-frozen cakes are best defrosted by giving them an overnight stay in the refrigerator.) When the mousse is defrosted but the cake is still cool, top with the streusel, using your fingers to lightly press it in an even layer on top of the mousse.

2. Cut two bands of parchment or wax paper, each about 1 inch wide and at least 9 inches long. Place the bands across the cake on a bias and dust the top of the cake with confectioner's sugar; remove the bands. Serve immediately.

VARIATIONS

If you'd like, you can omit the griottes and spread the cake layer with about 1 cup of Twenty-Hour Apples (page 33), or enough to form a thin (no more than ¼-inch-thick) layer, before adding the cream-cheese mousse in a single layer. Alternatively, you can substitute about 2 cups of fresh raspberries for the griottes, placing them in an even layer between the two layers of mousse. If you're using raspberries, there's no need to macerate them.

199

Keeping

Without the streusel, the cake can be wrapped airtight and kept frozen for 2 weeks. Once topped with streusel, the cake can be kept covered in the refrigerator for up to 2 days. Apply the confectioner's sugar decoration right before serving.

TARTE
tropézienne

Not really a tart, but truly from Saint-Tropez, this dessert is unique in the lexicon of sweets. Its base is a brioche, an egg-and-butter-rich yeast bread that, in this case, is not as eggy, buttery, nor rich as brioche can be. (On the other hand, with five eggs, a stick and a half of butter, and some milk tossed in for good measure, you'll hardly mistake it for diet fare.) Topped with fine sweet crumbs and baked in a dessert ring until it's light, puffy, and invitingly golden, the brioche is sliced in half and generously filled with a kirsch-flavored mixture of buttercream, pastry cream, and whipped cream. (Told you this wasn't for calorie counters.) In fact, there's almost as much of this ethereally light cream filling as there is brioche, so the finished cake is majestically tall and beautifully proportioned.

Since the brioche needs a long mixing, a two- to three-hour rise, and at least a six-hour chill before it's shaped, left to rise again, and then baked, you should plan to make the dough the day before. You can also prepare the buttercream, pastry cream, and crumbs in advance, so your dessert-day schedule will be as light as the Tropézienne's filling.

« *This dessert is a classic. I'm sure there are as many recipes for Tarte Tropézienne as there are pastry chefs in France, but this wasn't easy to develop. It took me two months to get a recipe I liked, during which time people kept bringing me cakes from Saint-Tropez. The topping on my Tropézienne isn't the traditional large crystals of sugar. I created the crumbs for the top because I like the added texture and taste they give. But it's the cream that's my favorite. It has an incredible lightness. In fact, it's so light that it has the sensation of being cold even when it's not.* » — P.H.

Makes 10 to 12 servings

The brioche recipe produces enough for two cakes, but you won't be successful with the brioche if you make a smaller amount. (The dough for the second dessert can be rolled out and frozen.) If you want to have two of these treats for a large party, it's easy — the basic buttercream and pastry cream recipes turn out enough for two cakes, and the recipe for the sweet crumbs can be doubled. Of course, the extra brioche dough can be used to make a loaf (page 204) just right for French Toast (page 45) or a special snack (page 43).

the brioche

- 3¾ cups all-purpose flour
- Scant ⅓ cup sugar
- ¾ ounce fresh yeast (1¼ cubes compressed yeast), crumbled
- ⅓ cup plus 2 tablespoons whole milk, at room temperature
- 5 large eggs, at room temperature
- 1 teaspoon salt
- 1 stick plus 4½ tablespoons (6¼ ounces) unsalted butter, softened

I. Put the flour, sugar, and yeast in the bowl of a heavy-duty mixer fitted with the dough hook and mix on low speed just to combine. With the mixer at its lowest speed, add the milk, eggs, and salt in succession, mixing until the flour is moistened. Stop the mixer and, with a rubber spatula, scrape down the sides of the bowl and incorporate the dry crumbs that in all likelihood will be at the bottom of the bowl.

2. Increase the mixer speed to medium and beat until the dough comes together and cleans the sides of the bowl, 5 to 10 minutes. Scrape the sides of the bowl as needed. When you start this beating process, the dough will look hopeless — persevere and it will smooth out.

3. Cut the butter into 6 or 7 pieces. (If the butter is at all hard, smear it against a work surface with the heel of your hand. Ideally, the butter should have the same consistency as the dough.) Increase the mixer speed to medium-high and add the butter a couple of pieces at a time, mixing until it is incorporated. Continue to mix until the dough detaches itself from the sides and bottom of the bowl, curls around the dough hook, and makes a gentle slapping noise as it hits the bowl. The process of incorporating the butter and beating the dough until it detaches might take as long as 15 minutes. When the dough is properly beaten, it will be silky and voluptuous.

4. Transfer the dough to a large bowl and cover the bowl tightly with plastic wrap. Allow the dough to rest in a warm place (about 72°F) until it doubles in bulk, 2 to 3 hours.

5. Gently deflate the dough and press a piece of plastic wrap against its surface. Cover the bowl well with plastic wrap and place it in the freezer until the dough almost doubles in bulk again, 2 to 3 hours. Deflate the dough, remove it from the bowl, wrap it tightly in several layers of plastic wrap, and refrigerate it for at least 6 hours. *(The dough can be prepared to this point and kept in the refrigerator overnight.)*

the crumbs

- 2½ tablespoons (1¼ ounces) unsalted butter, softened
- ¼ cup sugar
- ⅓ cup plus 2 tablespoons all-purpose flour

Working with a rubber spatula, cream the butter in a small bowl until it is smooth. Stir in the sugar and then the flour. By the time you add the flour, you'll probably find it easier to mix the ingredients together with your fingers. Just blend the ingredients until their texture resembles fine meal. Cover the bowl and refrigerate until needed. *(The crumbs can be made up to 3 days ahead and kept well wrapped in the refrigerator.)*

to rise

1. Line a baking sheet with parchment paper and butter the inside of a 10¼-inch/26-cm dessert ring; set aside.

2. Cut the chilled dough in half and return one piece to the refrigerator. Working on a lightly floured surface, form the dough into a tight ball and then press or roll the ball into a 10¼-inch/26-cm circle. Lift the circle onto the parchment-lined baking sheet and fit the dessert ring around the dough, pressing and pinching the dough as needed in order to have it fit into the ring. Cover the ring with plastic wrap and allow the dough to rise in a warm place (about 72°F) until it almost doubles in bulk, about 2 to 3 hours. (You have several options for the second piece of dough: You can make a second Tarte Tropézienne now; you can roll the dough out into a 10¼-inch/26-cm circle and freeze it until you want to make another Tarte Tropézienne, within 1 month; or you can make a loaf of brioche to serve at any time or to use for French Toast [page 45]. To make a brioche loaf, see the varation on page 204.)

to bake

- Egg Wash (page 40)

1. Center a rack in the oven and preheat the oven to about 420°F.
2. Remove the plastic wrap from the risen brioche and gently apply a coat of egg wash to the top, taking care not to let any of the egg wash dribble down the sides of the dessert ring (it would glue the brioche to the ring and keep it from rising evenly in the oven). Sprinkle the

crumbs over the top of the dough and use your fingers to lightly pat them in place. Slip the baking sheet into the oven and bake the brioche for 12 minutes, until it is puffed and golden. (The brioche will be very soft — that's perfect.) Transfer the brioche to a cooling rack, keeping the dessert ring in place, and allow the brioche to cool to room temperature. Leave the ring in place until you are ready to slice and fill the brioche.

the filling

- 1⅓ cups heavy cream
- 1¾ (slightly rounded) cups Vanilla Buttercream, (page 29)
- 1 (rounded) cup or (about ½ recipe) Vanilla Pastry Cream, (page 27)
- 1½ tablespoons orange flower water
- 1½ tablespoons kirsch (imported cherry brandy)

I. Whip the heavy cream until it holds medium-firm peaks; set aside.

2. Stir the buttercream and the pastry cream with a whisk to soften them. Using the whisk, fold the pastry cream into the buttercream. Stir in the orange flower water and the kirsch, then gently fold in the whipped cream. The filling is now ready and should be used immediately. (If it must wait just a few minutes, cover it with plastic and refrigerate.)

to assemble

Remove the dessert ring by running a slender blunt knife between the ring and the cake. Wash and dry the ring and center it on a cardboard cake round. Slice the brioche horizontally in half and fit the bottom piece, cut side up, into the dessert ring. Using an offset spatula, spread the filling evenly across the brioche; you'll have a thick layer. Position the top of the brioche over the cream, jiggling it lightly to settle it into place, and put the cake in the refrigerator for 2 hours to chill and set the filling. (At this point, the cake can be wrapped airtight and kept in the refrigerator for up to 1 day or in the freezer for up to 2 weeks). The cake should be served cold.

VARIATION

BRIOCHE LOAF

To make a Brioche Nanterre, a loaf comprised of six mounds, generously butter an 8½ by 4½-inch loaf pan. Divide the fully risen and chilled dough (half of the recipe for Tarte Tropézienne) into six equal pieces. Working with one piece of dough at a time on a clean, unfloured work surface (marble is ideal), roll the dough under your cupped palm to form it into a tight ball: Push the dough around and around with the heel of your hand and press down gently with your palm to form a ball. Repeat with the remaining pieces. Place the pieces side by side in the pan (you'll have two rows each with three balls of dough), cover the pan loosely with wax paper, and allow the loaf to rest in a warm place (about 72°F) until the dough doubles in volume, 2 to 3 hours.

Center a rack in the oven and preheat the oven to 375°F. Glaze the top of the loaf with the egg wash. Holding a pair of scissors so that the points are perpendicular to the top of the loaf, snip a cross in the center of each of the balls. Work as quickly as you can and, as you finish each snip, draw the scissors up so that you draw up a little of the dough as well.

Bake the loaf for 20 to 22 minutes, or until deeply golden and an instant-read thermometer plunged into the center of the loaf reads 190°F to 200°F. Unmold the loaf and cool to room temperature on a rack.

205

Keeping

All of the cake's elements can be made ahead, but once the filling is mixed, it must be used immediately. The cake is best served chilled on the *day it is made, but it can be kept overnight in the refrigerator. Make sure to wrap it well.*

COFFEE and *walnut*
CAKE

Nothing in the name prepares you for what happens when this sleek cake's four elements come together. There's the base, a soft brown sugar and walnut cake (a variation of the recipe used in the Philadelphia Almond Cake, page 195). And then the three toppers: a gloss of chunky sweet orange marmalade; a layer of potent, syrupy, paper-thin Chinese ginger; and an airy, deeply coffee-flavored, lightly coffee-colored cream. On its own, each component has its charms, but stacked one on top of the other, their powerful flavors and intriguing textures melded, they defy characterization and define teamwork: Each player brings out the best in the others.

The idea to mix ginger and coffee came to me in a Chinese restaurant — I ordered a cup of coffee and it was served with a piece of crystallized ginger on the side. Adding the orange to the cake just seemed like a good idea. — P. H.

the cake
- ⅓ cup ground walnuts (see page 277), plus 1 tablespoon finely chopped walnuts
- ⅓ cup ground blanched almonds (see page 277)
- ½ cup confectioner's sugar, sifted
- 2½ tablespoons all-purpose flour
- 3 large egg whites
- ¼ cup (packed) light brown sugar, pushed through a strainer

Makes 8 to 10 servings

1. Center a rack in the oven and preheat the oven to 350°F. Line a baking sheet with parchment paper and place an 8¾-inch/22-cm dessert ring on the sheet; set aside.

2. In a medium mixing bowl, stir the ground walnuts, chopped walnuts, ground almonds, confectioner's sugar, and flour together just to combine. Place the egg whites in an impeccably clean, dry mixing bowl, preferably the bowl of a mixer fitted with the whisk attachment, and beat on medium-high speed just until the whites form soft peaks. Mixing all the while, add the brown sugar a little at a time. Increase the speed to high and beat until the whites form firm, glossy peaks.

3. Working with a large flexible rubber spatula, gently fold the nut mixture into the meringue in three additions, taking care to maintain as much of the meringue's volume as possible. Turn the batter into the dessert ring and use the spatula to smooth the top.

4. Slip the baking sheet into the oven and, as you're closing the oven door, insert the handle of a wooden spoon into the oven so that the door remains slightly ajar. Bake the cake for 24 to 26 minutes, or until the top, which will look dry, is springy to the touch and honey brown. Transfer the baking sheet to a cooling rack and allow the cake to cool to room temperature. When the cake is absolutely cool, run a thin knife between it and the ring and lift off the ring. (Don't be concerned if, after you remove the ring, the cake shrinks a little — it's inevitable.) Wash and dry the ring — you'll need it to construct the finished cake. *(Wrapped airtight in plastic, the cake can be kept at room temperature for 4 days or frozen for a month.)*

the ginger and jam

- 3 to 4 pieces ginger in syrup (available in Chinese and specialty markets)
- ½ cup sweet orange marmalade with orange pieces (choose one that is neither too bitter nor too gelatinous)

1. Cut 3 pieces of ginger into the thinnest possible slices and then cut each slice in half. Set the slices aside until needed. (You want to cover the cake with an even layer of ginger slices. If 3 pieces of ginger are not enough, you'll need to cut into another piece.)

2. If the marmalade is too thick to spread easily, loosen it by beating it with a spoon or, if necessary, heating it gently (perhaps with a teaspoon or two of water) in the microwave oven; let it come to room temperature before using it. Set aside until needed.

the cream

- 1⅓ cups whole milk
- 3 tablespoons ground-for-espresso coffee
- 1 teaspoon instant coffee

- 1 cup heavy cream
- 1¼ teaspoons gelatin
- 4 teaspoons cold water
- 4 large egg yolks
- ¼ cup sugar

1. Line a strainer with a double thickness of dampened cheesecloth. Bring ⅓ cup of the milk to a boil in a medium saucepan. Add the ground coffee and the instant coffee, stir, and then remove the saucepan from the heat. Strain immediately and set the mixture aside. Wipe out the saucepan.

2. In a medium bowl, whip the heavy cream until it holds medium peaks. Cover the bowl with plastic wrap and refrigerate until needed.

3. Sprinkle the gelatin over the cold water and allow it to soften. Dissolve the gelatin by placing it in the microwave oven for 15 seconds or heating it over gentle heat.

4. Bring the remaining 1 cup milk to a boil. While the milk is heating, whisk the yolks and sugar together in a heavy-bottomed 2-quart saucepan until thick and pale. Still whisking, add about one third of the hot milk, a little at a time, to acclimate the yolks to the heat; whisk in the rest of the milk. Place the pan over medium heat and, stirring constantly with a wooden spatula or spoon, cook until the mixture thickens and reaches 180°F as measured on an instant-read thermometer — which will take less than 5 minutes. (Alternatively, you can stir the cream and then draw your finger down the spatula or the bowl of the wooden spoon — if the cream doesn't run into the track you've created, it's done.) You now have a crème anglaise.

5. Immediately remove the saucepan from the heat and allow the crème anglaise to rest, or "poach," for about 2 minutes. While the crème anglaise is resting, fill a large bowl with ice cubes and set aside another bowl that can hold the finished cream and be placed in this ice bath. Strain the crème anglaise into the reserved small bowl and stir in the dissolved gelatin and the reserved coffee infusion. Place the bowl in the ice-filled bowl, add some cold water to the cubes to make an ice bath, and stir constantly until the cream mixture is cool and mounds gently when stirred, about 2 to 3 minutes. Immediately remove the mixture from the ice bath and delicately fold in the reserved whipped cream. The cream is ready and must be used now.

to assemble

Center the 8¾-inch/22-cm dessert ring on a cardboard cake round and set the walnut cake into the round. Smooth the marmalade over the cake layer and cover with the ginger slices.

208

(If you don't have enough slices to cover the cake, cut more slices as needed.) Spoon the coffee cream into the ring and level the top with an offset spatula. Place the cake in the freezer for about an hour to set the cream. *(The cake can be made ahead to this point and, once frozen, wrapped well and frozen for a month; defrost the cake before finishing it.)*

to finish

- 7 or 8 very thin orange slices (unpeeled)
- Orange marmalade, pushed through a strainer

Arrange the orange slices in a rosette in the center of the cake and brush the top of the oranges and the cake with the marmalade. Remove the dessert ring (see page 272) and serve or refrigerate until needed.

209

Keeping

The walnut cake base can be made ahead, wrapped airtight, and kept at room temperature for about 4 days or frozen for a month, while the assembled cake can be kept in

the refrigerator overnight or (if not finished with orange slices and marmalade) frozen for a month. To store in the freezer, freeze the cake unwrapped and then, when

completely frozen, wrap airtight in plastic. Thaw the cake, still wrapped, overnight in the refrigerator.

christmas L O G

Leave it to Pierre to come up with a combination that turns classic into cutting edge. The *bûche de Noël,* or Christmas log, is a holiday classic and, staying true to its name, Pierre has kept its form; his dessert looks like all other *bûches* and is, at its base, strictly traditional: a rolled cake covered with buttercream and made to look like a bumpy log. But tradition gets tossed with the first taste. Pierre flavors his log with an ingenious mix of chestnut, cassis, and rum. If you can't find cassis packed in syrup (they are a rarity in the States), you don't have to give up on this cake — you can use dried currants macerated in rum (see page 214) and get every bit of the play on flavors Pierre was after.

Like so many holiday sweets, this is not a cake you should decide to make on the spur of the moment. Depending on where you live, you may have to go to specialty shops to find the chestnut purée, chestnut spread, and, if available, cassis, and the (optional) *marrons glacés* (candied chestnuts) are a treat with a short season — they're often only sold from November until January (see Mail-Order Sources, page 282). But then, Christmas comes but once a year and this cake's worth the wait.

« *The flavors in this cake are in opposition. You have one fruit that's not very strong, that's the chestnut, and another, the cassis or currant, that's hyperacidic, so the cassis wakes up the chestnut. I assembled the cake in my head and when I actually made it, I was delighted with the way the chestnuts' mild flavor was enlivened by the other ingredients and underscored by the rum.* » — P.H.

Makes 6 to 8 servings

the syrup

- ⅓ cup water
- ⅓ cup sugar
- ⅓ cup dark rum

Bring the water and sugar to a boil in a small saucepan, stirring until the sugar is dissolved, or use the microwave oven. Remove the syrup from the heat and, when it is absolutely cool, stir in the rum. *(The syrup can be made ahead and kept tightly covered in the refrigerator for at least a week.)*

the cake

- 1 recipe Ladyfinger Batter (page 7)

1. Position a rack in the center of the oven and preheat the oven to 450°F. Using a pencil, draw a rectangle 16 inches long by 10 inches wide on a piece of parchment paper. Turn the paper over (if you can't see the lines now that the paper is flipped over, make them darker) and place it on a baking sheet. (To keep the paper in place, you can "glue" the corners down with a dab of batter.)

2. Turn the batter out into the center of the rectangle and, using a long metal offset spatula, spread the batter evenly across the rectangle. Don't worry if the edges are a little ragged or if you overshoot the lines by a bit; it's more important that the batter be spread to an even thickness (about ¼ inch) than that the edges be neat. (You may have some batter left over.) Slip the baking sheet into the oven and, as you're closing the door, insert the handle of a wooden spoon into the oven to keep the door slightly ajar. Bake for just 8 to 10 minutes, or until the cake is lightly golden. Remove the baking sheet from the oven and lift the cake, still on the parchment paper, onto a cooling rack. Allow the cake to cool to room temperature and then place a piece of parchment over the top of the cake, turn the cake over, and carefully peel away the piece of parchment paper you used for baking. Cover the cake with a sheet of plastic wrap until you're ready to fill and roll it. *(The cake can be made ahead, wrapped airtight in plastic, and stored at room temperature for a day or two or frozen for up to a month.)*

the fruit

- ½ cup cassis (packed in syrup), bottled or canned (or see page 214 for variation using dried currants)

At least 2 hours before you plan to fill the cake, drain the cassis and gently pat them dry between sheets of paper towels.

the filling

- 1 cup chestnut purée (stir before measuring)
- ⅓ cup chestnut spread (stir before measuring)
- 2 tablespoons plus 2 teaspoons unsalted butter, softened
- 2 tablespoons dark rum
- ¾ cup plus 2 tablespoons very cold heavy cream

Working in a bowl that's large enough to hold all of the filling ingredients and using a mixer or a whisk, beat the chestnut purée, spread, and butter together until well blended. Stir in the rum. In another bowl, whip the heavy cream until it holds firm peaks. (In order for the filling to hold its own when it's rolled in the cake, the cream needs to be whipped until it is very stiff.) Delicately fold the cream into the chestnut mixture. Don't be discouraged if the mixture looks curdled — this is the way it's supposed to be, so don't overmix it. And don't worry — it won't taste or feel curdled in your mouth. *(It's best to use the cream immediately, but, if necessary, you can cover it tightly and refrigerate it for about an hour.)*

to fill and roll

- 5 to 6 *marrons glacés,* broken into crumbs (optional)

1. With the cake still on its sheet of parchment paper, transfer it to a work surface; the short sides of the cake should be at the top and bottom and the underside of the cake should be face up. Using a pastry brush, moisten the cake with the rum syrup. The cake should be evenly moistened but not soaked, and you may have some syrup left over.
2. Using a long metal offset spatula, spread the filling evenly across the cake, smoothing it to within ½ inch of the bottom edge. Scatter the cassis and the bits of candied chestnuts evenly over the filling.
3. Starting at the top short edge of the cake and using the parchment paper to move things along, roll the cake into a spiral that is as tight and neat as you can make it. Wrap the cake very tightly in plastic to help it keep its shape, and chill it, seam side down, in the refrigerator for at least 6 hours. *(The cake can be made ahead to this point and refrigerated overnight.)*

the buttercream

- 2½ tablespoons chestnut purée (stir before measuring)
- 2 tablespoons chestnut spread (stir before measuring)
- 1½ cups Vanilla Buttercream (page 29), whisked and ready to use

213

Whisk the chestnut purée and chestnut spread together just until they're smooth and then whisk them into the buttercream.

to finish

1. Unwrap the cake, place it on a large cardboard cake round or cutting board, and, using a long thin knife and cutting on the bias, cut off the ends of the cake; the widest part of these pieces should be about an inch thick. Use these pieces, placed flat side down on the cake close to either end, to form the bumps on the log. Cover the log and its bumps with an even layer of the buttercream. To make the log look as if it's covered with bark, run a fork down the length of the log and around the outer edges of the bumps, wiping the fork frequently so that you get clean lines. (While clean lines are nice, you needn't be too neat — wavy lines, knots, and gnarls will only make the cake look more log-like.) Use the fork to make a circular pattern on the top surface of the bumps. Put the cake back into the refrigerator to firm the buttercream.

2. At serving time, carefully transfer the log to a serving plate. Pierre suggests that the plate be covered with a lacy napkin and decorated with pine cones and gilt holly leaves. The cake should be cut and served while it is cold.

VARIATION

CHRISTMAS LOG WITH CURRANTS

Replace the cassis with ½ cup dried currants. Place the currants, 3 tablespoons dark rum, and 3 tablespoons water in a small saucepan over low heat and cook, stirring, just until the currants are soft and plump, about 2 minutes. Remove the pan from the heat and allow the currants to macerate for at least 2 hours, or for up to 1 day. About 2 hours before you plan to fill the cake, drain the currants well and pat them dry between paper towels.

Keeping

You can make the cake and the buttercream ahead (the buttercream can be stored in the freezer, then thawed, whisked to smooth, and mixed with the chestnut flavorings right before you need to use it), but the fully assembled cake is best served the day it is made.

RIVIERA

As elegant as the high-rent, high-life area it's named for, this Riviera offers pleasure in triplicate — three flavors in three textures. Composed of layers of dark flourless chocolate cake, thin and chewy; darker bittersweet mousse, deceptively light and unmistakably rich; and sunshine-yellow lemon cream, buttery, custardy, and terrifically tart, the neatly constructed cake is given a mantle of mousse and a lemon-slice fillip, a hint of the surprise within.

Mixing up flavors and textures is one of Pierre's hallmarks, as is the trick of putting together tastes bitter and acidic. But, as Pierre cautions, mixing chocolate and lemon only works when the balance, always a delicate matter, is perfect. Of course it's perfect here, but you do need to pay attention. To attain perfection, use only as much lemon cream as specified and, if you can, make this stunner with the same chocolate Pierre uses, Valrhona Manjari. Once the balance is right, show it off to advantage by serving the cake one hour out of the refrigerator (cut the time if your kitchen is warm). Taking the chill off the mousse and cream brings out the high notes in their flavors.

215

《 *Bitter and acidic flavors don't make an easy marriage. To make the relationship work in this cake, it's important to have a chocolate that's more sweet than bitter.* 》 — P. H .

the cake
- 1 recipe Flourless Chocolate Cake Batter (page 10), piped into four 9-inch circles, baked, and cooled

Makes 8 to 10 servings

Trim 3 of the disks to fit inside an 8¾-inch/22-cm dessert ring. (The cake can be trimmed easily with scissors.) The fourth disk can be wrapped airtight and frozen for another use. Wrap the layers in plastic and set aside until needed. *(Freshly baked layers can be wrapped airtight and kept at room temperature for 2 days or frozen for a month.)*

the lemon cream

- 1½ cups Lemon Cream (page 31)

Place a piece of parchment paper on a cardboard cake round and center an 8¾-inch/22-cm tart or dessert ring on the cardboard. Spoon in the lemon cream and use an offset spatula to smooth the top. Freeze until firm, about an hour. *(The cream can be wrapped and frozen for up to 2 weeks. Note that you'll need an 8¾-inch/22-cm dessert ring to assemble the cake, so if you must use your one and only dessert ring for the lemon cream, freeze the cream in the ring until firm, then remove the ring and keep the cream covered in the freezer until needed.)*

the mousse

- 1¾ cups heavy cream
- 2 large eggs, at room temperature
- 4 large egg yolks, at room temperature
- 10 ounces bittersweet chocolate (preferably Valrhona Manjari), coarsely chopped
- ½ cup sugar
- 3 tablespoons water

1. Beat the cream until it holds medium-firm peaks, then cover and chill it until needed. Place the eggs and yolks in the bowl of a mixer fitted with the whisk attachment and beat at the lowest speed for a few seconds, just to break up the eggs; set them aside while you prepare the chocolate and sugar syrup.

2. Melt the chocolate in a microwave oven or in a bowl over a pan of simmering water. Remove the chocolate from the heat and, if necessary, pour it into a bowl large enough to hold all the ingredients for the mousse. Cool the chocolate to 114°F, as measured on an instant-read thermometer.

3. While the chocolate is melting and cooling, place the sugar and water in a small heavy-bottomed saucepan. Bring the mixture to a boil, stirring occasionally and washing down the sides of the pan with a pastry brush dipped in cold water. Boil the syrup over high heat without stirring it until it reaches 257°F, as measured on an instant-read thermometer, about 8 to 10 minutes, then immediately remove it from the heat.

4. With the mixer on the lowest speed, beat the eggs for a few seconds, then very slowly add the syrup in a thin, steady stream. To avoid splatters, try to pour the syrup down the side of the bowl, not into the spinning whisk. (Inevitably, some will splatter, but don't attempt to scrape the hardened syrup into the eggs — you'll get lumps.) Increase the mixer speed to high and beat the eggs for about 5 minutes, or until they are pale and more than double their original volume. If the mixture is still warm, reduce the speed to medium and continue to beat until the eggs are at room temperature.

5. Using a large rubber spatula, fold about one quarter of the whipped cream into the chocolate. Fold in the rest of the cream and then, very delicately, fold in the whipped egg mixture.

to assemble

1. Center an 8¾-inch/22-cm dessert ring on a cardboard cake round and lay one chocolate cake disk in the ring. Using an offset spatula or a flexible rubber spatula, spread 1½ cups of mousse over the cake and smooth the top. Position a second layer of cake over the mousse, pressing down gently and jiggling the cake to settle it in place. Give the top of the cake a light coating of mousse, just enough to help glue down the next layer. Remove the ring (see page 272) from the frozen lemon cream (if necessary) and, using two wide spatulas, lift the cream onto the cake. Spread a little mousse over the lemon cream to act as glue, and position the third cake layer over the cream. Using an offset spatula, cover the top layer of cake with a smooth coating of mousse, sweeping the spatula across the mousse to level it with the edge of the dessert ring.

2. Refrigerate the cake for about 1 hour to set the mousse; cover the leftover mousse with plastic wrap and refrigerate it as well.

to finish

- Cocoa powder
- 1 lemon
- About 1 tablespoon lemon, quince, or apple jelly, warmed, optional

1. Spoon the reserved mousse into a pastry bag fitted with a ½-inch plain tip. Starting at the center of the cake, and rotating the cake as necessary, pipe spokes of mousse over the top of the cake. The spokes should start in the center of the cake and thicken little by little until they finish at the edge of the cake. Pipe a dollop of mousse in the center of the cake so that the pattern resembles a daisy. Transfer the cake to the refrigerator for another hour. *(At this point, if it's more convenient, you can freeze the cake for up to 2 weeks. Wrap the cake airtight once the decoration is set.)*

2. To complete the decoration, remove the dessert ring (see page 272). Run a spatula around the top of the cake just to smooth the exposed sides of the decorative spokes you piped. Dust the top of the cake lightly with cocoa powder.

3. Cut off one third of the lemon; reserve the remainder for another use. Brush the cut surface of the lemon with a little of the warmed jelly, if desired, and place the lemon, cut side up, into the center of the cake.

4. Allow the cake to rest at room temperature for an hour (less, if the room is warm) before serving. This rest brings the mousse and the cream to their best texture and fullest flavor.

Keeping

The cake circles and the lemon cream can be made ahead — indeed, the cream needs to be frozen — but it may be just as convenient to prepare the Riviera up to (but not including) its final dusting of cocoa powder and the positioning of the lemon, and then to store it, wrapped airtight, in the refrigerator for 2 days or in the freezer for up to 2 weeks. To defrost the cake, allow it to rest, still covered, overnight in the refrigerator. In all cases, remember to give the cake a room-temperature rest before serving.

MOZART

One look at this grand chocolate cake is enough to set you thinking that Mozart would have been pleased to have this inspired gustatory divertimento in his repertoire. It's the confection's cinnamon-almond pastry, or, more exactly, the way it's made, that connects this cake with the famed Austrian composer. The pastry, buttery, fragile, and friable, gets some of its textural interest from the inclusion of sieved hard-boiled egg yolks, a typically Austrian touch. That layers of this pastry are alternated with layers of dark, sweet chocolate mousse shot through with chunks of cinnamon-scented apples is a flight of imagination that goes beyond national borders or musical musings.

You can make the pastry layers early in the day, but the cake needs to be assembled as soon as the mousse is made and should be served the same day, so plan ahead.

This cake is completely different from the Melody [page 179] even though both cakes have apple, cinnamon, chocolate, pastry, and a play on textures. What makes them so different is the way you experience the flavors. Take some of the Mozart and see if you don't taste chocolate first, cinnamon next, and apple at the end. — P. H.

the pastry

- 1 recipe Cinnamon Dough (page 18), chilled

I. Cut the dough into thirds. Working with one piece of dough at a time, and keeping the work surface and the dough well floured, roll the dough into a round about ⅛ inch thick. Cut an 8¾-inch/22-cm circle from each piece (use a dessert or tart ring to get the size right) and

Makes 8 to 10 servings

221

carefully transfer the dough to two or three parchment-lined baking sheets. (The dough is very fragile and is transferred most easily — and safely — by slipping the removable bottom of a metal tart pan under the dough. If necessary, dust the metal round with flour for extra insurance.) Prick the dough all over with the tines of a fork, cover with sheets of plastic wrap, and chill for at least 30 minutes. *(The dough can be kept, well covered, in the refrigerator for several hours.)*

2. Center a rack in the oven and preheat the oven to 350°F. Remove the sheets of plastic and bake the disks for about 18 to 20 minutes, or until they are honey brown. (If you are baking two sheets at a time, rotate the sheets front to back and top to bottom halfway through the baking period. Alternatively, you can bake the sheets one at a time.) Transfer the pastry, parchment paper and all, to racks to cool to room temperature. *(The pastry can be kept at room temperature for up to 8 hours, but it should be used the day it is made.)*

the mousse

- 1 large Granny Smith or other tart apple, peeled and cored
- ¼ cup sugar
- ⅛ teaspoon cinnamon
- 1 tablespoon (½ ounce) unsalted butter
- 2 tablespoons dark rum
- ⅓ cup heavy cream
- 1 cinnamon stick, broken
- 8 ounces bittersweet chocolate (preferably Valrhona Caraïbes), coarsely chopped
- 6 large egg whites, at room temperature

1. Cut the apple into very small cubes (about a scant ¼ inch on a side) and toss in a bowl with 1 tablespoon of the sugar and the cinnamon. Melt the butter in a large skillet, preferably one with a nonstick finish, over moderately high heat, and when the butter is pale brown add the apple. Cook the cubes over high heat, tossing and turning them, until they develop a light crust, a matter of a few minutes. (Keep the heat high so that the apples brown but retain their shape. If the heat's too low, you risk ending up with applesauce.) The apples should be glistening, brown, and caramelized — they'll resemble a batch of terrific hash browns. Add the rum, carefully set it aflame, and stir the apples to coat. Turn the apples out onto a plate to cool to room temperature.

2. Pour the cream into a small saucepan, add the cinnamon stick, and bring to the boil; remove from heat. (Alternatively, you can do this in a microwave oven.) Cover and allow the cream to infuse for 10 minutes.

3. Meanwhile, melt the chocolate over simmering water or in the microwave and pour it into a large bowl. Strain the hot cream over the chocolate, discard the cinnamon stick (or wash, dry, and reserve for decoration; see page 224), and gently stir the chocolate and cream together. Allow the mixture to cool to a temperature of 104°F, as measured on an instant-read thermometer. Pay attention to this step — it's vital to the texture of the finished mousse that the chocolate be the correct temperature.

4. In an impeccably clean, dry bowl, whip the egg whites until they start to mound. Still whipping, add the remaining 3 tablespoons sugar little by little and continue to beat until the meringue forms stiff glossy peaks.

5. Using a large rubber spatula, fold one quarter of the meringue into the chocolate. Fold in the remaining meringue and then the cooled apples, mixing gently. (Temperature is important here. If the meringue or apples are too cold when they're added to the chocolate, the chocolate will block and the mousse will be too thick. If the chocolate and cream are too warm, they'll produce a thin, runny mousse.) Once the mousse is mixed, the cake must be assembled immediately.

to assemble

Center an 8¾-inch/22-cm dessert ring on a cardboard cake round. Using the removable bottom of a metal tart pan as a transporter, place one round of cinnamon pastry in the dessert ring, positioning it with the flat side down. Spread the pastry with half of the chocolate mousse. Top with another layer of pastry, pressing against it very gently to settle it into the mousse, and then spread over the rest of the mousse. Finish the cake with the last layer of pastry. Transfer the cake to the refrigerator and chill for at least 30 minutes or for up to 8 hours.

223

to finish

- Chocolate curls or shavings (see page 270), optional
- ½ Granny Smith or other tart apple
- Freshly squeezed lemon juice
- ¼ cup quince or apple jelly
- Cocoa powder
- 2 cinnamon sticks

1. Remove the dessert ring (see page 272). Place the chocolate curls or shavings on a baking sheet and, holding the cake over the sheet, pat a thin layer of curls or shavings against the side of the cake. (If the curls don't stick to the mousse, warm the mousse gently with a hair dryer — see page 275.)

2. Cut about 6 paper-thin slices of apple, cutting the apple from stem to blossom end, and rub the slices with a little lemon juice to keep them from discoloring. Arrange the apple slices, each slice slightly overlapping the preceding slice, in the center of the cake. Warm the jelly in a saucepan over direct heat or in the microwave and brush a thin coat of jelly over the apples.

3. Dust the edges of the top of the cake with a little cocoa powder, and transfer the cake to a serving platter. For the last touch, place the cinnamon sticks on top of the cake, positioning them so that they form an X with one set of points touching the apple slices. The cake is ready to serve. If necessary, you can refrigerate the cake before serving.

Keeping

Because of the cooked eggs in the pastry and the raw egg whites in the mousse, this cake has very limited keeping qualities. It should be prepared and served the same day.

chocolate temptation

For the past few years, one-to-a-person-size warm chocolate cakes, the kind that are just set around the edges and still runny in the center, have been bestsellers on dessert menus in both France and America. Their popularity is not surprising: They're the most-chocolate chocolate dessert you can get short of a candy bar; their oozy centers, like chocolate lava, are dramatic; and they're easy to make — the batter, which is put together quickly, can be prepared ahead, and the cakes can be baked and served at the last minute without the typical last-minute fuss.

Pierre's version of this cake has all the warmth, softness, and fluidity of the best of the genre, and then it's got a spin — it's spiked with habanero pepper and sauced with an avocado-banana purée. When Pierre introduced this dessert at a class in New York, he confessed that he always has problems telling people about this offbeat combination. "It's better to taste it first and deconstruct it later," he suggests. With so many out-of-the-ordinary elements, you can understand his hesitancy to reveal all before the first mouthful.

The small sliver of hot pepper that's warmed with the butter before it goes into the batter is just enough to add a little heat and a subtle kick to the chocolate. The cake, sporting a crunchy (and optional) orange tuile, is circled with caramelized bananas and set on a bed of citrusy avocado and banana purée, a pale green, super-creamy topping that keeps guests guessing. Do as Pierre does: Let them guess until they've tasted.

« When people tell me they're shocked by the idea of chocolate and spice, I remind them that the Aztecs did it centuries ago. » — P.H.

Makes 6 servings

While the thrill of this dessert is in its brilliant mix of flavors, if you're serving less adventurous types, there's nothing to stop you from omitting the habanero and making the chocolate cake straight — it makes an excellent "plain" cake and a good palette for your own variations.

the sauce

- 1½ ripe bananas
- 1 medium-size ripe avocado
- ½ cup freshly squeezed lemon juice
- 3 tablespoons freshly squeezed orange juice
- 2 tablespoons sugar
- Zest of ¼ lime — removed with a zester (see page 281) and finely minced

1. Peel and coarsely chop the bananas and avocado. Place all of the ingredients in the container of a blender or a food processor and whir until you have a smooth purée, scraping the sides of the container as necessary. The sauce should be creamy and thick, but not heavy. If, at serving time, you think the sauce is too thick, you can thin it with a little water.

2. Scrape the sauce into a bowl and cover the sauce with a sheet of plastic wrap, pressing the plastic against the top of the sauce to create an airtight cover. The plastic wrap will help keep the sauce from turning black, a natural problem with both banana and avocado. Chill until needed. *(The sauce can be made early in the day and kept refrigerated until needed.)*

the bananas

- 2 ripe bananas
- 2 tablespoons freshly squeezed lemon juice
- 1 tablespoon (½ ounce) unsalted butter
- 2 tablespoons sugar

1. Peel the bananas and cut them on the diagonal into slices about ¼ inch thick. Toss the slices with the lemon juice to keep them from discoloring.

2. Melt the butter in a large skillet, preferably one with a nonstick finish. Turn the heat up to high, add the bananas, and sprinkle them with the sugar. Cook, turning the bananas, for about 2 minutes, or until they are lightly caramelized on both sides; remove the pan from the heat. (Ideally, the bananas should be cooked just before the cakes go into the oven or even while the cakes are in the oven, so that they can be served warm. However, if it's more convenient, you can make the bananas a few hours ahead, store them uncovered at room

temperature, and either reheat them in the skillet before serving or serve them at room temperature.)

the cakes

- 1 stick (4 ounces) unsalted butter
- 1 sliver habanero or Scotch bonnet pepper
- 4¾ ounces bittersweet chocolate (preferably Valrhona Manjari), finely chopped
- 1 large egg, at room temperature
- 3 large egg yolks, at room temperature
- 2 tablespoons sugar

1. Center a rack in the oven and preheat the oven to 350°F. Butter six 4-ounce ramekins (small soufflé or custard cups are perfect) and dust the insides with sugar; tap out the excess sugar and place the cups on a baking sheet.

2. In a small saucepan or a microwave oven, melt the butter with the sliver of hot pepper; remove the pepper from the butter and discard. Melt the chocolate in the microwave oven or in a bowl over, but not touching, simmering water. Cool both the butter and the chocolate until they measure 104°F on an instant-read thermometer.

3. In a medium bowl, gently stir together the egg, yolks, and sugar with a small whisk. Whisk only until the sugar is blended into the eggs, and take care not to beat air into the mixture. Gently stir in the melted chocolate little by little and then the butter, again little by little. You'll have a smooth, glossy ganache. *(The ganache can be used now or it can be stored, covered airtight, in the refrigerator for about 12 hours. If you've refrigerated the chocolate mixture, bring it back to room temperature by warming it in the microwave oven or over a pan of simmering water before proceeding.)*

4. Pour the ganache into the prepared molds and bake for 10 minutes without opening the oven door. Resist the temptation to bake these any longer — even though their tops will be just slightly dull and their centers will shimmy at the slightest shake, this is the way they're supposed to be. Remove the baking sheet from the oven and set aside while you arrange the plates — the cakes need to be served just minutes from the oven.

to assemble

- 6 Orange Tuiles (page 101), optional

For each dessert, make a pillow of sauce in the center of a large plate. Turn a cake over onto a plastic pastry scraper or a broad metal pancake turner — don't unmold the cake yet — and then slide the cake onto the sauce; remove the ramekin. Place a few caramelized bananas on the plate and, if you're serving them, press an orange tuile into the cake. Serve immediately, passing the remaining sauce in a sauceboat.

228

Keeping
Although all of the components can
be prepared a few hours in advance,
once the cakes are baked, there's
no time to lose between pulling them
from the oven and serving them.

GOLDEN PEARL
brownie
CAKE

A thin, profoundly chocolaty, very American brownie forms the base of this cake, which, when complete, bears no resemblance to American cakes past or present. Topped with a featherweight Cognac cream polka-dotted with Cognac-drenched golden raisins — the pearls — and finished with more raisins and a gloss of citrus-fresh glaze, this cake, whose elegance belies the ease with which it is made, is a brilliant combination of contrasts in color — dark cake against light cream; texture — crunchy, chewy cake against soft cream; and taste — sweet cake against rich, boozy cream. The cake is good on the first bite, even better on the next; its seductive power seems to build in a more-you-have-more-you-want way. Don't say you weren't warned.

« *I started making this cake with* marc de gewürztraminer, *a liqueur from my birthplace, Alsace. But I was working in Paris and no one there knew the liqueur, so the cake wasn't very popular. All that changed when I changed the recipe to include Cognac — the cake has been a grand success ever since. And by the way, it's good with rum, too.* » — P.H.

the raisins

- 1 cup (packed) golden raisins
- ¼ cup water
- ¼ cup Cognac

Bring the water and raisins to a boil in a medium saucepan. Boil for a minute or two, stirring until most of the water has evaporated, then remove the pan from the heat. Add the Cognac

Makes 10 to 12 servings

and carefully set it aflame. Stir until the flame dies out, and then transfer the raisins and their liquid to a refrigerator container. Cool to room temperature, then cover and chill until needed. This is best done a day ahead. *(The raisins can be packed into a jar with a tight-fitting lid and kept in the refrigerator for about 5 days.)*

the cake

- 2½ ounces bittersweet chocolate (preferably Valrhona Caraïbe), finely chopped
- 9 tablespoons (4½ ounces) unsalted butter, softened
- 2 large eggs, at room temperature, lightly beaten
- ½ cup plus 2 tablespoons sugar
- ⅓ cup plus 2 tablespoons all-purpose flour, sifted
- ¾ cup (3¼ ounces) pecans, coarsely chopped

1. Center a rack in the oven and preheat the oven to 350°F. Place a 10¼-inch/26-cm tart or dessert ring on a parchment-lined baking sheet and set aside until needed.

2. Melt the chocolate in a microwave oven or in a bowl over a pan of simmering water. Remove the chocolate from the heat and set it aside to cool to 114°F, as measured on an instant-read thermometer.

3. Working in a large bowl with a rubber spatula, beat the butter until it is smooth and creamy. (The purpose is to smooth it, not to beat air into it.) One by one, stir in the chocolate and then the remaining ingredients, in the order in which they are listed, stirring only until each ingredient is incorporated.

4. Scrape the batter into the tart ring and spread it evenly with a spatula. Bake for 10 to 13 minutes, or until the cake is just dry around the edges and only starting to dry in the center. (If you touch the cake, it will still be tacky.) Transfer the baking sheet to a rack and allow the cake to cool to room temperature, then run a small knife around the inside of the ring and lift off the ring. *(The cake can be wrapped airtight and kept at room temperature for 2 days or frozen for up to a month.)*

the cream

- 1⅔ cups heavy cream
- 1½ teaspoons gelatin
- 3 tablespoons cold water
- 3½ tablespoons Cognac
- ⅔ cup Vanilla Pastry Cream (page 27)

1. Whip the cream to medium-firm peaks and set aside at room temperature until needed.
2. Sprinkle the gelatin over the cold water and allow it to soften. Dissolve the gelatin by placing it in the microwave oven for 15 seconds or heating it over gentle heat. If necessary, transfer the dissolved gelatin to a bowl large enough to hold all the ingredients for the cream.
3. Using a flexible rubber spatula, stir the Cognac into the gelatin, followed by a quarter of the pastry cream. At this point, the mixture should not be warmer than 70°F, as measured on an instant-read thermometer. If it is too warm, cool it over ice. Stir in the remainder of the pastry cream and then fold in the whipped cream. The cream is now ready to be used.

to assemble

1. Drain the raisins and pat them free of excess moisture with paper towels.
2. Center a 10¼-inch/26-cm dessert ring on a cardboard cake round; lay the brownie layer in the ring. Spoon half of the Cognac cream over the cake and cover with a layer of the macerated raisins, using about three quarters of them; reserve the remaining raisins for the top of the cake. Spoon on the rest of the Cognac cream and smooth the top with an offset spatula. Transfer the cake to the freezer for an hour to set the cream. *(The cake can be made to this point and, when set, wrapped airtight and frozen for 2 weeks. If the cake has been frozen, defrost it in the refrigerator overnight before glazing and serving.)*

to finish

- About ½ recipe Transparent Glaze (page 38) or about ½ cup quince or apple jelly
- 1 green grape, optional
- 1 small piece gold leaf, optional

1. If you are using the glaze and it has cooled, or it has been frozen, liquefy it by warming it over gentle heat or in a microwave oven on low power. (Do not reheat the glaze to over 104°F.) The glaze should not be hot when you pour it over the cake. If you are using the jelly, warm it over direct heat or in a microwave oven to liquefy it, then allow it to cool before pouring it over the cake.
2. Top the cake with the reserved raisins and spoon the glaze over the raisins and the top of the cake. If you want to finish the cake as it's decorated in the photograph (page 230), brush a green grape with glaze and center it on the cake; drape a tiny shred of gold leaf over the grape. Chill the cake to set the glaze before serving. At serving time, transfer the cake to a platter and remove the dessert ring (see page 272).

Keeping
The brownie and, indeed, the brownie with the cream, can be made ahead and frozen, but once the cake is glazed, it is best eaten within a day or two.

CHOCOLATE dome

Dark, tight-grained chocolate cake, dense almond-studded chocolate mousse, and a shiny bittersweet chocolate glaze make up this gem, but it's the package — an impressive dome — that gets the first round of raves. Never mind that it's easier to construct than a simple layer cake, the dome has the look of a present fresh from the pâtisserie. If you're not in the habit of constructing gorgeous *gâteaux* get ready for gasps of glee (and a swell of well-deserved pride) when you serve this. Follow the directions carefully, and your very first Chocolate Dome will be as perfect as Pierre's. And if the thrilling sense of accomplishment doesn't make you giddy, the first shot of almost-straight chocolate will.

The best mold in which to construct this elegant igloo is a metal bowl (preferably with a rounded bottom) with a capacity of about 8 to 9 cups. The instructions for this cake are based on a bowl of that capacity that's almost eight inches across. You can use a bowl with different dimensions — just make the appropriate adjustments in the diameter of the chocolate cake. The remaining elements should be fine with whatever bowl you choose as long as its capacity and dimensions don't differ too drastically from the model. This will even work with a flat-bottomed bowl. Of course, you'll have a plateau rather than a dome on top — just think of it as a serendipitous mesa on which to pile chocolate shavings, berries, or both.

《 *This is the* gâteau *par excellence for the chocolate lover. Except for a couple of almonds, this cake is chocolate, chocolate, chocolate.* 》 — P. H.

Makes 12 to 16 servings

235

the cake

- ¼ cup Dutch-processed cocoa
- 2½ tablespoons all-purpose flour
- 2 tablespoons cornstarch
- 3 large egg whites
- ½ cup sugar
- 5 large egg yolks
- 3 tablespoons (1½ ounces) unsalted butter, melted and cooled to room temperature

1. Center a rack in the oven and preheat the oven to 350°F. Butter an 8-inch round cake pan, dust the interior with flour, and tap out the excess; set aside. (If the bowl you'll be molding the cake in has a diameter larger than 8 inches, here is where you'll have to make the necessary adjustments and choose a cake pan with a compatible diameter. Since the cake is thicker than you need it to be, you can bake it in a larger pan and still have enough for the dome.)

2. Sift the cocoa, flour, and cornstarch together and reserve. Place the egg whites in an impeccably clean, dry mixing bowl and whip until they form soft peaks. Gradually add ¼ cup of the sugar and whip until the whites hold firm, glossy peaks. Set them aside while you work on the yolks.

3. In another bowl, whip the yolks and the remaining ¼ cup of sugar together until the mixture pales, thickens, and forms a ribbon when you lift the beater. Working with a large rubber spatula and a light hand, fold about one third of the beaten egg whites into the yolks. Fold in all of the sifted dry ingredients. (This can be sticky business at the beginning, but press on — it gets better when you add the butter and nice when the rest of the whites go in.) Carefully fold in the cooled melted butter, followed by the remainder of the whipped egg whites.

4. Turn the batter into the prepared pan, smooth the top with the spatula, and bake the cake for 25 to 28 minutes, or until the cake is springy to the touch and starts to come away from the sides of the pan; a knife inserted into the center of the cake should come out clean. Transfer the cake to a rack, invert, and cool to room temperature right side up. *(The cake can be made ahead and kept wrapped airtight at room temperature for 2 to 3 days or frozen for up to a month.)*

the syrup

- ¼ cup sugar
- 2 tablespoons Dutch-processed cocoa
- ⅓ cup plus 2 tablespoons water

In a small saucepan, stir the sugar and cocoa together. Add the water and, stirring, bring the mixture to the boil. Remove the pan from the heat and set the syrup aside to cool completely. *(The syrup can be made a week ahead and kept in a tightly sealed jar in the refrigerator.)*

the mousse

- $10\frac{1}{2}$ ounces bittersweet chocolate (preferably Valrhona Guanaja), coarsely chopped
- 2 large eggs, at room temperature
- 5 large egg yolks, at room temperature
- Scant $\frac{2}{3}$ cup sugar
- 3 tablespoons water
- 2 cups heavy cream
- $\frac{1}{2}$ cup slivered almonds, toasted (see page 277) and finely chopped

1. Melt the chocolate in the microwave oven on medium power or in a bowl over, not touching, simmering water. Pour the chocolate into a bowl large enough to hold all the ingredients and set it aside until it cools to 114°F.

2. Place the eggs and yolks in the bowl of a mixer fitted with the whisk attachment, and keep close at hand. Put the sugar and water in a small saucepan and stir to moisten the sugar. Bring the mixture to a boil and continue to cook until the surface is covered with large bubbles and the temperature is 257°F, as measured on an instant-read or candy thermometer. Remove the saucepan from the heat. Start beating the eggs on low speed and slowly but steadily add the hot sugar syrup, trying to pour it down the side of the bowl, not into the spinning whisk. (Inevitably, some of the sugar will splatter onto the sides of the bowl — just leave it there and keep beating.) When all of the syrup is incorporated, increase the mixer speed to high and beat until the eggs pale, triple in volume, and cool to room temperature.

3. In a large bowl, whip the heavy cream until it holds medium peaks. Working with a large rubber spatula, fold a quarter of the whipped cream into the cooled chocolate. Fold in the remaining cream, followed by the whipped egg-sugar mixture. Work as delicately as you can — you want to keep as much of the bubble structure you've whipped into these ingredients as possible. Finally, fold in the toasted almonds. It is best to use the mousse now, while it is still soft and spreadable, but you can keep it covered in the refrigerator for up to a day if necessary.

to assemble

1. Slice the chocolate cake into three layers, each ½ inch thick. You'll only need two of the layers, so freeze the remaining layer for another use. To figure out what size your layers should be, use a tape measure to measure the interior diameter of the bowl halfway up the bowl and at the top; cut your two layers accordingly. Brush one side of each layer with the cocoa syrup, moistening the layers well.

2. Spoon enough of the chocolate mousse into the bowl to half-fill it; smooth the top. Place the smaller layer of cake on top of the mousse, moistened side down; jiggle it around a little so that it fits snugly against the mousse. Now brush the exposed side of the cake with syrup. Fill the bowl with mousse (you may have some left over — it makes a good dessert on its own) and settle the second cake layer, moistened side down, over the mousse. Moisten the top side of the cake with cocoa syrup (you may have some syrup left over) and jiggle it so that it fits flat against the mousse. Wrap the bowl well with plastic film and freeze for at least 6 hours. *(At this point, the cake can be covered and frozen for a up to a month. The cake, which can be glazed when frozen or thawed, must be frozen for unmolding. It should be thawed in the refrigerator before serving.)*

238

to finish

- Chocolate Glaze (page 37)
- Chocolate curls or shavings (see page 270)
- Chocolate Sauce, warm (page 36), optional

1. The ease with which you'll be able to unmold the mousse cake will depend on the shape of your bowl. No matter what bowl the cake is in, you'll have to plunge it into a basin of hot water for about 20 seconds before attempting to unmold the cake onto a cardboard cake round. If the bowl is completely hemispherical, the ideal, and the mousse sufficiently softened by its hot water bath, you should be able to press your hand against one side of the chocolate cake on top and have the whole creation slide out easily. If the bowl has a flat bottom, the push procedure won't work — you'll have to run a thin blunt knife around the sides of the bowl and nudge and cajole until you're successful. In either case, you may have to give the bowl another hot-water dunk.

2. To get the best coverage, the glaze should be about 114°F. If it's too cold, just warm it to the right temperature by putting it in a hot water bath or popping it into the microwave oven for a few seconds on low power. Pour the glaze over the dome, making certain that you cover the entire cake. If necessary, use a long offset metal spatula to smooth the glaze and cover the cake, but try to keep the smoothing to a minimum — the less work, the shinier the glaze.

This glaze sets quickly (and will set even more quickly since it is going over a cold cake), so work briskly. (If you find that the glaze sets too quickly and that it doesn't flow over the cake, reheat the glaze for just a few seconds in the microwave oven on low power or in a hot water bath.) Decorate the base of the cake with the chocolate curls or shavings. If the cake is thawed, it can be served now. If you refrigerate the glazed cake, the glaze will lose its brilliance — no problem. A little hot air from a hair dryer will bring back it's sheen in seconds (see page 275). *(The cake can be kept in the refrigerator, covered with a large bowl or cake dome, for up to 3 days.)* This is nice served with warm chocolate sauce.

239

Keeping

The components of this cake can all be made ahead with ease. The assembled but unglazed cake can be frozen for a month; the chocolate glaze, sauce, and decorations can be made ahead; and the finished cake can be kept covered in the refrigerator for up to 3 days.

carioca

The best-known carioca may be the sexy Brazilian dance, but the tastiest is Pierre's sexy French cake. As lively and intense as its namesake, this Carioca is thoroughly suffused with coffee and chocolate, the national flavors of Brazil. Constructed like an old-fashioned American layer cake, the Carioca has alternating layers of génoise and dark chocolate mousse, is finished with bittersweet ganache and glazed almonds, and gets its coffee kick from an extra-strength soaking syrup. To get the full coffee flavor this cake demands, make the syrup with a rich, very dark coffee ground powdery fine for espresso.

The technique of coating almonds with cocoa powder and simple syrup and then roasting them until they're browned and crunchy is one you can use to make an easy snack. Toss mixed nuts (or your favorite kind of nut) with the cocoa and syrup and toast, following the directions for the decorative almonds [see page 243]; then, when they're cool, mix them with small cubes of dried fruit and, if you want, tiny pieces of chocolate. — P. H.

the cake

- One 9-inch Génoise (page 2), cooled

Cut two layers from the cake, each between ¼ and ½ inch thick (these layers need to be extremely thin), and set them aside. (Leftover cake can be wrapped airtight and stored in the freezer — génoise crumbs are good in the base of fruit tarts; see page 137.)

Makes 8 to 10 servings

the syrup

- 1 recipe Simple Syrup (page 39)
- 2 cups water
- 5 ounces (2 packed cups) ground-for-espresso coffee (the coffee must be very finely ground)
- ½ teaspoon instant coffee

1. Spoon off 2 tablespoons of the simple syrup, cover, and refrigerate to use for the glazed almonds. Keep the remainder of the syrup at the ready. Line a strainer with a double thickness of dampened cheesecloth and place it over a small bowl; keep close at hand.

2. Bring the water to the boil in a medium saucepan. Add the coffee, stir, and immediately pour the mixture through the lined strainer. You should have about ¾ cup of very dark coffee. Stir in the instant coffee and the simple syrup. Set the syrup aside until needed. *(The syrup can be made up to a week ahead and kept covered in the refrigerator.)*

the mousse

- 1¾ cups heavy cream
- 2 large eggs, at room temperature
- 4 large egg yolks, at room temperature
- 10 ounces bittersweet chocolate (preferably Valrhona Manjari), coarsely chopped
- ½ cup sugar
- 3 tablespoons water

1. Beat the cream until it holds medium-firm peaks, then cover and chill it until needed. Place the eggs and yolks in the bowl of a mixer fitted with the whisk attachment and beat at the lowest speed for a few seconds, just to break up the eggs; set them aside while you prepare the chocolate and sugar syrup.

2. Melt the chocolate in a microwave oven or in a metal bowl over a pan of simmering water. Remove the chocolate from the heat and, if necessary, pour it into a bowl large enough to hold all the ingredients for the mousse. Cool the chocolate to 114°F, as measured on an instant-read thermometer.

3. While the chocolate is melting and cooling, place the sugar and water in a small heavy-bottomed saucepan. Bring the mixture to a boil, stirring occasionally and washing down the sides of the pan with a pastry brush dipped in cold water. Boil the syrup over high heat without stirring it until it reaches 257°F, as measured on an instant-read thermometer, about 8 to 10 minutes, then immediately remove it from the heat.

4. With the mixer on the lowest speed, beat the eggs for a few seconds, then very slowly add the hot sugar syrup in a thin, steady stream. To avoid splatters, try to pour the syrup down the side of the bowl, not into the spinning whisk. (Inevitably, some will splatter, but don't attempt to scrape the hardened syrup into the eggs — you'll get lumps.) Increase the mixer speed to high and beat the eggs for about 5 minutes, or until they are pale and more than double their original volume. If the mixture is still warm, reduce the speed to medium and continue to beat until the eggs are at room temperature.

5. Using a large rubber spatula, fold about one quarter of the whipped cream into the chocolate. Fold in the rest of the cream and then, very delicately, fold in the whipped egg mixture.

to assemble

Center an 8¾-inch/22-cm dessert ring on a cardboard cake round. Place one layer of génoise, cut side up, in the ring. Brush enough coffee syrup over the cake to moisten it thoroughly. Using an offset spatula or a flexible rubber spatula, spread 2 to 2½ cups of mousse over the cake and smooth the top. Position a second layer of cake on the mousse, pressing down gently and jiggling the cake to settle it in place. Brush on some coffee soaking syrup and spread on another 2 to 2½ cups of mousse; smooth the top level with the edge of the dessert ring. (You may have some syrup left over, and you will have extra mousse. The syrup can be refrigerated for another use or discarded, and the mousse — delicious on its own or with cookies — can be refrigerated for 2 days or frozen for a month.) Transfer the cake to the freezer and freeze for 2 hours to set the mousse. *(The cake can be made to this point and frozen for up to a month.)* If you're not going to freeze the cake for long-term storage, it should be transferred to the refrigerator to defrost after its 2-hour freeze.

243

the almonds

- 1½ cups sliced blanched almonds
- ½ teaspoon Dutch-processed cocoa
- 2 tablespoons reserved Simple Syrup

Center a rack in the oven and preheat the oven to 325°F. Toss the almonds with the cocoa, then toss with the syrup to coat, and spread them out on a parchment-lined baking sheet. Toast the almonds, stirring every 3 to 4 minutes, until they are deeply and evenly browned, about 10 to 12 minutes. Transfer the sheet to a rack and cool the almonds to room temperature. *(The almonds can be used immediately or packed into an airtight container and stored at room temperature for about 4 days.)*

the ganache

- $10\frac{1}{2}$ ounces bittersweet chocolate (preferably Valrhona Noir Gastronomie), finely chopped
- 2 tablespoons Dutch-processed cocoa
- $1\frac{1}{4}$ cups heavy cream

1. Place the chocolate and cocoa in a medium bowl. Bring the cream to a boil and remove it from the heat. Pour the cream into the chocolate in three additions, using a rubber spatula to stir the mixture in concentric circles, starting each time with a small circle in the center of the bowl and working your way out into larger circles. You'll have a smooth, glossy ganache. Allow the ganache to rest uncovered and undisturbed (don't stir it) at room temperature until it sets, 40 to 60 minutes, depending on the room's temperature. When the ganache is properly set, it will hold a ribbon for a second or two when stirred. It is ready to be used now or covered and refrigerated until needed. If the ganache is chilled, it must be brought back to its proper consistency by leaving it at room temperature until it's spreadable (the best method), or by heating it over hot water or in a microwave oven at low power. Do not beat it or otherwise overwork it, or it will lose its lovely — and characteristic — sheen.

2. While the ganache is setting up, transfer the cake from the refrigerator to the counter. (Working on a cold rather than a solidly frozen cake will facilitate applying the ganache.)

to finish

1. Remove the dessert ring (see page 272). Using a long metal offset spatula, spread ganache over the top and sides of the cake. If you need to repeat with another one or two layers of ganache, go ahead — you've got plenty of ganache to play with (in fact, you'll have ganache left over). If the ganache is set enough to hold a design, you can decorate the top now. If the ganache is still very soft, return the cake to the refrigerator for a few minutes to set it enough to hold a line drawn across its surface with a knife. (Keep the leftover ganache at hand so you can cover up any design attempts that don't pass muster.)

2. Decorate the top of the cake using the blade of a long serrated knife, such as a bread knife. Hold the handle of the knife with one hand and the tip with the other. Starting at one edge of the cake and holding the knife almost perpendicular to the cake, gently slide the knife from one edge to the other. Without "losing your place" at the edge of the cake, shift the blade about $\frac{1}{16}$ inch and slide it back to the opposite edge of the cake. You will have created the first V in a herringbone pattern. (See the photo on page 240.) Continue until you have decorated the entire top of the cake. If the knife blade becomes clogged with ganache, clean the blade before continuing the pattern. Return the cake to the refrigerator for a few minutes to set

the design. If you prefer, the cake can be finished with a flat-top — that is, a smooth coating of ganache — or you can decorate the top with swirls, ridges, or any other pattern that pleases you.

3. The last step is to press the toasted almonds against the sides of the cake. (If the ganache has set so it's very firm and the almonds won't stick to the sides, just warm the sides ever so slightly with a hair dryer — lightly melting the ganache will help the almonds to adhere.) The cake can be served now or chilled until serving time. If the cake is very cold and firm, let it rest at room temperature for 15 to 30 minutes before serving.

Keeping

Each of the elements of the cake can be made ahead and, in fact, the constructed cake — minus the almonds — can be stored in the refrigerator overnight or wrapped airtight and frozen for up to a month. A frozen cake is best defrosted, still wrapped, in the refrigerator overnight. If the cake has been chilled without the almonds, heat the ganache on the sides of the cake with a hair dryer to soften it and then press the almonds into the cake.

autumn MERINGUE
CAKE

With only three components — meringue disks, dark chocolate mousse, and a shiny chocolate glaze — this cake tantalizes, satisfies, and delights your five senses. First you see the cake (an invitation to indulgence), then you catch the wonderful aroma of chocolate, and then, as you cut into it, you hear the crackle of the meringue. When you take your first forkful, you both feel and taste it — you don't chew this cake as much as allow it to melt in your mouth. The meringue goes first, and it goes with a little effervescence, a slight pop, and then the mousse, softer, richer, and more slowly, leaving enough of its lovely chocolaty residue to set you up for the next forkful. All this, and it's the perfect party cake because it's best assembled a day or two ahead. (In fact, you might want to start working on this a little ahead since you'll need to have the chocolate sauce and chocolate glaze on hand.)

Pierre uses two different chocolates to make the mousse filling, but if you can only get one extra-high-quality dark bitter chocolate, carry on — it will still be delectable.

« This cake is based on a great classic recipe. It is at its most intriguing when the meringue is really well done — so well done that there isn't a speck of white in the center. This may be contrary to the popular idea of meringue — some people say the best meringue is white all the way through — but I think a well-baked meringue has more flavor than one with no color. » — P.H.

247

Makes 8 to 10 servings

the meringue

- 1 recipe Meringue Batter (page 5), piped into three 9-inch rounds, baked, and cooled

If necessary, trim the meringue disks so that they are all the same size. The easiest way to trim meringue is to shave off the excess using a small sharp knife as you would a saw. *(The meringue disks can be made up to a week in advance and stored in a metal tin in a cool, dry place.)*

the mousse

- 9 ounces bittersweet chocolate (preferably 6½ ounces Valrhona Noir Gastronomie and 2½ ounces Valrhona Guanaja), finely chopped
- 1½ sticks (6 ounces) unsalted butter, at cool room temperature
- 4 large eggs, separated
- 3 tablespoons Chocolate Sauce (page 36)
- 1 tablespoon sugar

1. Melt the chocolate in a metal bowl over, but not touching, simmering water (or do this in the microwave oven). Set the chocolate aside to cool to 104°F, as measured on an instant-read thermometer.
2. Put the butter in a mixer fitted with the whisk attachment and beat on high speed until it is light and fluffy. Lower the speed and add the chocolate in three additions, increasing the speed and beating well after each addition, then lowering it again before the next addition. You want to beat as much air as possible into this butter-chocolate mixture. Whisk the yolks together with the chocolate sauce and add this mixture to the bowl, beating it in well.
3. In an impeccably clean dry bowl with clean beaters, start whipping the egg whites, then add the sugar and whip until the whites hold soft peaks. (The whites needn't be as firm for the mousse as they were for the meringue.) Working with a large flexible rubber spatula, fold a quarter of the whites into the chocolate mixture to lighten it, then, working with a light hand, fold in the rest of the whites. The mousse is now ready to use.

to assemble

1. Place one meringue disk, flat side down, on a cardboard cake circle. (To prevent the cake from slipping, you can "glue" the disk to the circle by placing a dab of mousse in the center of the plate and very gently pressing the disk into it.) Spread about two fifths of the mousse evenly over the disk. The meringue is very delicate, so work carefully. If the disk breaks — they really are fragile — glue it together with a little mousse. Cover with the second disk and

then another two fifths of mousse. Top with the remaining disk and spread the rest of the mousse over the top and sides of the cake, striving for an even coating but not fussing too much — it will be covered by the glaze or chocolate curls.

2. Refrigerate the cake until the mousse firms, about 2 hours. When the mousse is set, cover the cake with plastic if you're not going to glaze it immediately. *(The cake can be made to this point and kept covered in the refrigerator for up to 4 days.)*

to finish

- 1 recipe Chocolate Glaze (page 37)

1. To get the best coverage, the glaze should be about 114°F. If it's too cold, just warm it to the right temperature by putting it in a water bath or popping it into the microwave oven for a few seconds on low power.

2. Place the cake on a cooling rack and put a sheet of wax paper under the rack to catch drips. Pour the glaze over the top of the cake, letting it run down the sides. Using a flexible metal icing spatula, smooth the glaze, taking care not to work it too much. You can serve the cake now or allow the glaze to set in the refrigerator. If the cake has been refrigerated for 6 hours or more, it's good to give it a 1-hour rest at room temperature before serving. You can best appreciate the cake's taste and texture when it is just cool.

249

Keeping

The cake, glazed or unglazed, can be kept in the refrigerator for 3 to 4 days. If cut, make sure to cover the cut sides with plastic since both chocolate and meringue easily pick up refrigerator odors.

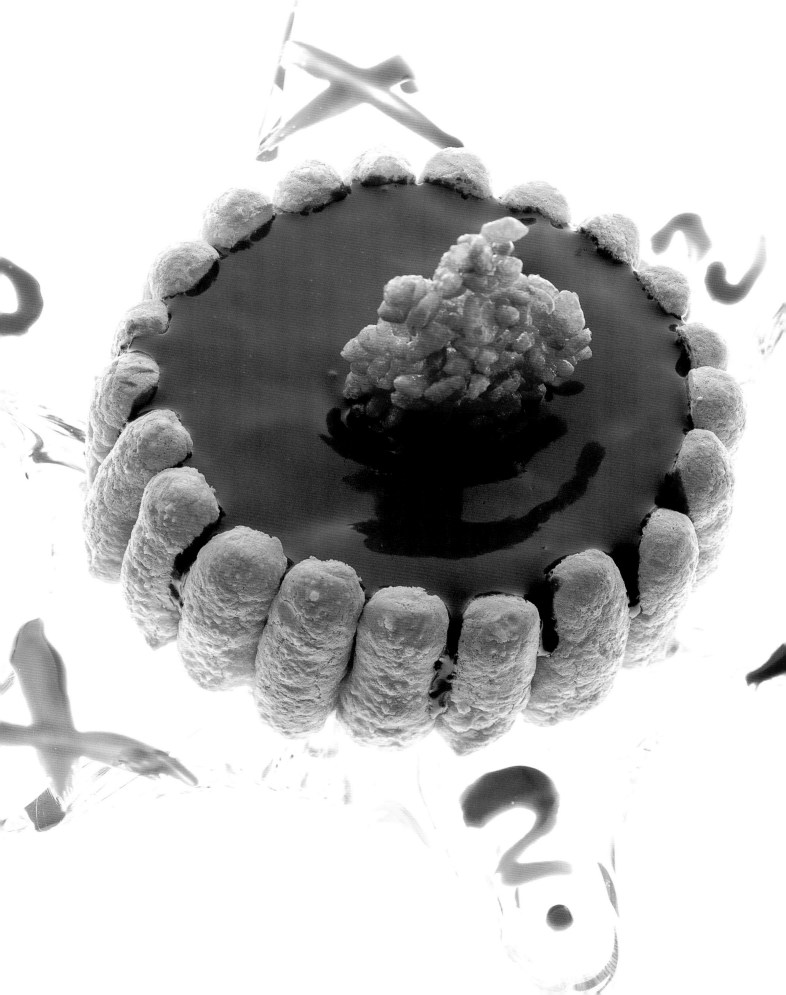

crispy and *creamy*
rice treat

Pierre calls this cake a *Régal au Riz Basmati,* which translates to a "Basmati Rice Treat." The fact that it contains chunks of Nestlé's Crunch and is finished with caramelized Rice Krispies (yes, Rice Krispies), makes it near-impossible not to recall those marshmallow snacks of American children's dreams.

Needless to say, the resemblance between this treat and that of childhood ends with the Rice Krispies. What you have here is a posh — but playful — dessert with a connoisseur's mix of flavors and textures. Because it is ringed with a band of lemon-soaked ladyfingers, it has the look of a classic charlotte, but the filling inside is neoclassic if not downright nouvelle. Composed of cinnamon-scented rice pudding, chunklets of Crunch, and small pieces of toasted hazelnuts, the filling is soft (except when it's crackly) and creamy, ricey, and lemony (except when it's chocolaty). The cake is finished with a thick layer of smooth chocolate cream and either a speckling of Rice Krispies or a shard of caramelized Rice Krispies, a great treat on its own.

《 *I've singled out the texture to play around with in this cake. It's really interesting when, in one mouthful, you experience the density of the cream and the crunchiness of the nuts and chocolate pieces.* 》 — P. H .

Makes 8 servings

the cake
- 1 recipe Ladyfinger Batter (page 7), or store-bought ladyfinger biscuits

If you're using the Ladyfinger Batter, following the recipe, pipe the batter into two 9-inch disks and two 8-inch-long, 4-inch-high bands of ladyfingers; bake, cool, and reserve. *(The ladyfinger disks and bands can be made ahead, wrapped airtight, and kept at room temperature for 2 days or frozen for a month.)*

the syrup
- $2/3$ cup water
- $1/4$ cup sugar
- Zest of 2 lemons — removed with a zester (see page 281)

Place all the ingredients in a small saucepan and bring to the boil. Remove from the heat, strain the syrup into a bowl or jar, and set aside to cool to room temperature. Once cool, the syrup should be refrigerated. *(The syrup can be made a week in advance and kept in a tightly sealed jar in the refrigerator.)*

252

the crunchies
- $3\frac{1}{2}$ ounces Nestlé's Crunch
- $1/3$ cup hazelnuts, toasted and skinned (see page 90)

Chop the Crunch into tiny cubes; coarsely chop the hazelnuts. Mix the chocolate and nuts together and set aside until needed.

the filling
- 2 cups whole milk
- $1/3$ cup imported basmati rice (avoid American basmati — it's too sticky)
- 3 tablespoons sugar
- Zest of $3/4$ lemon — removed with a zester (see page 281) and finely chopped
- $1/4$ cinnamon stick
- 2 large egg yolks
- 2 teaspoons gelatin
- $2\frac{1}{2}$ tablespoons cold water
- $1/3$ cup heavy cream

1. Place 1⅓ cups of the milk, the rice, 1 tablespoon of the sugar, the lemon zest, and the cinnamon stick in a 2-quart saucepan and bring to the boil. Lower the heat to a simmer and cook, stirring frequently, until the rice has absorbed all but the slightest bit of the liquid (each grain of rice will be surrounded by a film of milk), about 20 to 25 minutes.

2. While the rice is cooking, prepare an ice bath by filling a large bowl with ice cubes and setting aside another large bowl that will fit inside the ice-filled bowl.

3. Scrape the cooked rice into the reserved bowl, add cold water to the bowl with the ice cubes to create an ice bath, and let the rice cool, stirring occasionally, while you prepare the rest of the filling. The rice needs to cool at least to 70°F, as measured on an instant-read thermometer. (The next part of the filling — a crème anglaise — will also need to be cooled in an ice bath, so keep the setup in place after removing the rice. Also, keep a fine-mesh strainer close at hand.)

4. Bring the remaining ⅓ cup milk to a boil. Meanwhile, put the yolks and the remaining 2 tablespoons sugar in a heavy-bottomed 2-quart saucepan. Whisk the yolks and sugar together until well blended. Whisking without stop, drizzle in about one third of the boiling liquid. Add the rest of the liquid in a slow, steady stream. Place the saucepan over medium heat and, stirring constantly with a wooden spatula or spoon, cook the cream until it thickens ever so slightly, lightens in color, and, most important, reaches 180°F, as measured on an instant-read thermometer — all of which will take less than 5 minutes. (Alternatively, you can stir the cream, and then draw your finger down the spatula or bowl of the wooden spoon — if the cream doesn't run into the track you've created, it's done.) Immediately remove the saucepan from the heat and allow the crème anglaise to cool in the saucepan for 2 minutes.

5. Strain the crème anglaise into a bowl. Sprinkle the gelatin over the cold water and allow it to rest until softened, then heat it in the microwave oven for about 15 seconds, or cook it over low heat, until it dissolves. Stir the gelatin into the crème anglaise. Remove the rice from the ice bath if necessary and place the bowl with the crème anglaise in the bath, replenishing the ice if necessary. Cool the crème anglaise to about 70°F, stirring from time to time. Stir the rice and the crème anglaise together.

6. To finish the filling, whip the heavy cream until it holds medium peaks and then fold it into the rice mixture with a rubber spatula. The filling is ready and should be used immediately.

to assemble

1. Place a piece of parchment paper on a cardboard cake round and center an 8¾-inch/22-cm dessert ring on it; butter the inside of the ring. Cut the bands of ladyfingers lengthwise in half and fit the halves around the interior of the ring, making certain that the biscuits' flat

side faces in; you'll have a piece of band left over. Fit a ladyfinger disk into the bottom to form a base. (If you are using store-bought ladyfingers, cut the biscuits as necessary to form a base and band.) Brush the ladyfinger disk and band with the lemon syrup to moisten them.

2. Pour and scrape the filling into the lined mold (it should come up to just below the halfway mark) and top with the reserved Nestlé's Crunch and hazelnut mixture. Brush one side of the remaining ladyfinger disk with syrup and lay it on the dessert ring to cover the filling; brush the top of the cake with lemon syrup. (You may have some syrup left over.) Cover the cake loosely with plastic wrap and refrigerate for an hour.

the chocolate cream

- 3½ ounces bittersweet chocolate (preferably Valrhona Caraïbe), finely chopped
- ½ cup whole milk
- ½ cup heavy cream
- 2 large egg yolks
- 3 tablespoons sugar

1. Prepare an ice bath for the cream and set aside.

2. Place the chopped chocolate in a medium bowl and set aside. In a small saucepan or the microwave oven, bring the milk and cream to a boil. Meanwhile, whisk the yolks and sugar together in a heavy-bottomed 2-quart saucepan until thick and pale. Just as you did for the rice filling, you'll be making a crème anglaise: Whisking all the while, slowly drizzle one third of the hot liquid into the yolk mixture and then whisk in the remainder. Working over medium heat and stirring constantly with a wooden spatula or spoon, cook the cream until it reaches 180°F, as measured on an instant-read thermometer, or passes the draw-a-finger test (see step 4, page 253). Immediately remove the saucepan from the heat.

3. Strain about one third of the hot crème anglaise over the chopped chocolate and whisk gently, taking care not to beat air into the mixture. Whisk in the rest of the cream in two more additions and then allow the cream to cool in the ice bath until it reaches about 85°F.

4. Remove the cake from the refrigerator and pour the chocolate cream over the top. Don't worry if a little chocolate flows between the biscuits — it's unavoidable. Place the cake in the freezer for an hour to set. *(If you want, you can cover the cake airtight and freeze it for up to a month at this point. Thaw the wrapped cake overnight in the refrigerator before proceeding.)*

to finish

- ½ cup sugar, optional
- 3 tablespoons water, optional
- 2⅓ cups Rice Krispies, optional, or ½ cup Rice Krispies to sprinkle over the cake

1. If you want to caramelize the Rice Krispies, bring the sugar and water to the boil in a heavy-bottomed 2-quart saucepan. Swirl the ingredients around to dissolve the sugar and then allow the mixture to boil, without stirring, until it reaches 248°F, as measured on an instant-read thermometer. (If any sugar sticks to the sides of the pan, as might happen at the start of the cooking, wash it down with a pastry brush dipped in cold water.) Add the 2⅓ cups Rice Krispies and, working with a wooden spoon or spatula, stir the cereal into the sugar. Remove the pan from the heat and continue to stir until the cereal is coated with the sugar, about 2 to 3 minutes. The sugar will be white and sandy — don't expect an even coating at this stage. Turn the cereal out onto a plate.

2. Set a piece of parchment paper and a metal spatula or pancake turner aside on the counter. Wash and dry the saucepan and return it to the range. Heat the pan and then add half of the sugar-coated cereal. Using the wooden spoon or spatula, stir the cereal without stopping until the sugar caramelizes — you're looking for the sugar to turn a light amber color; this could take about 4 minutes. Turn the caramelized Rice Krispies out onto the parchment paper — try not to turn them out into a mound — and quickly flatten the cereal with the back of the metal spatula or pancake turner. Wash the pan and repeat with the remaining cereal. When the Rice Krispies are cool enough to handle, break them into uneven pieces. You'll only need one piece to decorate the cake, but the leftovers make a terrific snack. *(You can make the caramelized cereal up to 1 day ahead if it's not humid. Store the broken pieces of candy in a tin in a cool, dry place.)*

3. Transfer the cake to the refrigerator at least an hour before serving. (If the cake is deeply frozen, it will need a longer defrosting period — probably overnight — in the refrigerator.) Right before you're ready to serve, stand a large shard of the caramelized Rice Krispies candy in the center of the cake; serve the rest of the crunch alongside the cake, if desired. (If you just decorate the cake with one piece of candy, your guests, no matter how well behaved they are, will fight over it — Rice Krispies candy can do that. So, unless you plan on hoarding the candy to munch on its own, it's best to crack it up and give everyone some.) Alternatively, you can skip the candy and sprinkle the top of the cake with Rice Krispies straight from the box. Transfer the cake to a platter and remove the dessert ring (see page 272) before serving.

255

Keeping

The "un-Krispied" cake can be kept in the refrigerator for about 2 days or frozen for 1 month; in either case, wrap the cake airtight.

WEDDING
CAKE

Dubbing Pierre the "Dior of Desserts," as *Food Arts* magazine did, seems absolutely on the mark since Pierre, like his fellow designers in the fashion world, brings out a collection each fall and spring. And just as every couturier's show finishes with a wedding gown, so this collection of Pierre's desserts closes with a *gâteau de mariage,* a wedding cake.

To finish this collection with a flourish, Pierre has designed a cake that's exquisite in its simplicity, an aromatic almond cake layered with a light orange cream and covered with a thin veneer of almond paste, a palette that can be decorated in any style from baroque to modern-day minimalist. You can decide to trim the cake with royal icing swags and shells, as Pierre did; to encircle it with paste flowers and frilly petals or an array of marzipan fruits; to turn it into a bridal bouquet of fresh fragrant flowers; to shower it with silver dragées; to pipe it with icing in a dotted-swiss pattern; or to top it with a big candy heart, a treasured memento, or the traditional bride and groom. However you choose to decorate this cake, the finish will be both literally and figuratively the icing on the cake, the heart of the cake will be its sentiment: Handcrafting a wedding cake is an act of love and generosity.

For all its elegance, this cake is exceedingly easy to prepare and construct. The cake itself is straightforward to make and very well behaved. It bakes to a level-topped golden finish, its compact crumb slices cleanly, and you can multiply the recipe at will to make more tiers or to change the size of the tiers to match the size of your guest list. The orange syrup that moistens the cake layers is fresh, full flavored, and fast to make, and the orange cream that's smoothed between the layers is luxurious and accommodating — once it's been

Makes 30 to 35 servings

257

beaten, you can use it immediately, or store it in the fridge or freezer. In fact, each of the cake's elements can be made ahead and frozen, at the ready when you are for the great fun of constructing this tiered treat. Finally, there's the almond paste sheath, a neat, clean matte finish on which to play out your artistic whims or decorative fantasies. But even the veneer of almond paste isn't sacred — you can omit it and cover the cake with more silken rich buttercream, if you wish. No matter what you do, because you are making this cake yourself for one of life's greatest occasions, it will be a cherished memory for all who share it.

《 *Wedding cakes are often dry, but this cake is tender and moist and very appealing. If you'd like, you can add whole fresh raspberries or halved strawberries to the orange cream between the layers.* 》 — P. H.

the candied orange
- ⅓ cup candied orange peel, homemade (page 62) or store-bought
- Zest of 1 orange — removed with a zester (see page 281) and very finely chopped
- 2 tablespoons Cointreau or other orange liqueur

The candied orange will be mixed with the buttercream, but it should be made a day ahead. Cut the candied peel into very small cubes and mix all the ingredients together. Cover and allow to macerate overnight in the refrigerator.

the syrup
- ⅓ cup sugar
- ⅓ cup water
- Pinch of cardamom
- Pinch of freshly ground black pepper
- ⅓ cup freshly squeezed orange juice
- 1½ tablespoons Cointreau or other orange liqueur

Bring the sugar, water, cardamom, and pepper to the boil in a small saucepan. Pour the syrup into a heatproof jar or bowl and, when it's completely cool, add the orange juice and Cointreau. *(The syrup can be made a week ahead and kept covered in the refrigerator.)*

the cake
Pierre makes this cake in two layers, one 11 inches/28 centimeters in diameter, the other 7½ inches/19 centimeters. You may find it easier to use one 10- or 12-inch cake pan and one 6-

258

or 8-inch pan. Whatever pans you use, make certain that they have sides at least 1½ (prefer-ably 2) inches high.

In addition, in order to make this full recipe, you will need to use a stand mixer with a bowl that has a capacity of at least 4½ quarts; 5 quarts is preferable. If your bowl is smaller, you will have to make one cake at a time, dividing the batter accordingly.

- 1½ cups all-purpose flour
- ½ teaspoon double-acting baking powder
- Four 7-ounce rolls almond paste (see page 266)
- 12 large eggs, at room temperature
- 2 sticks plus 1 tablespoon (8½ ounces) unsalted butter, melted and cooled

1. Center a rack in the oven and preheat the oven to 350°F. Brush the insides of two round cake pans, one 11 inches and the other 7½ inches in diameter, with butter and set aside. (Or butter whatever size pans you choose.) Set out two cooling racks, one for each cake layer, and place a sheet of parchment paper over each rack.

2. Combine the flour and baking powder and set aside. Break up the almond paste and put it in the bowl of a stand mixer fitted with the paddle attachment. With the mixer set at low speed, add the eggs one at time, beating well after each addition, then beat the mixture until it is thin and smooth. It may take 10 minutes to reach this point.

3. While the almond paste and eggs are beating, bring a large skillet of water to the boil. When the almond mixture is smooth, remove the bowl from the mixer and place it in the skillet. Adjust the heat so that the water simmers and, whisking without stop, heat the mixture to a temperature of 140°F, as measured on an instant-read thermometer. Depending on how much water you have in the skillet and how hot it is, it will take about 10 minutes, plus or minus a few, to reach this temperature, at which point the almond paste will have metamorphosed into a smooth, pourable mixture with an essence-of-almonds aroma.

4. Return the bowl to the mixer, fit the mixer with the whisk attachment, and, working on high speed, beat until the almond mixture is light, airy, ribbony, and absolutely cool, about 10 minutes.

5. You need to fold in the butter and flour at this point. Depending on the size of your mixer bowl, you may find it easier to scrape the almond mixture out of the mixer bowl and into a big wide bowl for these next steps. In either case, remove the bowl from the mixer. Using a large flexible rubber spatula, fold the butter into the almond mixture a little at a time. Sift the flour-baking powder mixture over the batter in about three additions, folding each addition in delicately with the spatula.

259

6. Pour and scrape the batter into the prepared pans and slip the pans into the oven. Bake for about 30 minutes, rotating the pans at the midway mark, or until the cakes are golden brown and shrink slightly from the sides of the pan. A slim knife inserted in the center of the cakes should come out crumb-free. Remove the pans from the oven and invert the cakes onto the parchment-lined cooling racks. Lift off the pans and allow the cakes to rest on the racks (right side up or not) until they reach room temperature. *(The cakes can be made ahead to this point, wrapped airtight in plastic, and kept at room temperature for 2 days or frozen for a month.)*

the orange cream
This recipe makes exactly the amount of buttercream you'll need to fill and skim-coat the cakes. If you'd like to frost and/or decorate the cakes with buttercream, you'll need to increase the recipe.

- 8 large egg yolks
- ½ cup plus 2 tablespoons water
- ¾ cup sugar
- 1 plump, moist vanilla bean, split lengthwise and scraped (see page 281)
- 3 sticks plus 4 tablespoons (14 ounces) unsalted butter, softened
- Reserved candied orange (from above)

1. Put the yolks in the bowl of a mixer fitted with the whisk attachment; set aside. Bring a large skillet of water to the boil — you'll need it for the yolks.

2. Put the water, sugar, and vanilla bean (pulp and pod) in a small saucepan and bring to the boil; remove the pod (wash, dry, and reserve it for another use — see page 281 — if you wish). Start beating the yolks on high speed and then slowly add the hot syrup, pouring the syrup down the side of the bowl to avoid the spinning whisk. When all the syrup is incorporated, remove the bowl from the mixer and set it into the skillet of boiling water. Adjust the heat so that the water simmers and, whisking energetically and without stop, beat the yolks and syrup until the mixture is hot, voluminous, and thick enough to form a ribbon when dropped from the whisk (it will resemble a sabayon). Depending on how much water you have in the skillet and how hot the water is, it could take about 10 minutes for the mixture to thicken. Return the bowl to the mixer.

3. With the whisk attachment in place, beat the yolk mixture until cool, creamy, and pale, about 8 to 10 minutes. While the yolks are cooling, soften the butter by working it with a spatula in a bowl. When the yolks are ready, decrease the mixer speed to medium-low and add the butter in pieces, each about 2 tablespoons. Don't worry if the buttercream looks curdled; it will smooth out when all of the butter is added. When the last of the butter is incorporated, beat on medium-low speed for another 2 to 3 minutes. If the cream isn't smooth, increase the speed to high and beat just until it comes together. (You don't want to beat for too long on high speed because you don't want to beat air into the buttercream.) Remove the bowl from the mixer and fold in the reserved candied orange. The buttercream can be used now or stored in the refrigerator or freezer. *(The cream can be made ahead, packed airtight, and stored in the refrigerator for 2 to 3 days or the freezer for a month. If chilled, it will need to be whisked before using; see "Keeping," page 30.)*

to assemble

- Four 7-ounce rolls almond paste
- 4 large egg whites
- Cornstarch

1. Trim two cardboard cake rounds to the size of the cake layers. Run a thin metal spatula between the cake layers and the parchment and lift each layer onto a cardboard round, inverting each layer so it is right side up. (Don't be concerned if a bit of cake remains stuck to the parchment — it will be covered.) With a ruler, measure the height of each cake layer and mark it at intervals, making small slits with a thin knife, to divide each into thirds. With a long thin knife, cut each cake into three even layers.

2. Working with one cake at a time, brush the bottom layer with some of the orange syrup. There's no need to soak it — the point is just to moisten and flavor each layer. Spread an even layer of orange buttercream over the moistened slice and top with the middle layer. Moisten that layer with syrup and cover it with buttercream. Now, top with the upper layer. Use a dry pastry brush to whisk away any crumbs on the top or sides of the cake. Moisten the top of the cake with syrup and then mask the entire cake, top and sides, with a very thin layer of buttercream — think of this as a skim coat. Repeat with the other cake. When both cakes are coated, pop them into the refrigerator for about an hour just to set the buttercream. *(The cakes can be made ahead to this point. When the buttercream is firm, wrap the cakes in plastic and refrigerate for a couple of days or freeze for a month.)*

3. To cover the cakes in almond paste, you will probably need to use one to one-and-a-half rolls of paste for the small layer and two to three for the larger layer. It's best to start with three rolls for the larger layer and then incorporate the scraps from that into the paste you'll use for the top tier. To get the proper rolling consistency, each roll of almond paste must be mixed with 1 large egg white. Mix the almond paste and egg white together in a mixer fitted

with the paddle attachment. (You can work with the whole batch of almond paste and just keep whatever you don't need at the moment well wrapped in plastic.)

4. Work the almond paste into a ball and flatten the ball into a disk. Lightly dust a very smooth rolling surface (marble would be great) with cornstarch, place the disk on the rolling surface, and then dust the disk and your rolling pin very lightly with cornstarch. Roll the almond paste, working from the center out, turning the dough at intervals to keep it round and lifting it frequently to keep it from sticking, until it forms a thin (about $1/16$ to $1/8$ inch) circle that's about 4 inches larger in diameter than the layer you'll be covering.

5. Slip a large cardboard cake round under the rolled-out almond paste. Now, working gingerly, turn the cake layer, still on its cardboard round, upside down onto the center of the almond paste. (This is an unorthodox move, but because the almond paste is fragile, you'll have an easier time of wrapping the cake if you don't have to lift the almond paste off the work surface and onto the cake.) Gently lift the almond paste up and onto the sides of the cake, smoothing the paste with the palm of your hand as you work your way around the cake. To get a smooth finish, you can use a small piece of cardboard to give the almond paste a last press and buff. When you've fitted the almond paste around the cake, cut off the excess with a sharp knife. Now, carefully, get one hand under the bottom cardboard round and the other on the top cardboad, take a deep breath, and turn the cake over. One layer is done. Gather together the scraps of almond paste and work them into the paste for the second layer. Set the finished cake aside and cover the other layer in the same way.

to finish (optional)
- **2 cups confectioner's sugar**
- **2 large egg whites**

1. You can decorate each layer individually and then stack them or, before you begin the decoration, you can center the small layer on the larger layer.

2. To decorate the tiers with swags, polka dots, shells, rosettes, or any other kind of fine white decoration, you'll need to make a royal icing. Place the confectioner's sugar and egg whites in the bowl of a mixer fitted with the whisk attachment. Mix on low speed just until the ingredients are blended, then increase the speed to medium-high and beat until the icing is thick, creamy — marshmallowy, really — and white, 4 to 5 minutes. The icing is ready to use; if you need to hold it for a while, make sure it's covered. It's best to cover the icing with a damp paper towel and to cover the towel with plastic wrap, pressing down on the plastic to create a seal. To pipe the decorations, spoon the royal icing into a parchment paper decorating cone or use a very small pastry bag fitted with a very fine tip.

Keeping
The syrup, cake layers, and buttercream can be made ahead and refrigerated or frozen. Once assembled, the cake can be covered with plastic and kept in the refrigerator for 3 days before you decorate it with the royal icing. (The royal icing shouldn't be frozen.) If you're worried about humidity in the refrigerator, you can do what the pros do — brush the cake with a very, very thin layer of melted cocoa butter (see Sources, page 282). If the cake is coated with cocoa butter, there's no need to cover it with plastic wrap.

A DICTIONARY OF TERMS, TECHNIQUES, EQUIPMENT, AND INGREDIENTS

A la minute

Literally, this means "this instant," but when you're working in the kitchen, and need to translate the term into action, think of it as "at the last minute." Anything that's done *à la minute* is done just before a dish is served. While *à la minute* maneuvers are more common on the savory side of the kitchen than they are on the sweet, you'll find you'll need to put a few finishing touches on cakes and tarts and a few more on plated desserts. The key to doing things *à la minute* is preparation. Read the recipe through before you set to work, then organize your work space, and put your guests on alert — they should be at the table, forks at the ready the instant you present dessert.

Almond paste

A mixture of ground almonds, confectioner's sugar, and corn syrup or glucose, almond paste is available in supermarkets, where it is sold in cans under the Solo label and in tubes under the name Odense, from a Danish manufacturer. (The recipes were tested with both brands, although most testers preferred the logs of paste from Odense.) Both pastes can be stored at room temperature until you're ready to use them, but any leftovers will dry out quickly unless you wrap them airtight in two or three layers of plastic. Well wrapped, almond paste can be kept in the refrigerator for about six months. While almond paste is firmer than marzipan, you can use them interchangeably in these recipes.

Baking powder

Recipes using baking powder were tested with double-acting powder, a leavening agent that releases its first round of rising power when it's mixed with liquid and its second when it's heated in the oven. Keep baking powder tightly covered in a cool, dry cupboard and, regardless of the use-before date stamped on the tin, replace opened tins every six months.

Baking sheets

As used in these recipes, a *baking sheet* is what home cooks often refer to as a cookie sheet, that is, a large flat metal sheet with one or both of the short sides slightly raised. The raised sides give you something to hold on to when you're slipping the sheet in and out of the oven, and the long rimless sides make it easy to slide cookies and tarts onto and off the sheet. When buying baking sheets, buy the largest ones you can, making certain that there will be at least an inch, preferably two, of airspace between the sheet and your oven's walls. And because the sheets will often be used at high temperatures, you'll do well to buy the heaviest sheets available so they won't warp, and to buy at least two of them — four would be even better. Since nothing unbaked should ever go on a hot sheet, having two sets of sheets means that while one set is in the oven, you can be setting up another batch of cookies on the other.

It's a good idea to have at least one baking sheet with a nonstick finish. While in most cases you'll be lining the baking sheets with parchment paper, there are some cookies, tuiles for example, that do nicely on nonstick sheets.

Finally, while insulated baking sheets, the kind with a built-in air cushion, are not recommended for baking cookies — they don't let enough heat hit the cookies' bottoms — they're great under loaf cakes that need only gentle bottom heat. You can always double up on regular baking sheets or, if you're baking in a slow oven, put a piece of heavy corrugated cardboard on a regular sheet to get this kind of protection, but an all-in-one insulated sheet is a nice, if optional, addition to your *batterie de cuisine*.

Baking times

Baking times are usually given as a range (such as "bake for 30 to 35 minutes") because even the same cake won't bake in the same amount of time every time. To be on the safe side, you should always start testing your dessert for doneness at the lowest end of the range (or even a few minutes before, especially if the cake or tart has been in the oven for 30 minutes or more), and always pay attention to the visual clues, such as browning, rising, or shrinking — often they're your best indicators.

Batterie de cuisine

This French term refers to all the tools, gadgets, and pots, pans, tins, and molds used to prepare food.

Bench or dough scrapers

Used most often by bread bakers, a bench or dough scraper is a good tool for pastry chefs as well. The business end of a scraper is a square of metal. It's attached to a grip, either wood or plastic, and while it makes handling sticky bread doughs manageable, it's also very well suited to cleaning off a work surface after you've rolled out pastry dough. Once you get the hang of using a scraper, you'll think of it as an extension of your hand and find it's convenient to have close by for cutting doughs into portions or for transferring ingredients, like chopped fruits and nuts, from cutting board to work bowl.

Black pepper

Pierre keeps his pepper mill at the ready in his pastry kitchen, using the pungent spice to give spark to fruit desserts, like those that feature apricots, pineapple, and berries. Pepper should always be freshly ground — don't even think about buying ground pepper from the spice rack in the supermarket. Pierre's favorite pepper is Sarawak, a black pepper from Borneo, which he likes for its subtle heat and lovely fragrance. While it's not readily available everywhere, it is often on display in specialty shops since Flavor-bank, a spice company with national distribution, offers it in two-ounce plastic tubes. (See Mail-Order Sources, page 282.)

Blender

When a recipe says to put something in a blender, you can use a food processor or often an immersion blender in its stead. (However, the opposite is not true. For example, the food processor is great for pastry dough, while the blender is hopelessly inappropriate.) But there are times, particularly with sauces and recipes like Lemon Cream (page 31), when either a blender or a food processor can do the job, but the blender will do it better — the recipe will be your guide. If you're buying a new blender, look for one with a heavy-duty motor and a heavy, heatproof glass jar.

Blowtorch

Sure, you can get through life without a blowtorch, but having one is great fun and using it to finish meringue makes a great difference. With the pinpoint control you get with a blowtorch, you'll be able to give your meringue perfect color, and as much of it as you want. You'll find the blowtorch used to brown meringue, caramelize sugar over the Caramelized Cinnamon Tart (page 245), and make the brûlée part of crème brûlée. If you don't have a blowtorch or the courage to use it (it takes some practice), you can brown meringue in a hot oven. (You won't be able to burn the sugar for the crème brûlée or the tart in the oven, but both desserts will have virtues without these finishes.) Individual recipes will give you instructions for working with and without a torch. Hardware stores are a good source for household propane blowtorch kits, which, by the way, are small and inexpensive (about $20); Williams-Sonoma offers a sleeker, more compact (and more expensive — about $35) butane torch.

Brown butter

Brown butter is not a type of butter you can buy — it's what you get when you cook butter beyond the melting stage. After the butter melts, it goes from golden to nutty brown — and then to burnt — so you need to cook it over low heat and keep an eye on it. (If your pan is very dark, you might want to spoon a little of the butter onto a white plate — or look at it on a white spoon — to get a reading on its color.) Even under a watchful eye, brown butter always develops some very dark bits. You can strain these out before using the butter or, if they're not really burnt, add them to the recipe — it's an aesthetic call. Brown butter serves all the same functions as melted butter in a recipe and delivers a bonus: a full, warm, nutty flavor and aroma, the reason the French refer to it as *beurre noisette,* or hazelnut butter. In fact, it's usually true that the instant you catch a whiff of hazelnuts wafting from the saucepan, it's time to check the color of the butter — it will probably be done or close to it.

Butter

Butter has no substitute, not for flavor, not for texture. In his pastry kitchen, Pierre uses about nine hundred pounds of butter a week, all of it artisanally made, and none of it refrigerated — he stores his butter at 66°F, the temperature at which it remains stable and maintains its texture, perfume, and fresh flavor. And he uses it in about four days, knowing that its sterling qualities start to diminish as soon as the butter is made. Pierre uses unsalted butter for most of his cakes, pastries, cookies, and desserts; "dry butter," a butter with almost no moisture, for making puff pastry; and salted butter for some of his cookies and most of his caramel desserts.

Dry butter, usually only produced during the winter when the cows are feeding on hay, is, for all intents and purposes, unavailable in the States. All of these recipes were tested with nationally available Land O'Lakes butter from the supermarket.

Measuring butter: Depending on quantity, you'll find the measurements for butter given in tablespoons or sticks (or parts thereof), and usually in ounces as well. It's helpful to know that 3 teaspoons equal 1 tablespoon and that there are 8 tablespoons of butter in a stick; these measurements are usually marked on the wrapper. Each stick weighs 4 ounces, and there are four sticks to a pound.

Softening butter: When a recipe calls for softened butter, it means the butter should be malleable but not gooey or oily. You can leave butter at room temperature to get to the soft stage; you can give it a few good bashes with the heel of your hand or the end of a French-style no-handles rolling pin; or you can place the unwrapped sticks of butter on a paper towel and soften them for about 10 seconds in the microwave oven (the quickest but riskiest method).

Buttering pans: Pans should be buttered with softened, not melted, butter. Apply a thin coating of butter to all the interior surfaces of the pan, paying particular attention to the oft-neglected and hard-to-get-to corners. The easiest way to get an even coating is to apply the softened butter with a pastry brush, although a scrunched-up paper towel works well too. Alternatively, you can coat the pans with vegetable oil spray.

When a recipe instructs you to butter and flour a pan, you should butter the inside of the pan as usual, then toss in a couple of spoonfuls of flour. Shake the pan to get the flour across the bottom and tilt and tap the pan to get a light dusting of flour on the sides. Working over a trash bin, turn the pan upside down, and tap out the excess flour. *The amount of butter and flour you need to prepare pans is never included in a recipe's ingredient list — it's always extra.*

Cake crumbs

Cake crumbs or trimmings (preferably a tad stale) are an antidote to the problem of soggy tart crusts. Sprinkled in the bottom of a baked tart shell, they're great at keeping crusts crisp. When you've got an extra slice of génoise or some leftover ladyfingers, or trimmings from either, whir them around in the food processor or blender and use them immediately, or pack them airtight and keep them in the freezer; they'll keep for at least a month.

Cake pans

For the recipes in this book, you'll need conventional cake and loaf cake pans, dessert or cake rings (see page 272), and tart or flan rings (see page 280). Most of the cakes that form the foundations for Pierre's *gâteaux* are either assembled or baked in dessert or tart rings. The exceptions are the génoise, which should be baked in a 9-inch round cake pan that has sides that are at least 2 inches high; the Wedding Cake, which calls for two pans, one between 10 and 12 inches across and the other 6 and 8 inches, both at least 2 inches high; the chocolate cake for the Chocolate Dome, which is baked in an 8 by 2-inch round cake pan; and the Ligurian Lemon Cake, which needs a 10-inch round cake pan with 2-inch-high sides. Because of their high sides (and their high quality — they're usually heavy-gauge), these are often considered professional pans, but they are available in many specialty stores as well as by mail order (see Mail-Order Sources, page 282). Each recipe calls for just one pan (or one of each size), but in the case of the 9-inch round, you'd do well to buy a pair because you'll use them often when you make American-style layer cakes. These pans should not have a nonstick finish.

Translating the loaf cakes from their French forms to their American equivalents was particularly difficult because of the great differences between French loaf pans, called *moules à cake,* and American pans. The French pans are long thin affairs with sides that often slant out, while American pans are, for the most part, shorter, stouter, and straighter. However, with a collection of American loaf cake pans, you'll have no problem producing a collection of simple French loaf cakes. To work your way through the loaf cake recipes, you'll need: two 7½ by 3½ by 2½-inch pans; one 8½ by 4½ by 2½-inch pan; and two 9 by 5 by 3-inch pans. For loaf cakes, avoid dark metal pans — the cakes bake for a long time, and dark pans, which attract and maintain heat, will make their crusts too dark. Whether or not you purchase a pan with a nonstick finish is a matter of personal preference, but for these loaf cakes, some of which should be baked in parchment-lined pans regardless of the pan's finish, a nonstick coating is unnecessary.

Cake rings
See Dessert rings.

Cardboard cake rounds
There are lots of small jobs in the pastry kitchen that are made easier with a stack of cardboard cake rounds at your disposal. The rounds, available at baking supply houses, specialty shops, and by mail order (see Mail-Order Sources, page 282), are made of corrugated cardboard, have one smooth white paper side, and come in various sizes, the 12-inch rounds being the most convenient since they're big enough for everything, including cutting them down to size. All of the recipes that are assembled in dessert and tart rings are best put together on a cardboard cake round. If you do not want to purchase rounds, however, you can use the removable bottom of a fluted metal tart pan or the base of a springform pan.

Chocolate
Chocolate is the fruit of the gods — at least that's the translation of the ancient Greek word for the genus of cacao, *Theobroma,* from which chocolate is derived — and it comes in varieties from so-bitter-one-taste-makes-you-shiver to so-sweet-it's-cloying; its colors range from mahogany to ivory.

All chocolate starts with chocolate liquor, the ground nib of the cacao bean. Chocolate liquor is pure chocolate — it's about half cocoa butter and half cocoa — and it's all there is in unsweetened chocolate, sometimes called baking chocolate in America. To make the gamut of chocolates from bittersweet to semisweet to sweet, sugar is added

and, usually, more cocoa butter (especially if the chocolate is meant for melting or dipping), and, sometimes, cocoa powder. Since it is the chocolate liquor that gives chocolate its depth of flavor — its chocolatiness — the higher the percentage of chocolate liquor, the more chocolaty and the less sweet the chocolate will be.

In the United States, the minimum (but not maximum) amount of chocolate liquor that must be used in chocolate is regulated by the Food and Drug Administration. So, while one manufacturer's bittersweet may taste like another's semisweet (the FDA makes no distinction between the two names), both must contain at least 35 percent chocolate liquor. Sweet chocolate, a designation often used by large commercial American producers, indicates at least 15 percent chocolate liquor, and milk chocolate must have at least 10 percent.

For the most part, American chocolates, especially those popular brands found at supermarkets, are much sweeter and less deeply chocolaty than premium-quality imported chocolate. How much sweeter and less chocolaty by the numbers? Who knows? Manufacturers are not required to list the percentage of chocolate liquor in their products. In fact, percentages are listed only on the packages of selected very high quality imported chocolates, such as Valrhona, the first company to go public with its chocolate liquor, cocoa butter, and cocoa percentages.

Valrhona, made in France, is Pierre's chocolate of choice for these desserts, and all of the chocolate recipes were tested with Valrhona and carry a recommendation for which of Valrhona's several chocolates you should use. If you've never tasted Valrhona chocolates (or other chocolates of similar superior quality and high chocolate liquor percentages), you're in for a surprise. They are so chocolaty that they may not even "read" like chocolate on first taste. The best of them have layers of flavor and inspire a vocabulary usually reserved for wine. And as with wine, you should use what you like best.

Pierre is adamant on this point. He says, "The best chocolate is the one you like." As he points out, you may taste a chocolate with 70 percent chocolate liquor and find that it's not bitter at all because it has additional cocoa butter and less

269

cocoa. The percentage is just an indicator. Be that as it may, the percentage is a pretty good indicator of the chocolate's depth, particularly when you're just starting out on the premium chocolate path.

To complicate matters, percentages aren't everything. Where the cocoa beans come from affects the finished chocolate's taste too. Connoisseurs consider the *criollo* and *trinitario* beans from Central and South America and the Caribbean to be superior to the less aromatic (and higher yielding) *forestero* beans from Africa and Brazil. To find out what pleases you, taste, taste, and taste some more.

The following are the Valrhona chocolates used in Pierre's recipes:

Guanaja	70.5 percent cocoa
Caraïbe	66.5 percent cocoa
Manjari	64.5 percent cocoa
Noir Gastronomie	61 percent cocoa

These chocolates are available at specialty stores and directly from Valrhona (see Mail-Order Sources, page 282).

Storing chocolate: It's best to keep chocolate in a cool, dry cupboard away from light. In fact, chocolate benefits from being wrapped in aluminum foil, which will not only block the light, but will shield the chocolate from odors. Like butter, chocolate picks up odors from neighboring foods. Don't store chocolate in the refrigerator or freezer — you risk having it come in contact with its archenemy, humidity — and don't worry if your chocolate develops "bloom," a cloudy or grayish look. Bloom isn't attractive — it's a sign that the chocolate was stored in a warm place and an indication that the cocoa butter has separated — but it doesn't affect the chocolate's flavor or its melting properties. In fact, when the chocolate is melted, the cocoa butter reincorporates itself and the bloom disappears. Stored properly, unsweetened, bittersweet, and semisweet chocolates can be kept for a year or more.

Melting chocolate: Chocolate melts evenly and safely over hot water or in the microwave oven. No matter which method you use to melt chocolate, you should always start with chocolate that has been chopped into small, evenly sized pieces. To melt the chocolate over water, place the chocolate in a heatproof bowl and fit the bowl into a saucepan containing a small amount (about an inch) of simmering, not boiling, water — make sure the bottom of the bowl doesn't touch the water. (Alternatively, you can put the chocolate in the top of a double boiler over simmering water.) Keep the heat very low and stir the chocolate often. As soon as the chocolate is melted, remove it from the heat; stir to smooth.

To melt chocolate in the microwave oven, place the chipped chocolate in a microwave-safe container. Cook on medium for a minute, stir the chocolate, and continue to cook for 30-second intervals, until melted. (If you're melting four or more ounces of chocolate at a time, you can start with 2 minutes in the oven and then go to shorter intervals.) It's important to keep checking the chocolate because the microwave oven has a way of allowing the chocolate to keep its shape even though it's thoroughly melted — a deception that can cost you the batch. To avoid mishaps, press on the chocolate to check that it's melted.

Whether you melt over water or in the microwave, remember that water is chocolate's enemy. Even one drop of water splashed onto the chocolate while it's melting is enough to cause it to seize and go dull. However, if a recipe specifies melting chocolate with a liquid (butter, for example), don't worry — it's only moisture added mid-melt that will give you problems.

Chocolate shavings and curls: To make the decorative chocolate shavings and curls that give cakes a professional finish, you need a block of chocolate, a vegetable peeler, and, if you're new to this, time and patience to practice the technique. Start with a block of chocolate that's large enough for you to hold it at an angle and long and broad enough (on at least one side) to allow you to slide the vegetable peeler down its length and get a healthy amount of chocolate. So that you get shavings and curls, not flakes and chunks, the chocolate must be at warm room temperature — 75°F is just right. If you can't set your chocolate out to warm in a 75°F room, then you can take both chocolate and courage in hand and pass the block of chocolate very quickly (in fact, very, very quickly) over a flame or electric burner. Wait two minutes and then repeat this act of daring. At this point, the chocolate should be warm enough to shave.

Working over a piece of parchment or wax paper, hold the block of chocolate at an angle and scrape down the side of it with the vegetable peeler to produce short, fat curls or small shavings. This is not hard, but it does take practice to find the right angles for the chocolate and the peeler and the right pressure for the scraping. (For broader shavings and curls, use the same technique but substitute a dough scraper for the vegetable peeler.) Failures can be eaten or used in recipes that call for melted chocolate, and successes can be lifted off the paper with a dough scraper and used immediately or covered with another piece of paper and set aside at room temperature until needed.

Cinnamon

Pierre is unusual among French pastry chefs in that his affection for cinnamon rivals that of Americans. Not particularly admired by the French, cinnamon is a spice Pierre finds appealing and uses often in stick and powdered forms. Pierre's preference is for cinnamon from Ceylon, not readily found on your supermarket shelves, but available through the Penzeys catalog (see Mail-Order Sources, page 282). According to Pierre, "People who say they don't like cinnamon taste Ceylon cinnamon and change their minds." He attributes this to Ceylon cinnamon's mild flavor.

Most cinnamon on the market comes from China and is actually not true cinnamon but its cousin, cassia. Cassia is darker, sweeter, and stronger than real cinnamon. You can use either kind of cinnamon for any of these recipes, but if you can get your hands on cinnamon from Ceylon, do a comparative taste test — you'll find it interesting.

Cinnamon sticks, also called quills, can be stored at room temperature indefinitely; cinnamon powder, like all ground spices, loses its flavor and fragrance in the tin or jar. It's best to replace opened jars of ground cinnamon every six months.

Cocoa powder

These recipes were tested with Dutch-processed cocoa powder, which is cocoa powder treated with alkali. "Dutched" powder is darker and less acidic than cocoa powder that has not been treated with alkali. When a recipe in this book calls for cocoa powder, it always means unsweetened cocoa powder.

Coconut

All the recipes that use coconut — and there are several, since this is one of Pierre's pet flavors — call for unsweetened finely grated dried coconut. Available in some supermarkets, unsweetened coconut is easily found in health food or natural food stores. In France, unsweetened coconut is grated so fine as to be almost a powder. To get the best results with American coconut, use a food processor or blender to pulverize the coconut with a small amount of sugar (use a spoonful of the sugar called for in the recipe).

Coconut milk

Rich and thick, coconut milk is available, canned, in most supermarkets and Asian food stores. Always use unsweetened coconut milk and don't confuse it with coconut cream (seen most often under the Coco Lopez label), which is fine for piña coladas but not for pastry.

Cooling racks

Cooling racks with closely spaced metal wires are a must in the pastry kitchen. Whatever size racks you buy, make certain that they are sturdy and have feet that put them at least half an inch above the counter — you need room for air to circulate around the cake or pastry that's cooling on the rack. It's nice to have three round racks for cakes and tarts and at least one large rectangular rack for cookies.

Coulis

This French term, pronounced "coo-lee," refers to sauces made from puréed fruits or vegetables; think raspberry coulis.

Cream

Cream is what gives desserts richness, smoothness, and, when whipped, lightness. All of the recipes that use cream specify heavy cream, but if your market stocks only whipping cream (as is the case in some parts of the country), buy it and carry on. The difference between the two creams is in their butterfat content. Heavy cream contains between

271

36 and 40 percent butterfat, while whipping cream weighs in at between 30 and 36 percent. Their differences are less important than their major similarity: Unlike light cream, both can be whipped.

Whipping cream: Cream whips best when it is cold. It's also easier to whip cream when the bowl and beater are cold too. If you're using an electric mixer, start whipping the cream on low speed and then increase the speed when the cream begins to thicken a bit. Because the line between perfectly whipped cream and over-whipped cream (the kind that's on the verge of turning into butter) is thin, it's always best to whip the cream to a softer-than-it-should-be stage and then finish it by hand, giving it a few turns with a whisk. Although whipped cream is best whipped *à la minute*, it can wait a short time if necessary — just keep it refrigerated and make sure that it's well covered with plastic wrap, since whipped cream is a magnet for refrigerator odors.

Crème fraîche

Crème fraîche is sour cream's French cousin. It has sour cream's smooth, thick texture and tangy taste, but unlike sour cream, it can be heated without separating and whipped just like heavy cream. Commercially made crème fraîche is not easily found in the States and what is available is expensive. Fortunately, crème fraîche can be made simply and inexpensively at home. To make a cup of crème fraîche, pour 1 cup heavy cream into a clean jar, add 1 tablespoon butter-milk, cover the jar tightly, and then shake it for about a minute. Leave the jar on the counter for between 12 and 24 hours, or until the crème fraîche thickens slightly. How quickly the mixture thickens will depend on the temperature of your room — the warmer the room, the quicker the thickening action. When it's thickened, store the crème fraîche in the refrigerator and let it chill thoroughly before you use it. Crème fraîche can be kept covered in the refrigerator for about two weeks and it will get tangier and tangier as it ages.

Dessert or cake rings

The majority of Pierre's cakes are constructed (and some are baked) in dessert or cake rings,

known as *cercles d'entremets,* bottomless stain-less steel bands that are 1½ inches/4 centimeters high. Most cakes are assembled in 8¾-inch/22-centimeter rings and a few in 10¼-inch/26-centimeter rings. (Actually, Pierre prefers 9¾-inch/25-centimeter rings, but these are, for all practical purposes, unavailable in the United States.) With a dessert ring as the "mold" in which you build a cake, you'll get a straight-sided, polished, professional-looking cake every time. Using a ring is easier (and neater) than filling and stacking layers freehand, and if you've never used one, the first time you lift it off and get a look at your layers of cake and cream, mousse, or fruit, stacked up with military precision, you'll be thrilled.

Since dessert or cake rings (and tart or flan rings, see page 280) are essentially pieces of European and/or professional equipment, the measurements are given in centimeters as well as in inches. Indeed, in many stores you'll find only the metric measurements listed and, in fact, you'll do best to purchase the rings by their metric sizes if you can. Dessert rings are available in profes-sional baking and restaurant supply stores (Bridge offers rings by mail or Internet order; see Mail-Order Sources, page 282) and in well-equipped housewares stores (see Sur la Table in Sources).

Rings cost about $10 to $15 and it's worth having two of the 8¾-inch/22-centimeter rings, especially if you're planning to serve more than one cake at a time. Don't be seduced by those adjustable rings that can be sized from very small to larger-than-you'll-probably-need. The band that makes these rings adjustable also makes a dent in the side of your cake. Also, don't buy a ring in black metal — it can turn whipped creams and fillings an unpleasant color and give an off taste to anything acidic, such as lemon cream.

If you do not have a dessert ring, you can sub-stitute the ring of an appropriately sized spring-form pan, but you'll never get the perfectly smooth side that's a hallmark of the dessert ring.

To remove dessert rings, heat is the key. Since most desserts constructed in rings are chilled or frozen, you need to apply heat so that the dessert softens sufficiently to allow you to lift off the ring without damaging what's inside. A hair dryer is what makes this delicate operation quick, easy, and foolproof: Just blow hot air around the ring and presto — you've achieved liftoff. (See page 275 for other nifty things you can do with a hair dryer.) If you don't have a hair dryer, you can remove dessert rings by soaking a kitchen towel in hot water, wringing it out, and then wrapping it around the ring, although it may take a couple of soaks to warm things up. Similarly, you can use a sponge that's been dipped in hot water. Finally, if all you've got is a knife at your disposal, run it between the ring and the dessert, but be forewarned — the side of your dessert might suffer (only a minor problem if you can dust it with nuts or chocolate shavings).

Dried fruits

Pierre loves using dried fruits in his desserts and was delighted when he came to America and found such a wide variety of high-quality fruits available. In fact, there are more kinds of dried fruits available in American markets than in French markets. Indeed, it was during a visit to a New York market that Pierre discovered dried cherries, a discovery that inspired him to create the wildly aromatic Coconut–Dried Cherry Flan (page 124).

No matter what the variety of dried fruit, it should always be soft and moist. If you start out with hard fruit, it won't get soft and moist after you mix it into a batter, dough, or cream; instead, it will spoil your creation. If your fruit is not soft and moist, you can "plump" it by placing it in a strainer over boiling water. Steam the fruit for a short time — sometimes a minute is all it takes — until it's soft and plump. Remove it from the heat, pat it dry between sheets of paper toweling, and proceed with your recipe.

Eggs

The recipes in this book were tested with US Grade A large eggs, which come as close as possible to the size of the eggs Pierre uses in Paris, eggs that weigh 60 grams: 30 grams for the whites, 20 grams for the yolks, and 10 grams for the shells.

Eggs should be bought from a reliable market and handled with respect, since there is evidence that eggs can contain salmonella, a bacteria that causes unpleasant, flu-like illness. Salmonella is rarely fatal among healthy people, but the very young, the very old, ill people, pregnant women,

and anyone with a weakened immune system could be at risk, and so you should pay particular attention when you're baking for them. However, if you handle eggs properly, you should never encounter a problem. Here are some points to keep in mind:

- Always buy your eggs from a market that keeps them refrigerated at all times.
- Always keep eggs under refrigeration at home. If a recipe calls for eggs at room temperature — and most of these do — take the eggs from the fridge twenty minutes ahead of time. Never leave eggs at room temperature for more than two hours.
- Never use an egg that has a cracked shell.
- Wash your hands after you handle eggs and make sure to scrub your work surface and utensils after working with eggs.
- To kill salmonella bacteria, eggs must be brought to an end temperature of 160°F or held at a temperature of 140°F for three and a half minutes.

Egg whites: Eggs separate most easily when they are cold, but egg whites whip to their fullest volume when they are at room temperature or warmer, so it's best to separate eggs as soon as they come from the refrigerator, then whip the whites after they've had a few minutes to lose their chill. Whites must be whipped in an impeccably clean, dry bowl — even a speck of fat of any kind, including a drop of yolk, is enough to stand in the way of whipping whites to maximum capacity. While many bakers insist on whipping their whites in a copper bowl — there's an interaction between the copper and the whites that pushes the whites to extreme fullness — whites can be whipped beautifully and easily in a mixer fitted with the whisk attachment. The key to whipping whites is not to overwhip them. Pay attention to the changes in texture and sheen as the whites whip. Your ideal whipped-to-firm-peaks white is, indeed, white, smooth, and glossy. When the whites turn dull, it means you've gone too far. Ditto for when the whites break up into puffs and clouds. When you lift up some whites on a whisk, the whites should, in fact, peak, and the peak, while it might bend over a little — a very little — should stay, as though it's been lacquered. As firm and proud as the peaks may be, it's only a show: Whipped egg whites are wimps — they'll collapse under the slightest pressure. Keep this in mind when you're folding the whites into another, heavier mixture — use a flexible rubber spatula and a very light hand, and stop as soon as the whites are incorporated.

Yolks and sugar: There'll be many times when you'll have to whisk yolks and sugar together, often until they turn pale and thicken. Keep in mind that as soon as you add sugar to egg yolks, you've got to start stirring immediately — otherwise the yolks will "burn," a term bakers use to describe the lumps that develop when sugar is added to, but not mixed into, yolks.

Flan rings
See Tart or flan rings.

Flour
All but one recipe in this book was tested with all-purpose flour, that is, bleached and enriched flour, the kind found in the supermarket under national brand labels such as Gold Medal and Pillsbury — the Lemon Loaf Cakes were made with cake flour, a flour particularly low in protein. (While all-purpose flours have between 10 and 12 grams of protein per cup, cake flour has only about 8 grams.)

Regardless of the type of flour you're using, you should store it in an airtight tin in a cool, dry cupboard. Stored properly, white flours should keep for about six months.

In most cases, there's no need to sift all-purpose flour. Not so with cake flour, which is always lumpy and always needs to be sifted before it is added to a batter. In Pierre's recipes, flour is measured before it is sifted.

Always use the scoop-and-sweep method to measure flour (see page 277).

Folding
When you're instructed to fold one ingredient into another — usually a light, airy ingredient, such as meringue or whipped cream, into a heavier mixture, such as a batter or, often, a crème anglaise — you're meant to do so very gently.

It's a delicate maneuver, one most easily achieved by using a flexible rubber spatula, a roomy bowl, and a soft touch.

If a batter is particularly thick and heavy, it's a good idea to stir a little of the lighter ingredient into it before folding in the rest. No matter what you're folding into what, the motion is always the same. Put some of whatever you're folding in on top of the mixture in the bowl, putting it in the center of the bowl, and then use the edge of your spatula to cut down through both ingredients. As you hit the bottom of the bowl, do three things — give the bowl a quarter turn, simultaneously turn your wrist slightly (to angle the spatula), and draw the spatula against the bottom of the bowl and then up the side, finishing with the edge of the spatula breaking the surface first. Continue just until the two mixtures are combined — no farther. If you're new to folding, you might be so happy to get it right that you might overdo it — resist that temptation.

Food processor
Having a food processor on your counter is like having an assistant. It's the tool you should use when you need to grind nuts or pulverize dried coconut, and it's a terrific tool for making pastry dough. If you're buying a food processor for the first time, buy the best one you can afford (they last for years) and the one with the largest capacity. When you're making pastry, having a large work bowl is key.

Freezing
Many of Pierre's cakes, tarts, and cookies can be frozen, either at some point in their production or as finished desserts. You'll find information on a specific recipe's freezability in the recipe (as appropriate) or in the "Keeping" notes at the end of the recipe. At whatever stage you freeze something, you must always make certain to freeze it airtight. Double-wrapping in plastic bags or plastic film and finishing the package off with an aluminum foil wrap is not overkill. Use your judgment when freezing decorated cakes; often it's best to put the cake in the freezer uncovered until it's firm, and then wrap it airtight. If you have the time, the best way to defrost a cake is the slowest: Keep it in its wrapper and give it a leisurely overnight rest in the refrigerator. This is a particularly good way to defrost mousse and cream

cakes — they're not shocked into defrosting, as they are when you leave them at room temperature, and you don't risk the unpleasant surprise of biting into a seemingly soft and luscious cake only to find that the center is colder and harder than the sides.

Ganache
Always chocolate and always rich, a traditional, simple ganache is a mixture of melted chocolate and heavy cream. (There are other ganaches that use eggs and some that have butter too.) Depending on the proportion of chocolate to cream, ganache can be thick enough to use as a cake filling or thin enough to pour over a cake as a glaze. Because ganache is essentially an emulsion, like mayonnaise, Pierre advises that you mix it the same way you would mayonnaise, slowly and gently. When you add the hot cream to the chocolate to make a classic ganache, add a little of the cream to the center of the bowl with the chocolate and blend it in by stirring in small circles; then, as you add more cream, continue to stir gently in increasingly wider concentric circles.

Gelatin
In the French pastry kitchen, gelatin is used as a stabilizer in much the same ways as meringue and whipped cream are. Used in very small amounts (so small that they're almost unnoticeable in the texture and totally undetectable in the taste), gelatin is the secret weapon that gives a feather-light mousse the strength to work as a layer in a fancy *gateau,* a *chibouste* the structure to stand up, and a crème anglaise the muscle to make it as a filling. While Pierre and most other professional pastry chefs use sheet gelatin (leaves of gelatin that look like shiny plastic), these recipes were tested with the more commonly available powdered gelatin. (Knox gelatin was the brand used.)

The easiest way to prepare gelatin for incorporation into a dessert is to sprinkle it over the specified amount of cold water, allow it to rest until it is softened (a minute or so), and then pop it into the microwave oven for 15 seconds to dissolve it. It can also be dissolved over very low direct heat.

Hair dryer
This is one of Pierre's favorite pieces of kitchen equipment and it will become one of yours as soon as you see how it makes short work of removing dessert rings. Almost all of Pierre's cakes and desserts are constructed in dessert rings and then chilled or frozen, processes that cause whatever is at the edge of the dessert to stick to the ring. Running a knife around the edge of the ring is one way to release the ring, but it's not the best way, because you'll damage your dessert's sleek, smooth sides — the reason you used a ring in the first place. By blowing a little hot air around the outside of the ring, you'll warm the ring and the edges of the dessert just enough to allow you to lift off the ring cleanly. It's the perfect tool for the job.

But a hair dryer's not a one-job Johnny. You'll be glad to have it at hand when you want to press chocolate curls, cake cubes, or toasted nuts into the sides of a chilled cake. Hit the cake with a little heat and the unyielding mousse, cream, or glaze on the sides will become a model of stickability. And if your ganache or glaze looks a little dull, give it a quick (and gentle) puff of heat and watch it shine. All this work can be done with a travel-size hair dryer small enough to tuck into a kitchen drawer.

Immersion blender
You can manage in the pastry kitchen without this nifty tool, but once you've got one, you'll find lots of uses for it. The immersion blender does the work of a traditional blender, but it's portable — the blending blade is at the end of a grippable rod (the French call this machine a giraffe because it's all neck), which means you can blend, crush, purée, or liquefy a mixture in its mixing bowl or pot. (Think of the cleanup you save!) The immersion blender is good for puréeing lemon cream, a treat that needs a long blending; making coulis and sauces; and smoothing out anything that doesn't go exactly to plan. (You'll find it's also a wizard with soups — you can purée them in their stockpots.)

Instant-read thermometer
To succeed with Pierre's recipes, you need to have a thermometer at the ready frequently. As you work, you'll need to measure the temperature of a crème

anglaise, a sugar syrup, an egg mixture, or any number of preparations. All of these checks, and more, can be performed with an instant-read thermometer. There are three types of instant-read thermometer and any will do the trick. The simplest has a metal probe that finishes in a regular dial. This is fine, but in this age in which we expect instant to be immediate, its dial can seem a little pokey. The second model is constructed like the first, but its display is digital, and it measures ingredients up to 302°F (the analog only goes to 220°F). Finally, there's the digital thermometer made by Polder (available at Williams-Sonoma and New York Cake and Baking Distributors; see Mail-Order Sources, page 282). Its probe is attached to a long, flexible metal thread that, in turn, is attached to the digital display, a large-enough-to-read-easily affair. The separation of probe and display and the design of the probe — it is gently curved at the point at which it meets the thread — mean you can do a hands-free readout: The probe can rest in the saucepan while you stir the custard. In addition, you can set this ingenious instrument to beep after a certain amount of time or, more important, to beep when your mixture has reached its desired temperature — a boon when you've got chocolate cooling and you're doing other things.

Jelly-roll pans

Referred to as sheet pans by professional bakers, these pans are rectangular and, unlike baking sheets, have raised sides. They're good for making sheet and jelly-roll cakes (hence their name), transferring doughs from counter to refrigerator, toasting nuts, and similar jobs. However, they're not very good for cookies or for baking tart crusts in tart rings — their sides make sliding things on and off them tough. (Of course, if all you've got are jelly-roll pans, you can make do. Line the pans with parchment paper and, when you're finished baking, transfer the paper from pan to cooling rack, cookies or crust in situ.) Jelly-roll pans can be either 10½ by 15½ by 1 inch or 12½ by 17½ by 1 inch and can be purchased with nonstick finishes.

Marble

Rich, buttery pastry doughs (the best kind) can be finicky when it comes to rolling, but you can keep some of their finickiness in check if you roll them out on a smooth, cool surface; marble is one of the smoothest and coolest surfaces you can find. (Stainless steel, polished onyx, and granite are great too.) Ideally, you should have a large marble slab that you can slide in and out of the refrigerator so that if, while you're rolling, the dough gets a little soft or otherwise unwieldy, you can give it a quick chill, the secret to bringing it under control. (If you have access to a stone or marble supply house, have a marble slab custom-cut so that it is the exact size of one of your refrigerator shelves.) Of course, any surface can be cooled down by filling a pan with ice cubes and running the bottom of the pan over the area on which you'll be rolling.

Marzipan

Marzipan is a little softer and a little sweeter than almond paste, but the two ingredients can be used interchangeably. Wrapped airtight, marzipan can be kept in the refrigerator for up to six months.

Measuring

Accurate measuring is the cornerstone of success with these or any other pastry recipes — baking is not a little-bit-of-this, little-bit-of-that craft. Pierre's recipes, originally written with metric measures, have been adapted for the American measuring system, which is based on volume, not weight. It's for this reason that you'll come across some unorthodox measurements here, such as "1 cup plus 2 tablespoons," or "1 (slightly rounded) cup." Since the recipes have been adapted, in some cases changed, and in every case tested with these volume measures, you should not try to convert the measurements back to metric weights — you'll risk getting measurements with double rounding errors.

To measure accurately, you need accurate measuring cups and spoons for liquid and dry ingredients.

Liquids should be measured in clearly calibrated glass measuring cups. The surest way to get an accurate liquid measure is to place the measuring cup on a flat surface, bend down so that the calibrations are at eye level, and pour in the liquid. Don't lift the cup up to eye level — it will throw off the measurements; get down there and look. If you're measuring less than ¼ cup of liquid, you'd do better to measure the liquid in measuring spoons, remembering that 4 tablespoons equal ¼ cup.

Dry ingredients should be measured in metal measuring cups and spoons. Your *batterie de cuisine* should include cups to measure ¼, ⅓, ½, and 1 cup; ⅛-cup and 2-cup measures are optional, but nice. As for measuring spoons, your set should include ¼-, ½-, and 1-teaspoon measures as well as a 1-tablespoon measure. Actually, it's good to have two sets of both measuring cups and spoons.

Whatever you're measuring, it's important that, unless specified that the measure be "slightly rounded," as in 1 (slightly rounded) cup, the ingredients be level with the rim of the dry measuring cup or measuring spoon. For instance, if the recipe calls for ½ cup sugar, you should dip the ½-cup measure into the sugar bin, scoop up a rounded measure of sugar, and then sweep it level with a straight edge (the back of a knife or a ruler works well). Never use a measuring cup that's larger than the amount you need — you won't be able to level it.

When measuring flour, it's best to aerate the flour in the bin by fluffing it with a fork or whisk before you measure it. For flour, as for all dry ingredients, you should use the scoop and sweep method — scoop up (or spoon in) enough flour to overflow the cup and sweep the flour level with the rim of the measuring cup, taking special care not to tamp down the flour (which would really throw off the measurements). In these recipes, if flour needs to be sifted, it is sifted after it is measured.

Most sugar is measured like flour; brown sugar, the exception to the rule, should be packed snugly into its measuring cup. Confectioner's sugar needs to be sifted after it's measured, because it's always lumpy.

Milk

All of these recipes were tested with whole milk.

Mixers

A heavy-duty stand mixer is an invaluable kitchen tool, particularly when you're making cakes that depend on beaten eggs for their lift and structure, meringues that are heated with syrup and then need to be whipped until cool, or desserts that have several components or steps that must be

accomplished simultaneously or in quick succession. Pierre's fanciest recipes are easier and faster to make with a stand mixer, although they can be made with a strong hand-held mixer. Stand mixers are expensive, but good ones last for years and make light work of heavy jobs. (These recipes were tested with a twenty-year-old never-fail KitchenAid mixer with a 5-quart bowl.) In the best of all possible worlds, you would have two bowls for your stand mixer (extra bowls are usually available from the manufacturer and are an inexpensive but very useful addition to your *batterie de cuisine*) and a high-quality hand-held mixer at the ready for quick, light jobs and those times when you have to beat two things at once.

Mixing bowls

Equip yourself with a set (or two) of nesting stainless steel mixing bowls — available in all housewares stores and even many supermarkets — and you'll have what you need to mix up these recipes. While you can use plastic or glass bowls, it's important to have at least one metal bowl that can be set comfortably over a saucepan (preferably a 2-quart pan) to serve as the top of a double boiler.

Nuts

Nuts add incomparable flavor and texture to desserts, but they must be treated with care. The oils that make nuts delicious can also make them rancid, so taste before you buy (if that's possible) and then taste again before you bake. To keep fresh nuts fresh, it's best to wrap them airtight and store them in the freezer, where they'll keep for a few months. There's no need to thaw frozen nuts before you use them.

To toast nuts, place them in a single layer on a baking sheet or in a jelly-roll pan and either bake them in a 350°F oven for 10 to 12 minutes or do as Pierre does: Toast them in a 300°F to 325°F oven for 18 to 20 minutes. Toasting them at a lower temperature for a longer time ensures that the nuts are toasted evenly all the way through. (Long slow toasting also means nuts are less likely to scorch.)

To grind nuts, place the nuts in the work bowl of a food processor and pulse until the nuts are finely and evenly ground. Don't process the nuts continuously, and do check their progress regularly — if you go overboard, you'll end up with nut paste, not powder. To be on the safe side, grind the nuts with a spoonful of sugar (you can use some of the sugar from the recipe).

Oven thermometers

Even if you've just bought a brand-new oven that cost the earth and is the darling of world-class chefs, check its temperature with a reliable mercury oven thermometer before you bake. In fact, you'd do well to make the thermometer a permanent fixture in your oven — a few degrees higher or lower and your cake could be burnt or your crust tough.

Parchment paper

Professional pastry chefs never use wax paper — they depend instead on parchment paper, usually silicon coated and often sold in precut large sheets. (The sheets are available from specialty shops and through the King Arthur Flour Baker's Catalog; see Mail-Order Sources, page 282.) Parchment paper is just right for lining baking sheets, especially when you're baking in bottomless dessert or tart rings, and it's the perfect catch sheet for anything that you're sifting or grating. After you've sifted flour or grated zest, for instance, you have only to lift the parchment paper and turn up the sides a bit and you've got a funnel that makes easy work of transporting ingredients from counter to mixing bowl.

Pastry bags and tips

Making professional-looking ladyfinger biscuits and disks, meringues, and decorations requires a pastry bag and tip. The bags, cone-shaped and available in different sizes, are made of plastic-coated canvas, nylon, or plastic (disposable plastic bags are available from baking supply houses; see Mail-Order Sources, page 282), and can be fitted with metal or plastic tips that may be plain or decorative. At a minimum, you should have two pastry bags, one about 18 inches long and the other about 10 inches; a $\frac{1}{4}$-inch plain tip; a $\frac{1}{2}$-inch plain tip; and one star tip — but if you're interested in cake decorating, you'll want a collection of tips for sure. If you want to make the royal icing decorations on the Wedding Cake (page 257), you'll also need a small pastry bag with a plain tip, the kind

you'd use for writing with icing. (If you want to write with chocolate, it's best to fold a tiny cone from a triangle of parchment paper and then snip off a small hole at the tip.) Unless they're disposable, pastry bags should be turned inside out and washed well in soapy water, rinsed well, then hung up to dry after each use.

Pastry brush or feather

Bristle brushes, whether from a baking supply shop or the hardware store, are good to have on hand in narrow widths (about $\frac{1}{2}$ inch across) for applying an egg wash or glaze, and in wider widths (about 1 inch across) for brushing excess flour off pastry dough or softened butter onto the insides of baking rings and pans. For really delicate jobs, such as glazing a dainty petit four, it's nice to have a feather brush — one or two white plumes bound together at their quills. Whether they are brushes or feathers, it's important to wash them well after each use and allow them to air-dry.

Pie or pastry weights

Pie or pastry weights are used when you are baking a crust blind, that is, without filling. Line the crust with parchment paper or foil and then fill the bottom with weights to keep the crust from puffing during baking. When it comes to weighting a pie, a little is good and a little more is not. Pierre is firm in his disapproval of commercially available pie weights, pellets made from metal or ceramic: "They're too heavy. They leave pockmarks in the crust. They destroy the texture of the pastry. And," he adds, just in case his statements need clarification, "they're bad." Rather than pie weights, Pierre suggests you use good old (inexpensive) rice or dried pea beans. Set aside a jar of rice or beans for the exclusive use of weighting down pastry — when you remove the parchment or foil liner from the tart shell, let the rice or beans cool and then pack them into a jar or other container, ready to be used again and again. But don't try to use the rice or beans for dinner — once they've been baked they're good for nothing else but more weighting.

Piping

Piping is the term used to describe the act of pushing something — often a batter or a frosting — out of a pastry bag.

Rolling dough

The key to rolling dough is cold, cold, and more cold. Always make certain that your dough, whether it's tart dough, cinnamon, cookie, or puff, is well chilled before you start rolling, and, if it gets warm while you're rolling it, stop and put it back in the refrigerator to chill again (and again, if necessary).

You'll have an easier time rolling a dough out to an even thickness (important for tarts and other pastries) if the dough is the right consistency before you start rolling. You want the dough to be firm enough so that it doesn't stick to the rolling surface, yet soft enough so that it starts moving easily under the rolling pin. (Dough that cracks around the edges as soon as you start rolling is too cold and therefore too hard.) Let the dough sit at room temperature before you start rolling and then, if when you start, the dough doesn't get moving, you can help it along by pressing your rolling pin into it gently; just press a series of parallel indentations into the dough and it will soften up enough to roll. If the dough softens too much during the rolling process, pop it into the refrigerator for a quick chill before continuing.

Because Pierre's doughs are particularly short (the term used to describe doughs with a high proportion of butter) they can be fussy to roll. Always roll dough on a lightly floured surface with a rolling pin that's been rubbed with a little flour. Dust the top of the dough lightly (very lightly) with flour before you start rolling and, as you're rolling, lift the dough off the counter and toss a little flour under it from time to time. While you've got the dough up from the counter, you should rotate it too — giving the dough an eighth of a turn will help keep it round, as will rolling the dough from the center out. Always brush the excess flour off pastry before fitting it into a tart ring or baking it. If you've got the time, it's a good idea to chill the dough slightly after you've rolled it and before you fit it into the tart ring.

To fit the dough into a ring, roll the dough up and around your rolling pin and then unroll the dough over the ring. Gently fit the dough into the bottom and up the sides of the ring, always taking care not to stretch it. Remember: What you stretch on the work surface will shrink in the oven. Then chill the dough in its ring before baking it.

Rolling pin

The rolling pin of choice in the pastry kitchen is the one known as the French-style pin. It's 19 inches long, 2 inches across (straight along its whole length; it doesn't taper at the ends), weighs $1\frac{1}{4}$ pounds, and has no handles. The fact that it has no handles makes it easy to control, and its weight is ideal — not so light that it forces you to use pressure and not so heavy that it deflates rather than rolls the dough. Bring out the heavier pins only when you're rolling puffy yeast doughs.

Rotating pans

If you have pans on two oven racks, or even two pans on the same oven rack, it's best to rotate the pans halfway through the baking period in order to compensate for any hot spots or other inconsistencies in your oven. In fact, you should do a double rotation: Turn the pans front to back (so that the side of the pan that was facing the oven door now faces the back of the oven) and, if they're on two racks, switch their position in the oven by putting the pan that was on the upper rack on the lower and vice versa. If you have two tarts or cakes on one rack (which is fine as long as there's plenty of air space between the pans), turn the pans front to back and switch them left and right. Of course, if something will be in the oven for just ten minutes, it's better to leave it in peace than to open the oven door to do the rotations and have the oven's precious heat escape.

Rum

Pierre uses what is referred to in France as an old agricultural rum — it's dark, potent, and aromatic. Unless you're ready to spring for an expensive aged rum from Venezuela (Pierre's favorite is packed in leather and costs as much as a fine Cognac), you'll do well to use what many American bakers use, Myers's dark rum.

Salt

Salt may not be the first ingredient that springs to mind when asked what's most important in a pastry chef's pantry, but it's an ingredient that Pierre takes very seriously. Pierre's salt of choice is fleur de sel de Guerande. Fleur de sel means, literally, "flower of the salt," and de Guerande means it comes from Guerande, a town, famous for its salt, on Brittany's rugged coast. Referred to and used as a condiment, fleur de sel is moister, larger-grained, and less salty than common salt. It is not washed, iodized, or treated with anti-humidity chemicals; it is a natural sea salt that is rich in minerals and not easy to harvest. Fleur de sel is the finest salt that floats to the surface of salt ponds. It is harvested by hand and not always available — whether or not fleur de sel appears in the ponds depends on the season, the sun, the winds, the humidity, and, one has to believe, the whim of the salt gods. Its taste is distinctive and deliciously addictive — once you've tried it, you may take to doing what some Frenchmen do: carrying a cache at the ready to sprinkle on restaurant dishes that lack that certain *je ne sais quoi*. Not surprisingly, fleur de sel is expensive and not available in many specialty stores, although it can be purchased by mail (see Mail-Order Sources, page 282). Given its rarity, fleur de sel was not used to test these recipes — instead, table salt and fine sea salt were used. If you have fleur de sel and want to use it in these recipes, you may find it's best to increase the amount of salt ever so slightly.

Saucepans

It's important to have at least one heavy-bottomed 2-quart saucepan in your kitchen. You'll use it to make crème anglaise and pastry cream, caramel, and syrups. It will also come in handy when you want to make a bain-marie, or double boiler, for melting chocolate. However, you'll find it good to have a larger saucepan, too — one you can use as a bain-marie for larger quantities of chocolate as well as Pierre's lemon cream — and a tiny one, preferably with a spout, for boiling small quantities of sugar syrup to pour into meringues or custards.

Scale

While all of Pierre's recipes have been adapted for American volume measures, it's good to have a kitchen scale available for weighing bulky fare like chocolate and fruits. Whether you buy a balance scale or an electronic scale (more compact and more versatile since it can usually be switched easily between pound and metric measurements), look for one that, at a minimum, will be accurate to within a quarter ounce or five grams.

Spatulas

You'll need both rubber and metal spatulas to work your way through these recipes. When buying rubber spatulas, look for commercial-grade spatulas — they're more flexible, more durable, and usually have a larger blade than most supermarket-type spatulas. Ideally, you should have two each of small, medium, and large rubber spatulas.

You'll use metal spatulas to fill and finish cakes, smooth batter into dessert or tart rings, or lift cookies from baking sheets and cooling racks. Look for short, slim spatulas for small jobs; long ones for icing; wide ones for lifting; and offset spatulas in varying lengths and widths for smoothing. Specialty houseware and restaurant supply houses are the best sources for high-quality metal spatulas, especially offset spatulas, the ones with their blades set at an angle and slightly below their handles, like pancake flippers.

Sugar

If a recipe calls for "sugar," it's granulated sugar that you're meant to use. The only other sugars used in Pierre's recipes are light brown sugar and confectioner's, or 10-X, sugar. Granulated sugar should be measured using the scoop-and-sweep method (see page 277), brown sugar should always be packed into the measuring cup or spoon, and confectioner's sugar should always be sifted after measuring since it's always lumpy.

Tart or flan rings

All of the tart recipes were tested in tart or flan rings rather than tart pans. A tart ring is a bottomless metal ring that is placed on a parchment-lined baking sheet (which becomes its bottom); the ring serves as the mold or pan for the tart dough. A tart ring is straight-sided and only ¾ inch/2 centimeters high, shorter than a tart pan. To make these recipes, you'll need at least one tart ring that is 8¾ inches/22 cm in diameter and another one or two 10¼ inches/26 cm across. (Pierre prefers to use 9¾-inch/25-cm rings, but these are rarely available in the United States.) When you will be fitting tart dough into a ring, it's best to position the ring on a baking sheet rather than a jelly-roll pan so that, once the tart is baked, you can slide it off the sheet without lifting it — tart shells in general are fragile and shells that have no bottom support are more fragile still. In a pinch, you can use a fluted metal tart pan with a removable bottom instead of a ring, but because a tin is higher than a ring, your results will differ (the filling-to-shell proportions may seem skimpy in some cases). That said, it's better to bake a tart whose proportions are a little off than not to bake a tart at all.

Vanilla

Vanilla is one of Pierre's favorite flavors and fragrances and he uses it often, most frequently in bean form, in both starring and supporting roles. Until recently, Pierre's vanilla of choice was Tahitian, but currently the supply is extremely limited and the price extremely high, so this rare treat has become even rarer. In all likelihood the beans you'll find most readily will be Madagascan or Bourbon, and they'll be fine for any of these or other recipes. However, if you can find Mexican beans (see Mail-Order Sources, page 282), use them. Like Tahitian beans, Mexican beans are more expensive than Bourbon or Madagascan and they have a stronger and more distinctively floral fragrance. If you can, try a variety of beans and choose your own favorite.

No matter which beans you choose, they should be plump, moist, pliable, and, of course, fragrant. It's usually the soft, pulpy, aromatic seeds inside the pod that you're after, but the pod is a flavoring agent too and each recipe will tell you what part of the bean you're to use and how. If the recipe calls for a vanilla bean "split lengthwise and scraped," you're meant to split the bean in half from blossom to stem end with a small sharp paring knife. You may find it's easiest to do this if you lay the bean flat on a cutting board. Once the bean is split, use the point of the knife to scrape out the soft interior pulp. If you're infusing a liquid

with vanilla, you'll put the pod and the scraped pulp into the liquid and then, after the liquid has steeped, strain out the pod. Don't toss away these used pods. Wash and dry them well (in a slow oven or on a rack at room temperature) and use them to flavor sugar. You can either bury the pods in the sugar canister or pulverize them with sugar in the food processor.

Zest and zesters

Zest is the colorful outer rind of citrus fruit. Whether a recipe calls for broad strips of zest or for thin shreds, you should always avoid the cottony, bitter white pith that's just under the zest's surface. When you need broad strips of zest, as you will if you're infusing a liquid with the zest's bright flavor, you can remove the zest with a swivel-blade vegetable peeler or a small sharp knife. But when you need thin ribbons of zest or finely chopped zest, the fastest, cleanest, and most elegant way to get these ribbons (which can then be chopped) is to use a zester, a simple tool composed of a handle, wooden or plastic, in which is mounted a thin metal form with five holes at the top. Hold the zester so that the top of the holes rests against the top of the fruit, and then scrape it down the side of the fruit, applying gentle pressure to the zester as you move it down the fruit. Go around the fruit a second time, and the zester automatically settles onto the unzested part — lots of zest, no pith, very efficient.

281

MAIL-ORDER SOURCES

Bridge Kitchenware
214 East 52nd Street
New York, NY 10022
800-274-3435
Extensive stock of professional-quality baking, pastry, decorating, and cooking equipment and accessories, including tart and dessert rings, parchment, and cake rounds. Catalog available.

ECM, Inc./Valrhona
1901 Avenue of the Stars, Suite 1800
Los Angeles, CA 90067
310-277-0401
Valrhona chocolate. Catalog available.

Elk Candy Co., Inc.
1628 Second Avenue
New York, NY 10028
212-650-1177
Specializing in almond paste and marzipan.

Flavorbank
4710 Eisenhower Boulevard, #E-8
Tampa, FL 33614
800-825-7603
Spices, including Sarawak peppercorns.

King Arthur Flour Company
The Baker's Catalog
P.O. Box 876
Norwich, VT 05055
800-827-6836
Catalog offers wide variety of ingredients and tools, including fleur de sel, vanilla beans, thermometers, and scales.

La Maison du Chocolat
25 East 73rd Street
New York, NY 10021
212-744-7117
Marrons glacés.

Mushroom Man
800-945-3404
Fleur de sel.

New York Cake & Baking Distributors
56 West 22nd Street
New York, NY 10010
212-675-2253
General and specialized baking, pastry, and decorating equipment and tools, including tart and dessert rings, parchment paper, and cake rounds; chocolate in bulk; cocoa butter. Catalog available.

Penzeys Ltd.
P.O. Box 933
Muskego, WI 53150
414-574-0277
Spices and vanilla beans. Catalog available.

Sur la Table
1765 Sixth Avenue South
Seattle, WA 98134
800-243-0852
General baking, pastry, and decorating equipment and tools, including tart and dessert rings. Catalog available.

Williams-Sonoma
A Catalog for Cooks
Mail Order Department
P.O. Box 7456
San Francisco, CA 94120
800-541-2233
General baking and pastry equipment and tools, including tart and dessert rings as well as thermometers, available in stores and through catalog sales.

Zabar's
249 West 80th Street
New York, NY 10024
800-697-6301
General baking and pastry equipment and tools, including tart and dessert rings, thermometers, scales, parchment paper, and cake rounds; speciality ingredients, including Oetker Glaze. Catalog available.

INDEX

à la minute, 266
Almond Cups, Dainty, 106–107
almond paste, about, 266
Almond Philadelphia Cake, 195–
    199
Apple Galette, 126–127
Apples, Roasted, Caramelized Cin-
    namon Tart with, 141
Apples, Twenty-Hour, 33–34
Apricot Packets, 55–56
Autumn Meringue Cake, 247–249

baking powder, 266
baking sheets, 266
baking times, 266
Banana and Chocolate Tart, Warm,
    120–122
Basmati Rice and Fruits-of-the-
    Moment Salad, 81–83
batterie de cuisine, 266
bench scrapers, 267
Bittersweet Chocolate Sorbet, 79
black pepper, 267
blender, 267
    immersion, 276
blowtorch, kitchen use of, 267
Blueberry and Mascarpone Cake,
    189–192
Blueberry Sauce, French Toast with,
    45–46
Breton Sand Cookies, 95–96
Brioche Loaf (Nanterre), 204–205
brown butter, 267
Brownie Cake, Golden Pearl,
    231–233

butter, 267–268
    brown, 267
    measuring, 268
    softening, 268
Buttercream
    Chocolate, 30
    Vanilla, 29–30
buttercream variations, 29
buttering pans, 268

cake crumbs, using, 268
cake pans, 268–269
cake rings, 272–273
cake rounds, cardboard, 269
cakes
    Autumn Meringue Cake,
        247–249
    Carioca, 241–245
    Chocolate Dome, 235–239
    Chocolate-Nut Loaf, 173–174
    Chocolate Temptation, 225–
        228
    Christmas Log, 211–214
    Coconut Loaf, 165–167
    Coffee and Walnut Cake,
        206–209
    Crispy and Creamy Rice Treat,
        251–255
    Flourless Chocolate Cake Batter,
        10–11
    Fruit and Spice Loaf Cake,
        171–172
    Génoise, 2–4
    Golden Pearl Brownie Cake,
        231–233

Hazelnut-Carrot Loaf Cakes,
    169–170
Lemon Loaf Cakes, 163–164
Mascarpone and Blueberry Cake,
    189–192
Melody, 179–182
Mozart, 221–224
Pear and Fig Charlotte, 185–
    188
Philadelphia Almond Cake,
    195–199
Plain or Fancy Ligurian Lemon
    Cake, 177–178
Riviera, 215–218
Tarte Tropézienne, 201–205
Vanilla Bean Loaves, 164
Wedding Cake, 257–262
Candied Citrus Peel, 62–63
Caramel-Chocolate Mousse with
    Caramel Pears, 68–70
Caramelized Cinnamon Tart,
    137–141
Caramel Pears, Caramel-Chocolate
    Mousse with, 68–70
cardboard cake rounds, 269
Caribbean Tartlets, 149–150
Carioca, 241–245
Carrot-Hazelnut Loaf Cakes,
    169–170
Charlotte, Pear and Fig, 185–188
Cherries, Hot Sautéed, Rice Pud-
    ding Ice Cream with, 92–94
Chestnut and Pear Tart, 143–145
chocolate, 269–271
    melting, 270

storing, 270
chocolate circles, 60
chocolate shavings and curls,
    270–271
Chocolate and Banana Tart, Warm,
    120–122
Chocolate and Raspberry Tart,
    Warm, 122
Chocolate Buttercream, 30
Chocolate Cake Batter, Flourless,
    10–11
Chocolate-Caramel Mousse with
    Caramel Pears, 68–70
Chocolate Cream, Deep, with Rasp-
    berry Coulis, 43–44
Chocolate Dome, 235–239
Chocolate Glaze, 37
Chocolate-Nut Loaf, 173–174
Chocolate Sauce, 36
Chocolate Sorbet, Bittersweet, 79
Chocolate Tartlets, Passionately,
    157–159
Chocolate Temptation, 225–228
Christmas Log, 211–214
    with Currants, 214
cinnamon, 271
Cinnamon Dough, 18–20
Cinnamon Tart, Caramelized,
    137–141
Citrus-Mirliton Tart, 147–148
Citrus Peel, Candied, 62–63
cocoa powder, 271
coconut, 271
coconut milk, 271
Coconut Domes, 98–99
Coconut–Dried Cherry Flan,
    124–125
Coconut Loaf Cake, 165–167
Coconut Tuiles, 103–104
Coffee and Walnut Cake, 206–209
cookies
    Breton Sand Cookies, 95–96
    Coconut Domes, 98–99
    Coconut Tuiles, 103–104
    Dainty Almond Cups, 106–107
    Linzer Cookies with Homemade
        Raspberry Jam, 108–110
    Orange Tuiles, 101–102
    Sweet Grissini, 111–112
cooling racks, 271

coulis, 271. See also sauces
cream, 271–272
    whipping, 272
cream desserts. See also creams; Ice
    Cream
    Chocolate-Caramel Mousse with
        Caramel Pears, 68–70
    Deep Chocolate Cream with
        Raspberry Coulis, 43–44
    Faux Summer Pudding, 65–67
    Golden Lemon Fruit Layers,
        59–61
    Gourmandise, 49–51
    Lemon Crêpes, 88–90
    Tea-Flavored Crème Brûlée,
        73–74
creams. See also cream desserts
    Chocolate Buttercream, 30
    Crème Anglaise, 25–26
    Lemon Cream, 31–32
    Vanilla Buttercream, 29–30
    Vanilla Pastry Cream, 27–28
Crème Anglaise, 25–26
Crème Brûlée, Tea-Flavored, 73–
    74
Crème Brûlée Ice Cream, 84–86
crème fraîche, 272
Crêpes, Lemon, 88–90
Crispy and Creamy Rice Treat,
    251–255
Currants, Christmas Log with, 214

Dainty Almond Cups, 106–107
Deep Chocolate Cream with Rasp-
    berry Coulis, 43–44
dessert rings, 272–273
Dough
    Cinnamon, 18–20
    Inside-Out Puff Pastry, 21–24
    Perfect Tart, 12–14
    Sweet Tart, 15–17
dough, rolling, 279
dough scrapers, 267
Dried Cherry–Coconut Flan,
    124–125
dried fruits, about, 273

eggs, 273–274
Egg Wash, 40
equipment. See individual items

Faux Summer Pudding, 65–67
Fig and Pear Charlotte, 185–188
fillings and frostings. See creams;
    glazes
Flan, Coconut–Dried Cherry,
    124–125
flan rings, 280–281
flour, 274
    measuring, 277
Flourless Chocolate Cake Batter,
    10–11
folding ingredients, 274
food processor, 274
freezing, 274–275
French Toast with Blueberry Sauce,
    45–46
frostings and fillings. See creams;
    glazes
Fruit and Spice Loaf Cake, 171–172
fruit desserts. See also individual
    fruits
    Apricot Packets, 55–56
    Basmati Rice and Fruits-of-the-
        Moment Salad, 81–83
    Candied Citrus Peel, 62–63
    Faux Summer Pudding, 65–67
    Golden Lemon Fruit Layers,
        59–61
    Gourmandise, 49–51
    Grapefruit Fans and Fresh Mint
        Granité, 77–78
    Prunes in Sauternes, 71
    Salted, Peppered, and Sugared
        Pineapple Carpaccio with
        Lime Sorbet, 75–76
    Strawberry-Rhubarb Soup,
        53–54
Fruit Layers, Golden Lemon, 59–61
fruits, dried, about, 273
Fruits-of-the-Moment Salad, Bas-
    mati Rice and, 81–83

Galette, Apple, 126–127
ganache, mixing, 275
gelatin, using, 275
Génoise, 2–4
glazes
    Chocolate Glaze, 37
    Egg Wash, 40
    Transparent Glaze, 38

Golden Lemon Fruit Layers, 59–61
Golden Pearl Brownie Cake, 231–233
Gourmandise, 49–51
Granité, Fresh Mint, and Grapefruit
    Fans, 77–78
Grapefruit Fans and Fresh Mint
    Granité, 77–78

hair dryer, kitchen use of, 275
Hazelnut-Carrot Loaf Cakes, 169–170

Ice Cream. *See also* Granité; Sorbet
    Crème Brûlée, 84–86
    Rice Pudding, with Hot Sautéed
        Cherries, 92–94
    Strawberry, 87
immersion blender, 275
ingredients. *See individual items*
Inside-Out Puff Pastry, 21–24
instant-read thermometer, 275–276

Jam, Homemade Raspberry, Linzer
    Cookies with, 108–110
jelly-roll pans, 276

Ladyfinger Batter, 7–9
ladyfingers, piping and baking, 8–9
Lemon Cake, Plain or Fancy
    Ligurian, 177–178
Lemon Cream, 31–32
Lemon Crêpes, 88–90
Lemon Loaf Cakes, 163–164
Lemon Tart, 115–116
Ligurian Lemon Cake, Plain or
    Fancy, 177–178
Lime Sorbet, Salted, Peppered, and
    Sugared Pinepple Carpaccio
    with, 75–76
Linzer Cookies with Homemade
    Raspberry Jam, 108–110
loaf cakes. *See* cakes

marble, for rolling dough, 276
marzipan, about, 276
Mascarpone and Blueberry Cake,
    189–192
measuring, 276–277
    butter, 268
    flour, 277
    sugar, 277

Melody, 179–182
Meringue Batter, 5–6
Meringue Cake, Autumn, 247–249
meringues, piping and baking, 6
milk, for recipes, 277
Mirliton-Citrus Tart, 147–148
mixers, stand and hand-held, 277
mixing bowls, 277
Mousse, Chocolate-Caramel, with
    Caramel Pears, 68–70
Mozart, 221–224

Nut-Chocolate Loaf, 173–174
nuts, 277–278
    grinding, 277–278
    toasting, 277

Orange Tartlets, 153–155
Orange Tuiles, 101–102
oven thermometers, 278

pans, rotating, 279
parchment paper, 278
Passionately Chocolate Tartlets,
    157–159
pastry bags and tips, 278
pastry brush or feather, 278
Pastry Cream, Vanilla, 27–28
pastry weights, 278
Pear and Chestnut Tart, 143–145
Pear and Fig Charlotte, 185–188
Pears, Caramel, Caramel-Chocolate
    Mousse with, 68–70
Pears, Sautéed, Caramelized Cinna-
    mon Tart with, 140–141
pepper, black, 267
Perfect Tart Dough, 12–14
Philadelphia Almond Cake,
    195–199
pie weights, 278
pineapple, dried, 49–50
Pineapple Carpaccio, Salted, Pep-
    pered, and Sugared, with Lime
    Sorbet, 75–76
piping, 279
    flourless chocolate cake disks, 11
    ladyfingers, 8–9
    meringues, 6
Plain or Fancy Ligurian Lemon
    Cake, 177–178

Poached Pear and Walnut Tart,
    129–131
Prunes in Sauternes, 71
Pudding, Faux Summer, 65–67
Puff Pastry, Inside-Out, 21–24

racks, cooling, 271
Raspberry and Chocolate Tart,
    Warm, 122
Raspberry Coulis, Deep Chocolate
    Cream with, 43–44
Raspberry Jam, Homemade, Linzer
    Cookies with, 108–110
Rhubarb-Strawberry Soup, 53–54
Rice, Basmati, and Fruits-of-the-
    Moment Salad, 81–83
Rice Pudding Ice Cream with Hot
    Sautéed Cherries, 92–94
Rice Tart Impératrice, 132–134
Rice Treat, Crispy and Creamy,
    251–255
Riviera, 215–218
Roasted Apples, Caramelized Cin-
    namon Tart with, 141
rolling dough, 279
rolling pin, 279
rotating pans, 279
rum, 279
rum syrup, 167

Salad, Basmati Rice and Fruits-of-
    the-Moment, 81–83
salt, 280
Salted, Peppered, and Sugared
    Pineapple Carpaccio with
    Lime Sorbet, 75–76
Sand Cookies, Breton, 95–96
saucepans, 280
sauces. *See also* syrups
    Blueberry Sauce, 45–46
    Chocolate Sauce, 36
    fruit coulis, 61
    Raspberry Coulis, 44
    Strawberry Juice, 35
Sautéed Pears, Caramelized Cinna-
    mon Tart with, 140–141
Sauternes, Prunes in, 71
scale, kitchen, 280
scrapers, bench or dough, 267
Simple Syrup, 39

Sorbet
    Bittersweet Chocolate, 79
    Lime, Salted, Peppered, and Sugared Pineapple Carpaccio with, 75–76
Soup, Strawberry-Rhubarb, 53–54
spatulas, 280
Spice and Fruit Loaf Cake, 171–172
Strawberry Ice Cream, 87
Strawberry Juice, 35
Strawberry-Rhubarb Soup, 53–54
sugar, 280
    measuring, 277
Summer Pudding, Faux, 65–67
Sweet Grissini, 111–112
Sweet Tart Dough, 15–17
syrups. *See also* sauces
    lemon, 190
    rum, 167
    Simple Syrup, 39
    Strawberry Juice, 35

Tart Dough
    Perfect, 12–14
    Sweet, 15–17
Tarte Tropézienne, 201–205

Tartlets. *See also* tarts
    Caribbean, 149–150
    Orange, 153–155
    Passionately Chocolate, 157–159
tart rings, 280–281
tarts. *See also* Tart Dough; Tartlets
    Apple Galette, 126–127
    Caramelized Cinnamon Tart, 137–141
    Chestnut and Pear Tart, 143–145
    Coconut–Dried Cherry Flan, 124–125
    Lemon Tart, 115–116
    Mirliton-Citrus Tart, 147–148
    Poached Pear and Walnut Tart, 129–131
    Rice Tart Impératrice, 132–134
    Tropical Tart, 117–118
    Warm Chocolate and Banana Tart, 120–122
    Warm Chocolate and Raspberry Tart, 122
Tea-Flavored Crème Brûlée, 73–74

thermometer
    instant-read, 275
    oven, 278
Transparent Glaze, 38
Tropical Tart, 117–118
tuiles. *See* cookies
Twenty-Hour Apples, 33–34

vanilla, 281
Vanlla Bean Loaves, 164
Vanilla Buttercream, 29–30
Vanilla Pastry Cream, 27–28

Walnut and Coffee Cake, 206–209
Walnut and Poached Pear Tart, 129–131
Warm Chocolate and Banana Tart, 120–122
Warm Chocolate and Raspberry Tart, 122
Wash, Egg, 40
Wedding Cake, 257–162

zest, 281
zesters, 281

Copyright © 1998 by Societé de Créations Patissières-Socrepa and Dorie Greenspan

All rights reserved. No part of this book may be reproduced in any form or by any electronic or mechanical means, including information storage and retrieval systems, without permission in writing from the publisher, except by a reviewer, who may quote brief passages in a review.

First Edition

LIBRARY OF CONGRESS CATALOGING-IN-PUBLICATION DATA
Hermé, Pierre.
　　Desserts by Pierre Hermé / written by Dorie Greenspan ;
photographs by Hartmut Kiefer. — 1st ed.
　　　p.　cm.
　　Includes index.
　　ISBN 0-316-35720-0
　　1. Desserts — France.　2. Pastry — France.　3. Cookery, French.
　　I. Greenspan, Dorie.　II. Title
　　TX773.H43　1998
　　641.8'6'0944 — DC21　　　　　　　　　　　　　　　　　　97-46131

10　9　8　7　6　5　4　3　2　1

Book design by Julia Sedykh

Published simultaneously in Canada by Little, Brown & Company (Canada) Limited
Printed in Singapore